Teaching to Complexity

A Framework to Evaluate Literary and Content-Area Texts

quantitative

reader & task

qualitative

Authors
Mary Ann Cappiello, Ed.D.
Erika Thulin Dawes, Ed.D.

Image Credits

p.37 (Parrots Over Puerto Rico Text copyright © 2013 by Susan L. Roth and Cindy Trumbore Illustrations copyright © 2013 by Susan L. Roth. Permission arranged with LEE & LOW BOOKS, Inc., New York, NY 10016), Lee & Low Books; p.41 (A Splash of Red by Jen Bryan and Melissa Sweet. Used by permission of Penguin Group (USA) LLC All rights reserved.), 45 (Sky Boys: How They Built the Empire State Building by Deborah Hopkinson and James E. Ransome. Used by permission of Penguin Group (USA) LLC All rights reserved.), 151 (The Honeybee Man by Lela Nargi and Kyrsten Brooker. Used by permission of Penguin Group (USA) LLC All rights reserved.) Penguin Random House; p.65 (HERE'S A LITTLE POEM. Compilation Copyright © 2007 Jane Yolen and Andrew Fusek Peters. Illustrations Copyright © 2007 Polly Dunbar. Reproduced by permission of the publisher, Candlewick Press, Somerville, MA on behalf of Walker Books, UK.), (BEOWULF. Copyright © 1999, 2000, 2007 by Gareth Hinds. Reproduced by permission of the publisher, Candlewick Press, Somerville, MA.), 71 (ALMOST ASTRONAUTS. Copyright © 2009 Tanya Lee Stone. Reproduced by permission of the publisher, Candlewick Press, Somerville, MA.), 146 (IT'S OUR GARDEN. Text and photographs copyright © 2013 by George Ancona. Illustrations copyright © 2013 by the students of Acequia Madre Elementary School. Reproduced by permission of the publisher, Candlewick Press, Somerville, MA.), 151 (YUCKY WORMS. Text copyright © 2009 by Vivian French. Illustrations copyright © 2009 by Jessica Ahlberg. Illustrations Copyright © 2007 Polly Dunbar. Reproduced by permission of the publisher, Candlewick Press, Somerville, MA on behalf of Walker Books, UK.), (INSECT DETECTIVES. Text copyright © 2009 Steve Voake. Illustrations copyright © 2009 Charlotte Voake. Illustrations Copyright © 2007 Polly Dunbar. Reproduced by permission of the publisher, Candlewick Press, Somerville, MA on behalf of Walker Books, UK.) Candlewick Press; p.77–78 and 139 (From THOSE REBELS, JOHN & TOM by Barbara Kerley, illustrated by Edwin Fotheringham. Scholastic Inc./Scholastic Press. Text copyright © 2012 by Barbara Kerley, illustrations copyright © 2012 by Edwin Fotheringham. Reprinted by permission.), 145 (Cover illustration copyright © 2008 by Edwin Fotheringham from WHAT TO DO ABOUT ALICE? by Barbara Kerley. Scholastic Inc./Scholastic Press. Reprinted by permission.), (Cover illustration copyright © 2014 by Edwin Fotheringham from A HOME FOR MR. EMERSON by Barbara Kerley. Scholastic Inc./Scholastic Press. Reprinted by permission.), (Cover illustration copyright © 2001 by Brian Selznick from THE DINOSAURS OF WATERHOUSE HAWKINS by Barbara Kerley. Scholastic Inc./Scholastic Press. Reprinted by permission.) Scholastic; p.144 (Cover from ABRAHAM LINCOLN AND FREDERICK DOUGLASS: The Story Behind an American Friendship by Russell Freedman. Copyright © 2012 by Russell Freedman. Used by permission of Clarion Books, an imprint of Houghton Mifflin Harcourt Publishing Company. All rights reserved.), 151(Cover from THE BEETLE BOOK by Steve Jenkins. Jacket art © 2012 by Steve Jenkins. Used by permission of Houghton Mifflin Harcourt Publishing Company. All rights reserved.) Houghton Mifflin Harcourt; Back cover (photos courtesy of Lesley University); All other images Shutterstock.

Standards

© Copyright 2010. National Governors Association Center for Best Practices and Council of Chief State School Officers. All rights reserved. (CCSS)

Shell Education
5301 Oceanus Drive
Huntington Beach, CA 92649-1030
http://www.shelleducation.com
ISBN 978-1-4258-1460-1
© 2015 Shell Educational Publishing, Inc.

The classroom teacher may reproduce copies of materials in this book for classroom use only. The reproduction of any part for an entire school or school system is strictly prohibited. No part of this publication may be transmitted, stored, or recorded in any form without written permission from the publisher.

Weblinks and URL addresses included in this book are public domain and may be subject to changes or alterations of content after publication by Shell Education. Shell Education does not take responsibility for the accuracy or future relevance and appropriateness of any web links or URL addresses included in this book after publication. Please contact us if you come across any inappropriate or inaccurate web links and URL addresses and we will correct them in future printings.

Teaching to Complexity
A Framework to Evaluate Literary and Content-Area Texts

Table of Contents

Foreword...5

Dedication and Acknowledgments..7

Introduction...9

Chapter 1: The Complexity of Literacy Practices..................................15

Chapter 2: Evaluating the Quality of Literary and Informational Texts............31

Chapter 3: Evaluating for Instructional Purpose and Practice.....................83

Chapter 4: Considering Complexity...105

Chapter 5: Complexity in Context..137

Appendices

    Appendix A: References Cited...159

    Appendix B: Book Reviews Cited...165

    Appendix C: Children's Literature Cited....................................169

    Appendix D: Resources for Locating Children's Literature...................175

    Appendix E: Resources for Evaluating Texts.................................179

    Appendix F: Contents of the Digital Resource CD............................246

Foreword

Change is the only constant in education. If there is anything that I have learned as an educator, it is that teachers face change each and every year that impacts instruction and ultimately what and how students learn. With each school year, a teacher can face the adoption of new textbooks, a move to a new classroom, an increase in the number of students per classroom, and most recently, the integration of technology, including SMART Boards and 1:1 devices, and now the integration of Common Core State Standards (CCSS) and new assessments. Even with constant changes, teachers must ensure that the needs of all students are met, which now includes ensuring college and/or career readiness. This is not an easy yearly adjustment and requires a lot of flexibility and patience with what often feels like a lack of support. While change seems to be the only constant, it is important to take a moment to understand the why behind so many changes, particularly over the past few years.

The landmark 2001 No Child Left Behind (NCLB) Act was intended to be a step forward in federal policy, fostering inclusion in standards-based assessments and highlighting that all students must have access to mainstream curriculum. Unfortunately, what was and continues to be highlighted are major achievement gaps across the country. In fact, the 5.4 million English Learners (ELs) in our classrooms make up the lowest performing academic group in the United States (US) today (Adams, Robelen, and Shah 2012). Despite its good intentions, NCLB left behind the very students it was designed to help. Part of the problem, amongst other problems, has been the flexibility granted to states to teach to their state standards. This very lack of consistency and great variation in program content became major concerns for the quality of education that students were receiving across the country (Wiley and Wright 2004).

Among other staggering statistics are the major demographic shifts we are experiencing in the US. For the first time this past fall of 2014, the number of Hispanic, African-American, and Asian students in public PK–12 classrooms is expected to surpass the number of non-Hispanic whites (Maxwell, 2014). Additionally, the current projections are for children from racially and linguistically diverse backgrounds to make up more than 48 percent of total enrollment in public educational settings by 2020, and for one out of every four students to be identified as an EL by 2025 (Banks and Banks 2007; Berenyi 2008; Kihuen 2009). All of these major shifts coupled together pose a host of very complex challenges for educators, yet an imperative for change (Maxwell 2014). Improving the education of the ever-growing population of diverse students in the US will be important for continued domestic economic growth, the cohesion of society within the US, and for maintaining US competitiveness in the global economy (Faltis 2011).

The intention of CCSS is for students to learn the same content, not necessarily standardization, but standards for higher and similar expectations. The problem is that teachers, once again, feel alone during this time of shift and many are faced with questions, like, how is what I am teaching different from CCSS? Are my resources and texts CCSS-ready/approved? Very often teachers are told the why and the what, without the how. How can teachers select, evaluate, and implement texts and resources while teaching to new standards and plan engaging activities now? The careful balance is that teachers are also experts and know how to teach. Indeed, teachers are faced with "teaching to complexity."

Literacy, as we know, is the foundation that helps us make and express meaning in the real world. We make meaning about what we read and discuss based on our unique life experiences. That is what we want to help our students do in the real world; interact with text, make meaning of the text, and then give and listen to other opinions. *Teaching to Complexity* proactively guides teachers with selecting and evaluating texts for use in different content areas for a range of instructional purposes that are aligned to CCSS to help our students with these very skills. *Teaching to Complexity* directly and clearly defines some of the vagueness of CCSS terminology. This book, however, is not a step-by-step instruction guide to teach daily lessons. This resource has already differentiated an approach for teachers to evaluate a variety of CCSS-ready texts and aligns with how Tomlinson (2012) defines differentiation in that teachers proactively plan varied approaches to what students need to learn, how they will learn it, and/or how they will show what they learned in order to increase the likelihood that each student will learn as much as they can.

As this book is written with diverse learners in mind, it is also written with a diverse audience in mind to support teachers at all levels of experience and with varied levels of understanding of the CCSS, all with improving student learning at its core. Teaching to Complexity helps teachers help students have a more student-centered, inquiry-oriented focus on learning within and across the content areas. Authors Cappiello and Dawes are realistic in Text to Complexity in that teachers cannot do it alone, yet, do not claim to provide a one-size-fits all solution. Teaching to Complexity addresses the inherent complex road teachers face in efficiently delivering instruction to meet the needs of all learners and helps teachers make meaning of the CCSS. Faced with change, teachers have much-needed guidance in Teaching to Complexity with how to make daily instructional decisions to ensure equitable opportunities and equitable outcomes for all students.

Dr. Delia E. Racines
Visiting Research Scholar, Cornell University
Faculty, University of Southern California
USC Language Academy

Dedication

This book is dedicated to

Anne Dowd Geoffroy,

for the thirty-five years she spent teaching children in the community she loved so much
and her infectious sense of humor and joy,
all of which live on,

and to

Marian Brandt Schubauer,

whose gracious and giving spirit anchored, guided, and buoyed her family, friends, and neighbors for nearly a century.

Acknowledgments

Myra Zarnowski and Jennifer Bogard were careful readers of early versions of this manuscript and important sounding boards throughout the conceptualization and writing of this book. The final product is much stronger as a result of their feedback.

Our graduate work at Teachers College, Columbia University continues to inform and shape our work today. We are forever in debt to Dr. Barbara Kiefer for the introduction to the study of children's literature she provided, which serves as a set of lenses through which we view the role of books in classroom life across the curriculum. Ruth Vinz and Greg Hamilton grounded Mary Ann in the complex roles that texts of all genres can play at the secondary level and the significance of curriculum that grows out of ongoing work in individual classrooms. Marjorie Siegel introduced Erika to critical literacy and the role that teachers can play in guiding children to examine multiple perspectives embedded in texts. The selection of rich and engaging texts is a central component of literacy and language learning and we are grateful to have had our framework for text selection cultivated so deeply from the very early stages of our teaching lives.

This book could not have been written without the support of the Lesley University community. The conceptualization of this book took place during Mary Ann's sabbatical and much of the writing and revision during Erika's. The collaborative spirit that permeates the Graduate School of Education allows us to have conversations about our ideas with colleagues in our Language and Literacy Division and across the school. Our work is shaped by the many teachers we are privileged to teach and the schools, teachers, and librarians with whom we are lucky enough to collaborate. We particularly appreciate the support and advocacy of Division Director Margery Miller and Dean Jack Gilette, as well as Mary McMackin, Linda Dacey, and Dean of Faculty Lisa Fiore.

We would also like to thank the family, friends, and neighbors who helped us along the journey of this manuscript. For last-minute requests for childcare, to the cheerleading we needed along the way, we thank you!

Introduction

The texts we ask students to read matter. They influence students' knowledge of the world, their recognition of multiple perspectives, their ability to develop empathy, their understanding of how inquiry operates, and their perception of how people use literacies to express their understanding of the world around them, whether through a historic speech, a picture book, or a poem. Our goal in writing this book is to support you as you select texts that will make a difference in your students' learning today, next month, and in years to come.

We find ourselves at an important crossroads in public education in America. As we write this book, the Common Core Standards for English Language Arts and Content Literacy and Mathematics are no longer "new," but continue to be "newly important" as schools and districts across the country begin to implement them. The Next Generation Science Standards have also been introduced, and states are deciding whether or not to replace state-based curriculum standards with these new standards. Finally, the 3C Framework for Social Studies has also been introduced. Not every state will sign on to all four of these; some states may choose to develop their own Next Generation standards. However, the very idea of these standards, in addition to the content within them, has created a nationwide conversation about what content and skills should be taught in grades K–12 in the United States. It has also reintroduced the significance of integrating curriculum into the standards as much as possible, not only to parallel the "real-world" application of what we learn in school, but as a means of better achieving the standards, using one concept to reinforce and more deeply understand another. For example, the Next Generation Science Standards provide a pathway for all educators, at different grade levels, to consider the ways in which math, literacy, and science intersect. Those intersections are built into the standards, fostering a spirit of logical integration of curriculum and a more specific context for students to understand their literacy and mathematics instruction.

With the advent of the reauthorization of federal funding for elementary and secondary education in the United States set into motion by the 2001 No Child Left Behind Act, with mandatory annual testing in literacy and mathematics in grades 3–8 and accompanying punitive measures for schools failing to make "adequate yearly progress," we have witnessed the snowballing of isolated instruction of literacy and math. Each year, we have more and more students in the graduate programs in which we teach confessing to us that science and social studies play a very small role in the elementary curriculum regardless of what state standards have been put in place. We are hopeful that the new standards, taken collectively, will help schools to move towards a more student-centered, inquiry-oriented focus on learning within and across all the content areas from preschool to high school. Through a more carefully constructed study of science and social studies, as well as the arts, students will have the background knowledge they need when they confront the complexity of these subject areas at the secondary level.

When we wrote *Teaching with Text Sets*, we were excited about the potential that the Common Core State Standards had to transform schools into places where students, guided by their teachers, would use their developing literacy skills to explore our fascinatingly complex world through multimodal, multigenre text sets and inquiry processes. We believe that multimodal, multigenre text sets have an important role to play in the transition to new standards with renewed attention to the complexity of texts being read by our students. By nature, a multimodal, multigenre text set includes a range of texts that vary not only in complexity, but also in the perspectives they represent, and in the modalities (such as video and audio) and genres selected by the authors of these texts. As both digital and print texts continue to blend traditional genres, we can develop students' know-how in navigating across modalities and genres, reading and interpreting texts written by others, and selecting from a wide range of genre options when communicating their responses.

We also believe text sets are an ideal way to differentiate instruction for a diverse range of learners. Incorporating a wide range of texts for content-area study allows us to match each of these students with texts suited to their needs and that help them to grow as readers, writers, and thinkers. With digital resources that are growing by the day, and massive amounts of information available online in all fields, teachers and students can harness the potential these texts offer for bringing a range of content into the classroom. It's hard to imagine a more opportune moment for realizing the potential of *Teaching with Text Sets*. The materials we need to scaffold and layer content to effectively differentiate instruction are ours for the taking!

But we recognize that the process of transitioning to new standards for literacy and content-area learning is a turbulent one. Conversations about how to read the standards are fraught with different interpretations about expectations for students, the shape and flow of reading instruction, and what types and levels of texts students should be reading. We have been particularly struck by the conversations that focus on the issue of text complexity. While text complexity is defined and contextualized within the standards, local and professional group interpretations of this term highlight the ambiguity and problematic nature of "leveling" texts.

We believe that teachers have the capacity to make appropriate judgments in selecting texts that are accessible to their students, yet still offer space for students to stretch and grow as readers and writers through their analysis and response to the text's content. Making careful text selections, considering a constellation of factors, including the readability of the text, is an integral part of the teaching process. So, yes, this book *is* about text complexity and our desire to weigh in on and interpret this ongoing conversation, but it is also about so much more!

We also know that teachers can benefit from additional tools to help them implement text sets in the classroom. Since publishing *Teaching with Text Sets*, we have heard from many teachers in the process of implementing text sets on their own or as part of a team or school-wide effort. Here are just a few of the questions we've heard:

- There is a certain text I have always used in my curriculum that my students love. Can I still use it?
- My school has used basal readers for years. How can I become more confident in my own ability to select texts for classroom use?
- What is text complexity? I hear different things from my colleagues.
- How do I consider the text complexity of each text when I am putting together a text set?
- How might I select texts differently for language arts as compared to science or social studies?

We have written this book with multiple audiences in mind: new and veteran teachers, grade-level teams, professional learning communities, vertical subject-area teams, pre-service teachers, and literacy and curriculum coaches. We wrote this book for a broad audience because we understand that changes occur in schools in different ways. Sometimes, it is one teacher within a team that can serve as a catalyst for others, such as when a veteran faculty member shares new ideas gleaned from university coursework, or when a new hire shares practices from a previous school. Literacy or curriculum coaches are agents of change who need to provide their faculty with pathways to support their work as they transition from one set of standards to another.

We have also heard from teachers who don't feel as if they have the time and energy to research texts and consider their relationship to one another, the curriculum standards, and the students. But somebody in every school must make those decisions. We wrote this book to support you, in the midst of your very busy teaching life, as you seek to make effective text choices for your students. We want to encourage you to collaborate and cross-pollinate, working with your fellow educators, and equip you with the tools you need to research, curate, and utilize texts that are excellent matches with your curriculum and the needs of your students. What we gain from working together to carefully examine the potential of well-chosen texts for instruction in language arts and the content areas is far more valuable than the investment of time that this approach requires. With so many texts to choose from and the current emphasis on using multiple texts and text types espoused by today's standards, there are ways to divide the labor so that no single teacher has to feel alone and overwhelmed. We think, instead, that schools and districts can focus on building their own capacities to make important decisions about the texts students will read, in particular during this process of transition to new sets of standards. Building this capacity takes time and practice, but there is great potential for increased student achievement when text selection decisions are made by those who know the curriculum and students best—you and your colleagues!

The Common Core asks teachers and schools to pay closer attention to the texts offered to students. To facilitate students' growth as critical thinkers, we need to offer them texts of increasing complexity and immerse them in critical analysis and writing around these texts. The dilemma is that in order to accurately evaluate text complexity you have to consider so many contextual factors, including: the knowledge and abilities that students bring to the reading process; the content, clarity and structure of the text itself; and the classroom purposes and goals that shape how the text will be used. Considering these factors while keeping in mind the "big picture" goals for student learning is at the heart of constructing rich, curricular experiences.

Therefore, this book—an outgrowth of *Teaching with Text Sets*—focuses specifically on the process of selecting and evaluating texts for use in different content areas for a range of instructional purposes. This book will help you and your school to:

- consider the complexity of reading and the complexity of reading for different instructional purposes in language arts and the content areas in grades K–12;
- explore what makes a quality piece of literature or nonfiction/informational text;
- explore the meaning of text complexity and how aspects of a text's *quality* impact its *complexity*;
- consider texts and readers in the context of standards, curriculum goals, and instructional design; and
- consider the complexity of a text when it is used in a multimodal or multigenre text set.

We wrote this book to support you as you select high-quality, appropriate texts to teach in your classroom. Throughout the book, you will find guidance for evaluating texts with three criteria in mind:

- The book's quality—the literary and artistic value of a book.
- The book's utility as a teaching tool.
- The book's complexity—its appropriateness for the student reader(s) you have in mind.

In **Chapter One**, we consider the concept of text complexity in the larger context of literacy instruction, connecting the process of text selection to "big picture" goals for literacy and content-area instruction. In **Chapter Two**, we introduce the *Quality, Utility, and Complexity Chart*. This chart is an evaluation tool that offers a format for reviewing a particular text's quality, teaching potential, and appropriateness for a particular reader or class. We begin to equip you to use this chart by providing you with criteria for evaluating the quality of a text, offering both general and genre-specific considerations to support your review of potential texts. In **Chapter Three**, we consider how our purposes for teaching and different instructional practices influence our evaluation of a text as a teaching tool. In **Chapter Four**, we link the evaluation of a book's quality and its utility for our teaching purposes and practices with the evaluation of text complexity. We start with an interpretation of Reading Standard 10 of the Common Core State Standards and then connect the evaluation of complexity with a consideration of instructional purpose, practices, and particular readers. In **Chapter Five**, we further consider how complexity varies with instructional purposes and practices, and consider the different roles texts can play within a unit of study. The **Appendices** of this book list our favorite resources for locating children's literature and provide several completed samples of the *Quality, Utility, and Complexity Chart*.

This book will help you answer the following questions:

- What are the different purposes for reading in literacy and content curriculum? (Chapter 1)
- Is this book a quality book? Would I want to use it in my classroom? (Chapter 2)
- How is this book useful for teaching? What instructional goals can this book help me to meet? (Chapter 3)
- How do I consider the complexity of a book in the context of my classroom practice and readers? (Chapter 4)
- How can I use this book alongside other texts to support my students' understandings of complex content? (Chapter 5)

The Complexity of Literacy Practices

Another book about text complexity? Well, yes, and no. This book *is* about the complexity of texts, but it is *more* about the endlessly fascinating complexity of teaching. For years, we have followed a process for selecting texts for our classrooms. We want to share this process with you because we think it gives you the tools you need to teach with depth and authenticity in a time of high stress and high stakes. This is a book about making decisions as well as activating and applying your knowledge of students, standards, and strategies for instruction.

With the implementation of the Common Core and other state standards, teachers and administrators across the country have been grappling with the implications of higher expectations for student learning. These expectations involve an integration of the content areas into the standards, specifically focusing on the roles of reading, writing, speaking, and listening (the language arts) in science and social studies. Simultaneously, these standards ask teachers to explicitly consider how they build students' reading abilities—described as the facility to read increasingly complex texts in the interest of college and career readiness. Raising the bar yet higher, teachers are expected to guide students to critically analyze the texts they read and to express new knowledge and opinions in written responses.

Although the standards frame these expectations broadly, two components of the Common Core standards documents have generated much discussion and perhaps undue emphasis—Reading Standard 10: Text Complexity and Appendix A. Suddenly literacy organization discussion boards, reading specialists' and administrators' offices, and university classrooms are abuzz with talk about "text complexity." Although Appendix A makes it clear that evaluation of the complexity of texts is multifaceted, incorporating quantitative and qualitative analysis of text features, as well as a consideration of reader and task (who will read the text and how it will be used), the conversations we have been privy to in the education world tend to heavily emphasize quantitative readability levels. We wrote this book with the goal of extending these discussions because we see this moment as an opportunity to look more explicitly at exactly how teachers go about making text selections that are ideally matched to their curriculum goals, the readers in their classrooms, and their instructional activities.

In chapters two through five of this book, we will model the step-by-step process by which we evaluate and select books for instruction. But first, we think it is important to ground you in the larger conversation about literacy that informs the ongoing national dialogue about text complexity and the use of a wide range of diverse text types in PreK–12 classrooms. In order to make the best practical, everyday decisions about books for classroom use, you need to be grounded in the theoretical orientation that undergirds the choices we make in text selection and curriculum design.

"Big Picture Thinking": Considering Literacy and Instructional Goals

Understanding literacy as a socially situated dynamic communicative practice is at the heart of the *Teaching with Text Sets* (Cappiello and Dawes 2012) approach. Our discussion of text complexity is grounded in this broader picture of literacy and literacy practices. In this chapter, we will define literacy, discuss the interdependence of the language arts (reading, writing, speaking, and listening), and begin to look at how diverse readers, texts, and instructional practices interact to create a dynamic, complex instructional environment.

Moving Beyond "Reading": What is Literacy?

Our work as teachers, teacher educators, and professional development specialists centers on the use of multimodal, multigenre text sets for integrated literacy and content-area instruction. In our previous book *Teaching with Text Sets* (Cappiello and Dawes 2012), we describe a process for teaching with carefully curated collections of digital and print resources, including but not limited to children's and young adult literature, periodicals, and web-based texts. *Teaching with Text Sets* presents a process for locating appropriate texts as well as five instructional models that can serve as blueprints for constructing curriculum with text sets. These models grew out of our years of teaching elementary, middle, and high school, and our work as teacher educators. We are committed to supporting teachers to use the 'best of the best' resources to employ these models to meet their curricular goals.

When we talk about selecting texts for classroom use, it is easy to jump right into a conversation about reading. What texts *should* students read? *Who* will be reading *which* texts? In schools, we naturally talk a lot about reading. Are students "reading on grade level"? At what level is a student reading? Has a student achieved mastery of national, state, or district reading standards? Is he or she reading at a "level of complexity" deemed appropriate by the standards? Are students reading the literary canon? These questions are logical ones and they ground us in the nitty-gritty details of daily instruction; however, we always try to consider these questions within a broader framework of goals for student learning.

When we speak about our model for teaching with multimodal, multigenre text sets, we are always sure to emphasize the idea that "you don't teach a text set, you teach *with* a text set." This notion places the content of the text set, whether it be theme-, topic-, or genre-focused, at the heart of instruction. We believe that reading, writing, and speaking are tools for learning and communicating about the world around us. In other words, teaching with text sets involves so much more than teaching *reading*. When we teach with text sets, we develop students' *literacies* in order to improve their abilities to access knowledge, practice inquiry, and to convey what they have learned.

The distinction between *reading* and *literacy* is more than academic. This important distinction helps to remind us that students' ability to decode and comprehend words on a page is only one aspect of their abilities to learn and to effectively communicate. In other words, reading is only one facet of a spectrum of communicative skills and strategies. Equally important to the question, *"Can students read this text?"* is the question, *"What can students do with this text?"*

At a basic level, this conception of literacy comprises and extends reading, incorporating the communicative facilities of reading, writing, speaking, and listening. But beyond this listing, it is important to recognize the interdependence of these activities and the varied ways in which these activities are enacted in daily life. The National Council of Teachers of English (2013) on their website describes literacies as "multiple, dynamic, and malleable… inextricably linked with particular histories, life possibilities, and social trajectories of individuals and groups."

The continuum of expectations within the Common Core English Language Arts Standards (K–12) also highlights the interconnections of literacy processes:

> "Students who meet the standards… actively seek the wide, deep and thoughtful engagement with high-quality literature and informational text that builds knowledge, enlarges experiences, and broadens worldviews. They reflexively demonstrate the cogent reasoning and use of evidence that is essential to both private deliberation and responsible citizenship in a global setting. In short, students who meet the Standards develop the skills in reading, writing, speaking, and listening that are the foundation for any creative and purposeful expression in language" (Common Core State Standards 2010).

Literacy is the larger context that describes the meaning-making that happens when students are working in all of the modalities: reading, writing, listening, and speaking. We use the literacies of reading, writing, speaking, and listening in myriad ways to act on our world (Gee 1990; Heath 1982), using these communicative practices as tools for survival, learning, and advocacy. Grounded in this conceptual framework for literacy, we are guided in our daily teaching practice by several important concepts:

- **We are apprenticed into literacy practices by our parents, teachers, friends, and colleagues.** Babies learn to speak by listening. They develop an understanding of language and syntax by apprenticing themselves to the adults and children around them, experiencing exponential growth both in their ability to understand the world around them and to express that understanding. Teachers working with students of all ages can harness the potential of speaking and listening as tools for developing and refining conceptual understandings (Halliday 1975; Vygotsky 1986).

- **Literacy practices are purpose driven.** We read and write to communicate and to learn and express our understandings of the world. Teachers and students consider the purposes and audiences for all tasks they undertake, whenever possible, and communicate with authentic purposes and for real audiences (Lindfors 2008).

- **Literacies are highly contextual—situated within social contexts.** They express beliefs, values, and perspectives. We vary our manner of speaking, reading, and writing depending on who we are with, what we are doing, and what we hope to accomplish. Teachers apprentice students into academic literacies associated with different content areas and disciplines of study. What's more, teachers understand that students bring a set of beliefs, values, and perspectives that may be challenged by the texts they read and harnessed to critique those very texts (Gee 1990; Buehl 2011; Lee and Spratley 2010; Moje 2008; Rainey and Moje 2012).

- **Literacy practices, text types, and genres as we know them are constantly evolving.** The students with whom we spend time in the classroom are exploring ever-evolving forms of social media and communication tools. They tweet each other, build Pinterest boards, and connect with others who have similar interests through online forums and games, etc. These technologies provide the media through which students construct and express their lives and learning. As teachers, we can capitalize on students' interest in popular media, keeping current and using new technologies as learning tools (New London Group 1996; Mishra and Koehler 2006).

Taken as a whole, these foundational concepts suggest a model for practice that is multifaceted, multimodal, multigenre, and dynamic.

Embracing the Complexity of Reading

The aforementioned principles ground our approach to literacy instruction, but since this book is about text selection that supports students' growth as readers, learners, and thinkers, we also want to talk more specifically about reading. So what exactly is reading? While methods for teaching beginning reading continue to generate debate, many of the schools that we work with and in which our students work, currently name their approach to the teaching of reading as a "balanced approach." By this, they mean an approach that attends to the learning of decoding skills (phonics and spelling), the learning of language patterns (grammar), and the development of strategies for making meaning from text (comprehension). These three emphases begin to suggest the complexity of the reading process; however, naming them is just the tip of the iceberg. To understand the full picture, it is helpful to consider how reading processes have been theoretically conceptualized.

Louise Rosenblatt's seminal work, *The Reader, The Text, and the Poem: The Transactional Theory of the Literary Work* (1978) is foundational to the way we understand reading processes and reading comprehension today. She introduced the theory that reading is a dynamic process—a transaction between the reader and the text being read. She proposed that meaning does not reside in the text itself, or in the reader, but in the process of constructing meaning, which happens when a text is read by a reader. The construction of meaning is generated from the author's words on the paper and the reader's interpretation of these words, which is influenced by the life experiences and perspectives of the reader. Furthering her theoretical model, Rosenblatt described how readers' purposes for reading also influence the reading process, noting two stances that readers adopt toward text. Readers adopt an "aesthetic stance" when they read for pleasure, to enjoy a story, and/or to enjoy the language use within a text. When readers read with the explicit purpose of gaining information from text, they adopt an "efferent stance." We know that readers can use both of these stances when reading the same text and it may be helpful to you to think of these two stances as located on a continuum of purpose. Sometimes we read with a very specific informational purpose in mind (efferent stance), for example, to try to figure out how to get your new all-in-one printer to communicate wirelessly on a home network. Sometimes, we read purely for pleasure (aesthetic stance), for example, when we eagerly await the release of a favorite author's new novel. At other times, for example, when reading an essay in the newspaper or in a magazine, or a cookbook by a chef with a dynamic personality, we may appreciate both the information gained and the writing style employed by the author.

But knowing exactly all that is at play when a reader and a text meet is certainly a challenge, since comprehension is an "in the head" process. In 1999, the U.S. Department of Education charged the RAND Reading Study Group with the task of setting a research agenda for the study of reading comprehension. This group of experts in the field of reading developed a working model of reading comprehension processes and conducted a review of available research on the topic. While this review clearly identified comprehension as an area in need of further study, the model of comprehension processes developed by the group has strongly influenced conversations in the field about the instruction of reading, and most recently, about the readability of texts. Appendix A of the Common Core State Standards frames the issue of text complexity similarly to the RAND study group. This model of reading comprehension and its impact on the consideration of text complexity is multifaceted, and like Rosenblatt's work, highlights the dynamic and interconnected nature of reader, text, and task.

The RAND Reading Study Group, in *Reading For Understanding*, defines reading comprehension as "the process of simultaneously extracting and constructing meaning through interaction and involvement with written text" (2002, 11). The group's "Heuristic for Thinking About Reading Comprehension" is a model of concentric circles. The centermost circle has been divided into three wedges, labeled "Text," "Activity," and "Reader," suggesting that the interrelationship of these three dimensions comprises the heart of the comprehension process.

The Reader: When engaging with a text, a reader brings to the act of reading certain cognitive capacities, such as his or her ability to sustain attention to reading the text, memory for the text content, and ability to infer, analyze, and critique the text content. The reader also brings a certain level of motivation to the reading activity, dependent on his or her particular purpose for reading, interest in the content of the text, and sense of his or her capabilities to read a particular text. Finally the reader brings a body of knowledge and life experiences to the reading of the text. That body of knowledge includes what the reader knows about the world and the happenings of the world, and it also includes the reader's knowledge of language and how language is used. All these factors influence a reader's ability to construct meaning from a particular text at a particular moment in time.

The Text: When a reader interacts with the text, that reader works to construct an understanding of the text content. Once again emphasizing the dynamic relationships inherent in the process of reading comprehension, the RAND Reading Study Group (2002) states, "Texts can be difficult or easy depending on factors inherent in the text, on the relationship between the text and the knowledge and abilities of the reader, and on the activities in which the reader is engaged" (14). While reading a text, a reader seeks to make meaning from the "surface code," the exact wording of the text, while simultaneously tracking the bigger "idea units" of the text and constructing "mental models" of the perspectives on content embedded in the text as a whole.

The Activity or Task: Finally, we must also consider that the reader is reading a particular text at a particular moment for a particular purpose. The purpose for the reading either drives or is driven by the activity of the reading (or as worded by the Common Core State Standards Appendix A, the "task"). The reader comes to the activity of reading with a particular purpose in mind, either self-generated or imposed. As you can imagine, motivation and interest (reader characteristics) are at play in these processes. The way that the reader reads is also directly linked to the purpose—depending on what the reader's goal is he or she may read the whole text or part of the text, skim text or engage in close reading, and may or may not make notes while reading. What happens as a result of the reading of the text is also variable. The reader may leave the text with increased knowledge, or with the ability to do something new (if the purpose was to learn how to do something), or with the memory of having engaged with the text (as in the case of reading for pleasure).

Figure 1.1 reprises the many factors at play across the dimensions of the "Heuristic for Thinking About Reading Comprehension" offered by the RAND Reading Study Group (2002). Every time we review this listing, we are more than slightly awed by how complex the reading process is!

But you know this already. All you need to do is to think about the students in your classroom. Regardless of what community you teach in, you work with an incredibly diverse group of students. They vary in their home experiences, language practices, background knowledge, learning styles and aptitudes, and in their personal preferences and interests. This diversity is exactly why one-size-fits-all basal reading programs, or programs that are comprised by a series of pre-determined leveled texts, taken by themselves, cannot meet all of the needs of your readers. In order to effectively engage students in the reading process and to support students' goals as readers, we need to make text selections with our particular readers and our particular curriculum goals in mind.

Figure 1.1 RAND Study Factors at Play in Reading Comprehension

Reader	Text	Activity (Task)
Reader Brings: **Cognitive Capabilities**<ul><li>attention</li><li>memory</li><li>critical analytic ability</li><li>inferencing</li><li>visualization</li></ul>**Motivation**<ul><li>a purpose for reading</li><li>interest in the content</li><li>self-efficacy as a reader</li></ul>**Knowledge**<ul><li>vocabulary and topic</li><li>linguistic and discourse</li><li>comprehension strategies</li></ul>**Experiences**<ul><li>individual life experiences</li></ul>	Reader Constructs: **Surface Code**<ul><li>the exact wording of the text</li></ul>**Text Base**<ul><li>an understanding of the ideas, organization, and structure of a text</li></ul>**Mental Models**<ul><li>global meaning-making</li><li>a synthesis of the whole</li></ul>	Within Specific Contexts and For Varied Purposes, Readers Engage In: **Operations to process the text:**<ul><li>decoding the text</li><li>higher-level linguistic and semantic processing</li><li>self-monitoring for comprehension</li><li>shifts in purpose</li></ul>**Outcomes of performing the activities:**<ul><li>increase in knowledge</li><li>solution to some real-world problem (application)</li><li>engagement with the text</li></ul>

(Adapted from Reading for Understanding, RAND Reading Study Group, 2002)

The Importance of Sociocultural Context: When selecting texts for instruction, teachers think carefully about who their readers are and what they hope to accomplish with them in the classroom. The model of reading comprehension offered by the RAND Reading Study Group stresses the importance of the context in which the reading occurs. In the concentric circle model previously described, the outer circle is labeled "Sociocultural Context." The interaction of the reader, text, and the activity (or task) occurs within a particular socially- and culturally-influenced location. This location may be a home, a classroom, or a living room where a neighborhood book group is meeting, a library, or a variety of other locations set within a community of particular socioeconomic and cultural makeup. "The identities and capacities of the readers, the texts that are available and valued, and the activities in which readers are engaged with those texts are all influenced by, and in some cases, determined by, the sociocultural context" (RAND Reading Study Group 2002, 14).

The centrality of the sociocultural context for reading is at the heart of the theories of literacy development framed by James Paul Gee. Gee (1990, 2001) makes an explicit connection between students' experiences with language in social and cultural contexts—including, but not limited to, cultural heritage, languages spoken, socioeconomic status, and political affiliations—and their abilities to read and comprehend written text. His work reminds us that students need to learn to speak, read, and write, not one "language" but many different social languages. Think for a moment about how you vary your language use depending on your social context. You write an email to a friend or family member with a different level of formality than you use in an email response to a parent of a student in your class. You speak one way in the faculty lunchroom and with a different tone when participating in a district-wide professional development session. Similarly, there are different "discourses" associated with different disciplines and academic content areas. Through school experiences students can begin to be apprenticed in the ways of speaking, reading, and writing used by scientists, mathematicians, and historians. We will expand on this idea later in the chapter, discussing disciplinary literacy. Sociocultural context—the *where, with whom, how,* and *why*—is a key component of the reading processes.

These theories have implications in our daily lives as teachers. We know that the students in our class have unique strengths and needs and we know from years of experience that we need to shape our curriculum goals and instructional activities to align with our students' strengths and needs.

The Complexity of Instructional Contexts

Now that we've reviewed what makes literacy complex—the interdependence of reading, writing, listening, and speaking for meaning-making, the transactions that take place between the reader and the text during the act of reading—we want to discuss the different ways that literacy is at work within PreK–12 classrooms.

We, the authors, consider ourselves teachers of literacy. But we also consider ourselves teachers of many other things as well. When Erika taught first grade, she taught math, art, science, social studies, and more. When Mary Ann taught eighth grade language arts, she taught about literary genres, historical time periods, art history, and more. In all cases, we used literacy as a tool for learning. Literacy was the *means* by which students learned, and part of our job was to help them become better readers, writers, listeners, and speakers. But part of our job was also to help our students become better thinkers—to craft curriculum that gave them the opportunity to think independently and to foster a spirit of inquiry so that students could trust their ability to ask and answer their own questions as well as ours and their classmates'. Yet another part of our job was to teach them facts, theories, and constructs: the concept of subtraction, the political challenges of a particular event in history, the definition of a mammal, the motifs of fantasy fiction. Like literacy itself, each strand of our teaching was interdependent on the others. This interdependency is illustrated in Figure 1.2.

Figure 1.2 The Interdependent Nature of Literacy and Content Area Teaching

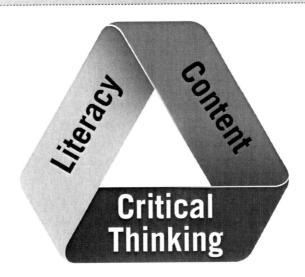

All teachers, at every grade level and content area, share this teaching triangulation of literacy, content, and critical thinking. We *teach* literacy, and we *use* literacy to *teach* content and critical thinking. You might teach middle school language arts, elementary art, or high school social studies. But you, too, teach and foster literacy, critical thinking, and content. This triangulation is also reflected in the Common Core State Standards, which ask students at all grade levels and content areas to pay attention to how texts are written; identify the content (the key ideas and details within those texts); and create new texts to demonstrate what they have learned, through inquiry, critical thinking, and research (Common Core State Standards for English Language Arts 2010).

Why is this so important to clarify? Because if we are talking about determining text complexity, and how to select texts appropriate for instructional use, we have to recognize that there are many different purposes for reading texts in the language arts alone, as well as across all of the different content areas. For example, students are asked to read and evaluate texts for different purposes and different outcomes. They *use* texts in different ways. All reading isn't the same.

The growing body of scholarship around disciplinary literacy supports this notion—not the mantra of "every teacher a teacher of reading" from the 1980s and 1990s, but rather, that every teacher apprentices students in disciplinary-specific literacy contexts. This includes behaviors that not only help those students access the facts and theories they need to learn in any discipline, but also the paths of inquiry and communication specific to that discipline, the kinds of questions that are asked and answered, and the types of texts written and produced within that discipline (Buehl 2011; Lee and Spratley 2010; Moje 2008; Shanahan and Shanahan 2008).

We know that as readers progress in their literacy proficiency, they progress to reading more specialized and sophisticated texts. Over the course of PreK–12 education, course materials also get increasingly more complex. For example, students move from an introduction to basic ideas and concepts in elementary school science, to an in-depth, year-long study of physics in high school. As students mature and become more seasoned learners, they are given more specialized elements of the academic disciplines to study. Any close academic study in the disciplines at the middle and high school level requires a precise and targeted approach to reading texts and writing in a framework recognized by each discipline.

Understanding Disciplinary Literacy

Right now, you are drawing upon your own disciplinary identity. You may be a teacher, teacher educator, literacy coach, reading specialist, or librarian. You draw on your specific knowledge of teaching, and therefore, you read this book as an "insider." A politician, policy maker, or parent would have a different reading of this book, an "outsider" stance. You are drawing on your own disciplinary understanding of education while reading this book; your purpose for reading is rooted in your professional role in a school.

As a teacher, you embody as many disciplinary identities as subjects that you teach. So think about what this kind of disciplinary identity means for your students who embody many disciplinary identities throughout the school day. Beginning in kindergarten and continuing through the middle and high school years, students are presented with increasingly more complex subjects of study and associated texts and tasks. Each subject area grows out of different fields of study with their own internal conversations. Until very recently, there was little attention paid to literacy learning at the middle and high school level. Other than the generic reading comprehension strategies, such as questioning, connecting, visualizing, and synthesizing that were applied to all the content areas, it was uncommon to find specific literacy instruction beyond language arts. Teachers instead focused on the other two strands: critical thinking and content learning.

But when looking at learning in highly specialized contexts, for example, studying global climate change in high school biology, generic strategies commonly taught to foster comprehension are not enough. According to Doug Buehl, secondary teachers of all content areas need to think of their students as apprentices in their disciplines. "As learners, students are expected to fine-tune generic comprehension strategies to accommodate the demands of each of these different subject areas…disciplinary literacy is not one thing but many things" (2011, 13–14). As Shanahan and Shanahan suggest, "[a] high school student who can do a reasonably good job reading a story in an English class may not be able to make much sense of biology or algebra books, or vice versa" (2008, 45). Furthermore, as Elizabeth Birr Moje asserts, "knowledge production in the disciplines needs to be understood to be the result of human interaction" (2008, 100).

Facts aren't simply facts. Theories get constructed. Ideas change. "Knowledge production in the disciplines operates according to particular norms for everyday practice, conventions for communicating and representing knowledge and ideas, and ways of interacting, defending ideas, and challenging the deeply held ideas of others in the discipline" (Moje 2008, 100). Secondary teachers need to make the purpose of reading explicit; model and teach discipline-specific ways of constructing, communicating, and critiquing knowledge; and "invite their students to expand the identities they bring to the classroom to include academic and specific disciplinary identities" (Buehl 2011, 30). So what does this mean for teachers at all levels on the PreK–12 continuum?

Reconsidering Disciplinary Literacy's Place Across the PreK–12 Continuum

Researchers and practitioners alike are focusing on content and disciplinary literacy as important components of the implementation of today's standards, such as the Common Core. Too often in the past, this conversation has focused only on the needs of adolescent students. However, we believe that the recommendations made regarding content literacy and adolescents in the Carnegie Corporations' report "Reading in the Disciplines: Rethinking Adolescent Literacy" are solid recommendations for teachers of any age group (Lee and Spratley 2010, 16–17); particularly the focus on using multiple texts and text types to "build knowledge and dispositions over time" (16). But we think "over time" really means the PreK–12 continuum, and focusing on the demands within adolescent disciplinary literacy provides us with another lens for looking at the ongoing work of literacy throughout the PreK–12 continuum.

Does disciplinary literacy really only start in middle school? We don't think so. For a long time, the adage was that you first "learn to read" and then "read to learn." But we think we're always reading to learn even as we are learning to read. Babies and toddlers show us this all the time as they pore over books, examine illustrations, and call for repeat reads. Furthermore, we believe that a robust and engaging early childhood and elementary learning environment fosters a spirit of inquiry, particularly in science, social studies, and the arts. Hands-on, student-centered, inquiry-oriented curriculum in science, social studies, mathematics, and the arts is essential. But within that environment, a great deal of literacy action is at work. Teachers and students are using literacy as a tool to learn, to ask and answer questions, and record what they find out through words and pictures. Often, texts of all genres are involved both in print and digital forms.

It is in these other areas of the school day—the immersive curricular experiences of science, social studies, mathematics, and the arts—that young children can practice their abilities to decode and encode, and to explore the world through speaking and listening. Literacy, even with our youngest students, can't be learned in the literacy block alone. Ideally, it is reinforced throughout the day. When it is reinforced throughout the day, students gain a sense of agency, an understanding that as learners, they "do" different things with reading in different contexts.

Consider primary grade students reading picture book biographies or life cycle books as part of social studies or science. These reading experiences can be contextualized within the fields of history and science. During read alouds, whole-class conversations, one-on-one conferences, and small-group explorations, teachers can model disciplinary-specific approaches to texts, so that students begin to understand the kinds of questions that scientists, mathematicians, and biographers pose and what constitutes an answer. From the very start of their school career, students can understand that reading is an act of discovery. With students experiencing this level of robust reading in and around the literacy block, there is greater potential to overcome the disconnect that has consistently surfaced when students reach adolescence. When students learn in a disciplinary-rich context from PreK onward, in developmentally appropriate, play- and inquiry-based contexts, the continuum can be seamless.

It is this multi-dimensional notion of reading to learn while learning to read across discipline areas that resonates with us in the Common Core State Standards, in particular the emphasis on reading more nonfiction and informational texts at the elementary level. With the increasing number of excellent nonfiction trade books being published, and the wide array of digital texts being produced, there are rich opportunities for using texts in all sorts of interesting and engaging ways. Finally, the Common Core English Language Arts Anchor Standards provide a continuum of thinking that pays attention to both literacy learning and disciplinary thinking—a promising pathway for opening doors of possibility for all our students.

Putting it All Together: Why Do We Read in School?

In this chapter, we have explored the complexity of literacy, and the interdependent nature of reading, writing, listening, and speaking. Reviewing the RAND Reading Study Group's "Heuristic for Thinking About Reading Comprehension," we have explored the multiple factors at play when a reader reads a text. We have stressed the importance of disciplinary literacy instruction in schools. Now, we want to suggest some of the most common purposes for text selection in the classroom. We know that we read for different purposes. Therefore, depending on our purpose, the texts that we choose may be very different. The purpose for student reading will shape how we consider the text, its role in the classroom, and the criteria we apply to determine both its quality and its complexity.

Figure 1.3 lists the most common driving forces behind our selection of texts for instruction. We see fostering a love of reading and healthy reading habits as a component of each of these different purposes.

Figure 1.3 Instructional Purposes for Text Selection

Understanding Content: Informational texts, such as trade books and digital texts are wonderful vehicles for finding out about the world. Sometimes, texts are selected for the curriculum because they are a good match for learning the information detailed in state or local curriculum standards. Teachers look for a match between the content they must teach and the details of the texts. In science, social studies, and mathematics such texts can be primary source materials, such as documents and artifacts from the past or brand-new research reports, as well as secondary source materials.

Developing Reading Skills: In preschool and the primary grades, texts will be selected for whole-class read alouds, shared reading, and guided reading groups in order to support individual students with the acquisition of literacy skills. When making selections, the match between the reader and the text will be the most important consideration. Books that are at a higher level than the books that students can read independently can be read aloud, in order to model language use, patterns, and fluency. As students develop as readers, teachers continue to select texts in language arts that they feel are a good match for the reader, and provide students the opportunity to continue to develop their comprehension strategies.

Developing Disciplinary Literacies: Across the grade levels, our goal is to introduce students to, and engage them with disciplinary literacies to apprentice them in the ways of reading, writing, speaking, and listening like they are scientists, historians, mathematicians, and artists. Teachers select texts that provide accessible models of disciplinary literacies across the content areas, considering the vocabulary used and how the texts demonstrate inquiry skills and strategies in the discipline.

Teaching Literary Analysis/Genre Study: Early on in the primary grades, students are grappling with emerging understandings of the differences between fiction, nonfiction, and poetry. Teachers can make selections for read alouds, whole-class and shared readings, guided reading, literature circles (book discussion groups), and independent reading that help students develop an understanding of the conventions of each genre. Teachers at the intermediate, middle, and high school level select texts that help students further develop their understanding of genre expectations and literary elements.

Analyzing Mentor Text for Student Writing: In language arts and the content areas, texts such as trade books and digital texts can serve as models for student writing. Such writing might be done in a literacy block, during which students are practicing an important aspect of genre or writing conventions. Or, such writing might be done during content-area instruction, and teachers select texts based on a combination of the content of the texts and the models of writing that they offer. In addition to reading and analyzing mentor texts, students use these texts as examples for their own writing, modeling what they write based on the array of examples they have been exposed to within a genre or text type.

Developing Critical Thinking: Teachers often plan curriculum around a theme or an essential question. When planning curriculum with this purpose in mind, teachers select texts that prompt thinking about an abstract understanding of theme or that get at the heart of the essential question. Focusing on critical-thinking skills is often one component of text selection, fused with one or more of the others mentioned on this list. Teachers pay close attention to the content as well as the perspective and point of view.

Engaging in Inquiry and Research: When conducting inquiry-based learning and research with students, teachers consider the source material that students might need as a catalyst for their research, and gather together materials relevant to the content of the research as dictated by state or local curriculum standards, or student interest. When selecting texts for research, teachers might look for "the literature of inquiry" (Zarnowski and Turkel 2011)—texts that model the process of inquiry. Or, they may simply look for books that cover the content at hand.

Fostering Habits and Love of Reading: An important component of teaching is fostering a love of learning. For literacy educators at every level, this includes a love of reading. But what makes one student love reading could be a very different text than what makes another student love reading. Teachers often are making selections for their classroom library or for individual students based on their understanding of the developmental levels of the students they teach, the enduring interests of those students each year, and individual interests and idiosyncrasies. Understanding student interests may also impact the ways in which teachers select texts for curriculum based on content standards.

Conclusion

We like to use the metaphor of the *teacher as juggler* when we describe the decision-making processes that teachers use to select texts for classroom use. When we make book choices, we are juggling the considerations of our curricular goals, the quality of the texts available to use, the complexity of these texts, the needs and interests of our readers, and the instructional purposes and practices that will shape our use of these texts.

As stated in the introduction, this book is about text complexity, but it is also about so much more. It is about how to make choices about instructional materials that will foster the kinds of critical reading, writing, thinking, and listening that we aspire to for our students. Understanding how literacy operates, the complexity of the reading process and reading comprehension, the ways in which literacy instruction has shaped PreK–12 classrooms, and the different roles texts can play in the classroom provides a foundation for understanding the purpose of text selection. In the next chapter, we outline the overall process for text selection, and then focus on determining the quality of a text, considering the questions: *Is it good?* and *How is it good?* (Stevenson 2006).

Questions for Reflection

1. How is literacy defined in your school? How does this definition influence literacy and content-area instruction in your school?

2. Think about your own instruction. What role does reading have in your instruction in relation to writing, listening, and speaking?

3. What else do you need to know about disciplinary literacy? What new questions do you have about it?

4. What are your most frequent purposes for selecting texts for your classroom?

Evaluating the Quality of Literary and Informational Texts

We wanted to write this book to provide teachers who we will never teach or work alongside the opportunity to learn some of the processes for text selection that we have learned and that we share with our graduate students. We want to give you a pair of lenses with which to view children's and young adult books in a new way, lenses which will not only help you make appropriate selections for your students, your curricular needs, and the Common Core or other state standards, but also help you internalize strategies for talking about texts that will help you be a better teacher.

During our teacher education coursework, we both had the opportunity to take survey courses in children's and young adult literature, opening our eyes to the range of wonderful teaching materials we have available across genres. During our graduate work, we continued to take more and more courses in children's and young adult literature, deepening our understandings of the processes of evaluating for quality and classroom use. We recognize that this focus is fairly unique. Many credential programs do not have separate courses in children's and young adult literature, even though a knowledge of this field is a valuable foundation for teaching all of the content areas, and is essential for teaching reading and language arts. Few education graduate programs provide courses that go beyond the survey. If you entered the field through an alternative program, you may have not had a course in children's or young adult literature. Unlike learning about science or history, it is difficult outside of formal coursework to learn about this body of work elsewhere. It is not something that gets covered in typical college-level content prerequisites required for licensure.

In Chapter One, we shared with you the theoretical orientation that grounds our work with teachers and children. When we select texts to use with students (whether they are early childhood, elementary, middle, high school, or college students), we hold our instructional purposes at the forefront of our selection process, but we are also thinking carefully about the students in our classroom—how they will read the text, and what they will be doing before, during, and after the reading. When we decide whether or not to present a book to our students, our decision-making process includes, but goes well beyond, the complexity of the text. We consider both the big picture *and* the nitty-gritty details.

When we pick up a book we:

- make judgments about the quality of the writing and illustration;
- think about our instructional goals and how they relate to the content;
- decide how we might offer the book to students, which instructional practice we might employ; and
- consider who our readers are and how well their knowledge and interests align with the content of the book.

These layers of consideration are illustrated in Figure 2.1. This book is meant to support you as you undertake a similar process for text selection for the students in your classroom. The process itself is complex and it will become faster and more facile over time as you seek to find and use the very best texts for your students.

Figure 2.1 Considerations for Text Selection

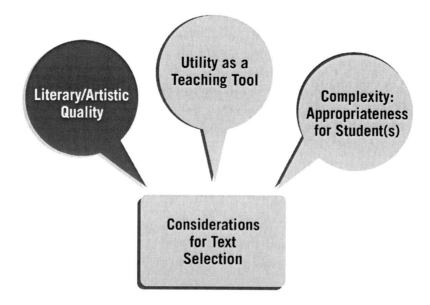

These considerations are not necessarily linear, as Figure 2.1 demonstrates. No single component is final without consideration of the others. But for the simplicity of sharing them with you, we will keep them separate. The consideration of these three areas can be captured in the following process, which has evolved for us over our years of teaching. When beginning a unit of study, we do the following:

1. Use resources and reviews to locate a range of potential texts

2. Read reviews and the texts themselves to identify the most promising texts

3. Take a closer look, using resources and evaluation criteria to consider:
   - What reviewers have said about the text
   - The quality of the written text and illustration
   - A range of instructional purposes and practices for the text
   - How the quality of the text impacts the text's level of complexity for the intended reader(s)
   - Quantitative measures of text complexity

Ultimately a consideration of this range of factors allows us to make an informed decision about whether and how to use this text for classroom instruction. This kind of thorough analysis takes time, but it also saves you time. The time spent planning allows you to better anticipate the successes and challenges that your readers will have in accessing, comprehending, and responding to a particular text. As you practice this kind of an evaluation, you will internalize the considerations. You will be able to pick up a book and more quickly consider all of these factors, making efficient and effective book choices for your students.

To equip you with selection tools, we have developed a template to use as you consider evaluation criteria, as well as a graphic organizer for your notes about the particular texts you are considering for use. As we walk you through the selection and evaluation processes in this chapter and beyond, we will provide a model of what we call the Quality, Utility, and Complexity Chart (Figure 2.2). This chart is designed to be a practice tool—a scaffold for you as you internalize the process of simultaneously evaluating a book's quality, utility, and complexity. We will introduce a blank version of the chart here, to capture the process in its entirety. Then, in each chapter, we will model how we consider different aspects of the evaluation process, which appear in separate portions of the overall template. As we review each step in the selection process, we will model our decision-making process.

Figure 2.2 is a blank version of the *Quality, Utility, and Complexity Chart*. This chart includes placeholders for notes about: (1) what professional reviewers have to say about the book; (2) aspects of the book's quality and the relationship between a consideration of quality and a consideration of complexity; (3) potential classroom uses for the book; (4) the appeal that the book may hold for the readers in your classroom; and (5) available quantitative measures of complexity. In this chapter, we will provide guidance for completing the sections of the chart that focus on reviews of the book and the quality of the text and illustration.

Figure 2.2 The Quality, Utility, and Complexity Chart Template

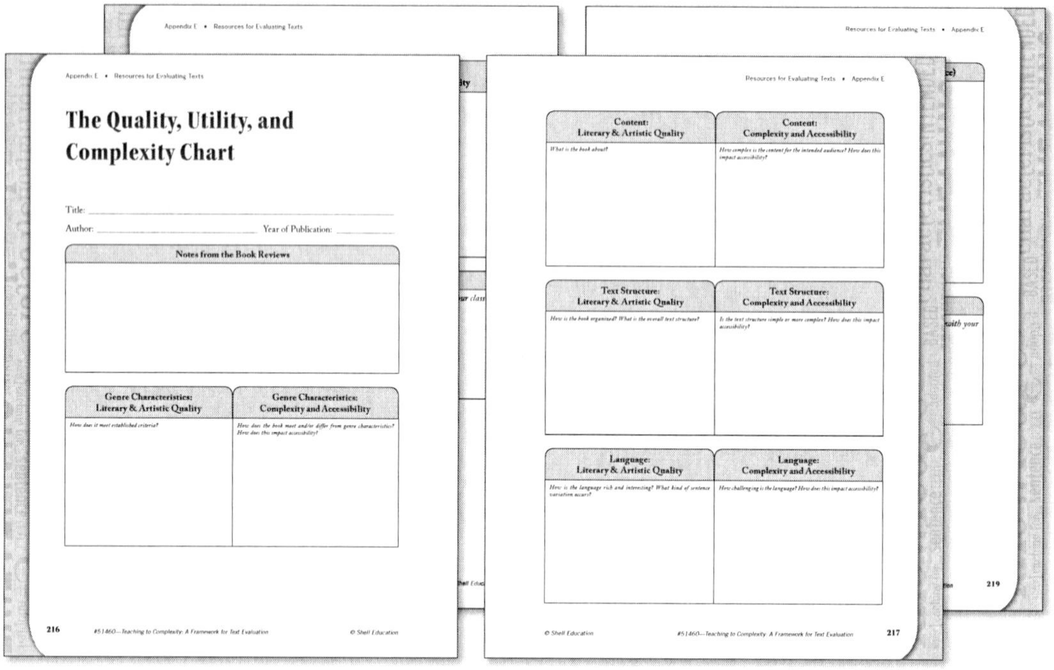

For the rest of this chapter, we will share some general practices for evaluating books for classroom use, and then walk you through, genre by genre, the particular qualities that are important to each. We will start by outlining a process for identifying books that seem appropriate, based on recommendations by others and your own sense of the text, publisher's criteria, etc., and give you a robust process for evaluating the book for its quality. We will also take a closer look at how to evaluate texts in the framework of genre characteristics.

Where to Begin: Finding and Considering Books

Where do *you* begin when you have to find books for your classroom? Do you have a set process that you follow for finding and locating books? A go-to teacher or media specialist colleague who always has something great to share? In so many ways, it is easier than ever to find and locate books because so many are published each year and so many resources exist to help identify and review children's and young adult book titles online. But that range of resources and the number of books published is also what makes it overwhelming.

Finding and locating curriculum materials may feel for some teachers like an added layer of responsibility that there isn't enough time for during the school day. Finding the right texts for one's students and curriculum standards indeed can be very time-consuming. But the time invested has tremendous payoff in many different ways. The wide range of topics covered by high-quality children's books allows us to locate appropriate and engaging books for the range of students in our classrooms. Ideally, the Common Core State Standards allow teachers in different states all over the country to support one another by positioning them as curators who share great ideas for teaching with selected texts and text sets at particular grade levels. The portability of the standards makes it even easier to "borrow" from one another. When teachers share which texts work well for different topics and units of study, other teachers can feel more empowered to make their own decisions.

In our first book, *Teaching with Text Sets*, we outlined some of the resources that we used to find and locate books. That list of resources again has been provided in Appendix B at the back of this book. We always recommend working as closely as possible with the school media specialist, if one is fortunate enough to have one, and one's local public librarians. They are experts at keeping abreast of new titles, and are always looking to grow their collection to meet the needs of the school and local community. Including a school librarian in your team's curriculum planning can help you find possible texts to consider more quickly, so that as a teaching team, you can spend more of your time thinking about how to use texts in the classroom, rather than which texts to use.

Before we go on, we also want to talk for a moment about libraries. Both of us have been lucky enough to spend most of our teaching time in public schools that had school libraries, some more robust than others, some staffed by a certified school librarian, others by aides. Now more than ever, a school library is not a guarantee. We also live in different states with different approaches to libraries. In Massachusetts, where Erika lives, there are incredible networks of libraries and a tightly-organized system for sharing books throughout those networks and the state as a whole. Within a few days to a week, she has access to almost any book she is interested in reading, without the burden of having to buy a book before considering it for classroom use. Some of you are lucky enough to live in a state with such a system. New Hampshire, where Mary Ann lives, is without such a network. Each town or city has its own separate library system, and while interlibrary loan exists regionally as a possibility, it is not as simple, quick, or plentiful as the Massachusetts systems. Mary Ann pays to belong to a larger library nearby, in order to benefit from its larger collection and complement what is available in her small town library. Some teachers may be in a similar situation. We understand that access to libraries makes a difference for teachers and are reminded of it all the time by the teachers with whom we work. Because of the uneven availability of public library systems, it becomes that much more important to support and advocate for a robust school library onsite that you can use and draw from in your planning, and for you to work with your school or district librarians to develop connections that provide resources for the key topics of study at your grade level.

What Book Reviews Tell You

Whether you work with your school librarian, identify books by walking the library stacks, or research books online, ultimately, you and your team members have to decide whether or not you think a book is good for whatever instructional purposes you are considering it for. To begin this evaluation, we recommend that you read a range of book reviews before reading the actual book. There are many professional bodies that review books for children and young adults, such as *School Library Journal* and *The Horn Book Magazine*. If your school does not subscribe to these print journals, digital versions of their book reviews are available through commonly-purchased databases made available through school and public library systems. Many are available for free on their websites as well. Furthermore, you can get a free username and password to Follett Library Resources Titlewave, which has a searchable database of full-text reviews for in-print children's and young adult books. Recently, Follett added "curriculum tags" to their book entries to help librarians and teachers identify books by content for curriculum, as well as different text structures, such as "compare and contrast" or "cause and effect." Details for all of these review sites are included in Appendix A of this book.

Regardless of how you find the reviews, they are really valuable to read. Because book reviews are short—a mere paragraph—reading them is not time-consuming. By reading a few at once, you begin to get a sense of the ways that other people have responded to the book. What do the reviewers generally agree on? What age ranges do they recommend it for? How do those ages differ from one another? Do the ages match the age range of students in your class? Are most of the reviews negative? If so, you may not want to bother reading it.

One disclaimer we like to make: there are books that get terrible reviews, but that the teacher knows some students are going to love. While we will talk more about instructional purposes later in this book, we want to say early on that even the worst-reviewed books can deserve space on the shelf of your classroom library, as for some readers they will be exciting and engaging.

Book reviews also offer a general introduction to evaluating books for children and young adults. By reading book reviews regularly, you begin to internalize the considerations of quality that cross genres, and get comfortable with the language used for talking about books for young people.

For instance, if we read the following book reviews of *Parrots Over Puerto Rico* (2013), a nonfiction picture book written by Susan Roth and Cindy Trumbore and illustrated by Susan Roth, what do we learn about the book and its potential for classroom consideration?

Horn Book (January/February 2014)

This gorgeously illustrated history of the critically endangered Puerto Rican parrot, along with the settlement and development of Puerto Rico, underscores the environmental consequences of human populations on indigenous animal species. The beautiful green and blue parrots witness early human settlement on the island, then suffer a decline in numbers over centuries of human population growth, colonization, and wars; invasive species that compete for resources; and natural disasters. The parrots were down to a population of only 13 in 1975; conservation efforts, located first in the El Yunque rainforest and then spread out to other locations across the island, have increased parrot numbers to several hundred. With stunning paper-and-fabric artwork on each spread, the book is laid out vertically to best give a sense of height. Ruffly feathered parrots, colorfully clothed people, and a series of Puerto Rican landmarks are located within dense, intricate illustrations in which layer upon layer of branches, leaves, ferns, and other greenery capture the lushness of the landscapes. An afterword includes additional details about conservation efforts, several color photographs of the parrots and the people working to save them, and a timeline of historical and environmental events in Puerto Rico.

Parrots Over Puerto Rico (2013)

—Danielle J. Ford *Horn Book* Review. January/February 2014. Copyright 2014.

School Library Journal (October 1, 2013)

Gr 3–6: Before humans arrived on the island, parrots numbered in the hundreds of thousands. By 1967, only 24 birds remained. Since then, scientists in the Puerto Rican Parrot Recovery Program (PRPRP) have established aviaries to raise the birds in captivity and release them in the wild. Using a vertical page orientation, Roth has plenty of space for detailed collages that depict the parrots' lives and struggles above human activities that have altered the island's ecosystem over the centuries. Tainos, Spanish explorers and settlers, African slaves, and others hunted parrots for food, cut down nesting places, and introduced animals that ate their eggs. After the United States took control, deforestation continued. Some military history and political questions such as the debate about Puerto Rico's commonwealth status slow the narrative. When the focus shifts to the strategies, setbacks, and successes of the PRPRP, the story soars. From constructing nesting boxes to training captive-bred birds how to avoid hawks, the program is slowly rebuilding the parrot population. After the main story, several pages of photos accompany further explanations of the group's work. In addition to their list of sources, the authors supply a detailed time line of events. Like this team's *The Mangrove Tree* (Lee and Low 2011), this title offers an engaging and hopeful look at environmental restoration.

—Kathy Piehl, Minnesota State University, Mankato (c) Copyright 2013. Library Journals LLC, a wholly owned subsidiary of Media Source, Inc. No redistribution permitted.

Reading these reviews, we marvel at all of the different possibilities this picture book presents for classroom work and all of the information it shares with readers. In terms of content, we know that by reading this book we can learn about the natural and human history of Puerto Rico and the many ways in which each impacted the other, as well as issues related to deforestation, conservation, and public policy. We learn about the birds themselves and their rainforest habitat. We know that the book contains rich language, including the literary elements of repetition and onomatopoeia. The unique ripped paper and fabric collage illustrations and the vertical book format contribute to the reader's understanding of the Puerto Rican parrot and its habitat. Finally, we learn that there is additional back matter that includes photographs, a timeline, resources, and an afterword.

Across the reviews, we can see that the reviewers are essentially focusing on the same strengths of the book, yet both focusing on different details. Through this combined portrait of the book, we can be confident that this is a book worth reading for a range of explorations in science, social studies, and language arts—from an exploration of animals and their habitats, to conservation and public policy, and as a mentor text for student research and writing. *Parrots Over Puerto Rico* was awarded the American Library Association's prestigious Sibert Medal for Nonfiction in 2014, so the reviewers were not alone in their praises. (For more in-depth teaching ideas for this book, see our Classroom Bookshelf blog entry at http://classroombookshelf.blogspot.com.)

Locating the Books

To actually get your hands on the books you are considering as teaching tools, you might use a variety of approaches. We usually start by using online databases (see Appendix D for recommended sites) as search tools, then we read the reviews of books that seem like good possibilities, and finally we use our local libraries and interlibrary loan systems to obtain the books so we can review them ourselves. But depending on your circumstances, the time you have available to you for planning, and your access to interlibrary loan systems, you may also begin your search with a trip to your school or local library. Perhaps you are consulting with the librarian or browsing the shelves to locate titles for potential use in your unit of study. Then, when you know what is readily available to you, you can use published reviews of the text (if they are available) in combination with your own evaluation of the book's quality.

The Book Itself: What the Book Tells You

Book Format

Whether you begin by reading a review, or with book in hand, one of the first things that you will consider is the format of the book. Reviewers will usually describe the book's format in a review if this is your starting point. If you are browsing the book before seeking a review, you can quickly assess the book's format by its physical appearance. Children's and Young Adult books generally fall into several format categories:

- picture book
- beginning reader
- chapter book
- graphic fiction or nonfiction

Picture Book: A picture book is defined as a book in which the illustrations and the text carry equal weight in conveying the content/meaning of the book. Traditionally, books in this format are 32 pages long and larger in size, to give full due to the art they contain. The number of pages in the book is less important, however, than the role that is played by the illustrations. Sometimes when people think about picture books, they think this format is less sophisticated and intended for young children. Or they think of picture books as storybooks, containing a fictional narrative. These are common misconceptions. Recently, there has been a proliferation of wonderful nonfiction picture books appropriate for audiences of all ages as well as sophisticated 'storybooks' for more mature audiences. We particularly appreciate the picture book format for use in reading aloud to students across grade levels.

Beginning Reader: Also known as leveled readers, the beginning reader book is probably the most clearly defined of the formats we discuss here. Books in this format have been specifically crafted to meet the needs of readers with limited sight word vocabularies and decoding skills. As such, they employ a limited range of vocabulary words or decodable text. Books in this format can vary in size, but are frequently organized in short chapters or sections (approximating books that young readers consider to be more "adult" in format).

Chapter Book: A chapter book is a book in which the content has been organized into sections or chapters to structure the lengthier text for readers. Novels are usually in this format, but so are many works of nonfiction. Chapter books are available for readers in a wide age range.

Graphic Fiction or Nonfiction: In recent years, there has been an explosion of interest in the format of the graphic novel. Think of comic books, where the images play out in a sequence of frames and the text appears in speech bubbles. The shifting of the term from graphic novel to graphic fiction and graphic nonfiction recognizes that nonfiction is available in this format, too. Because books in this format are highly visual, they appeal to a range of readers, including readers who can benefit from the comprehension support provided by the illustrations. But these books are anything but simple to read—in graphic fiction and nonfiction for the middle grades and young adults, the visual subtext is quite complex.

The Verso Page

When one picks up a book for children or young adults, one can quickly assess the format of the book, but there is also other information that can be identified before reading it. Much of this information is revealed on the verso page. The Latin origin of the word refers to the page to the left of the recto (right page), which serves as the title page. The recto would be read first, the verso second. Every book has a verso page, which is historically across from the title page, although now can sometimes appear on the last page of the book instead.

One of the most useful details the verso page can tell you is the genre of a book. Of course, if you grab a book at the library or research the book in advance, you will have been told the genre, either by its location in the stacks or the information in your resources. But if you pick up a book at a book fair or library sale, identifying genre at first glance can get tricky. Authors, illustrators, and book packagers are getting ever more creative in their work, with new formats, such as graphic fiction and nonfiction, continuing to emerge, and nonfiction picture story books being published in increasing numbers. Sometimes you really *can't* judge a book by its cover.

Without reading the book, you can get an initial designation on the genre by seeing the Cataloguing-in-Publication (CIP) information provided by the Library of Congress. Before a book is published, the publisher sends information to the Library of Congress; it creates the CIP and sends it back to the publisher. The CIP provides for easy and consistent classification in libraries.

What does the CIP information tell you? Here are three examples:

- In the picture book *In the Wild* (2010), written by David Elliott and illustrated by Holly Meade, the CIP says :"[1. Animals, Juvenile poetry; 2. Children's poetry, America.]." The CIP lets you know that the genre is poetry and that it is a book about animals.

- The CIP for the early reader novel *Mr. and Mrs. Bunny Detectives Extraordinaire* (2012), written by Polly Horvath and illustrated by Sophie Blackall, reads "[1. Human-animal communication, Fiction; 2. Kidnapping, Fiction; 3. Rabbits, Fiction; 4. Foxes, Fiction; 5. Marmots, Fiction; 6. Hippies, Fiction; 7. Hornby Island (B.C. Island), Fiction; 8. Mystery and detective stories]." In this case, the CIP tells us not only that humans and animals are characters in the story, the particular types of humans and animals, and that it is set in some part on Hornby Island in British Columbia, but that the story is fiction, and a particular genre of fiction—the detective story.

- Finally, for the picture book *A Splash of Red: the Life and Art of Horace Pippin*, written by Jen Bryant and illustrated by Melissa Sweet, the CIP reads "[1. Pippin, Horace, 1888-1946, Juvenile literature; 2. African American painters, Biography, Juvenile literature; 3. Painters, United States, Biography, Juvenile literature]." This lets us know that this is a biography of the African American painter Horace Pippin, who lived in the 19th and early 20th century. The designation "juvenile literature" lets us know that it is nonfiction, as does the designation of the particular genre of nonfiction, biography. We don't use the term juvenile much anymore, and it may feel antiquated to you, but it is an essential part of the cataloguing world.

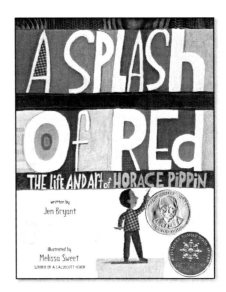

The verso page also provides the ISBN number, which stands for the International Standard Book Number. A book will have a different ISBN for different versions: library binding, trade binding (for book stores), hardcover, paperback, and audio. You will often need an ISBN when ordering a book. Make sure you have the correct ISBN number, or you may wind up with an audio book when you wanted a paperback.

If a book is illustrated, the verso page may also tell you what materials were used. For instance, *A Splash of Red's* verso page explains that illustrator Melissa Sweet used "watercolor, gouache, and mixed media." The verso page in *Mr. and Mrs. Bunny Detectives Extraordinaire* reveals that the illustrations were "rendered in ink," while *In the Wild's* reveals that the illustrations are "woodblock prints and watercolor." If a book uses photographs from another source, those photo credits are also often, but not always, listed on the verso page.

If the author or illustrator had someone check the manuscript for accuracy, a "thank you" may be listed as an additional piece of information on the verso page. This is helpful information to know if you are considering a piece of researched nonfiction, since you would want to know it was vetted by outside authorities for accuracy. Such an acknowledgement may also appear in an author's or illustrator's note. Finally, the verso page also gives the publisher's name and address.

Now that you've learned about what the book reviews, book format, and verso page can tell you about a book, it's time to dive into general evaluation criteria that you yourself can apply to any children's or young adult book.

Evaluating Books for Quality

General Criteria

Once you have decided a book seems good enough or interesting enough to read and evaluate further, what is it that you pay attention to *while you read*? How do you adopt the mindset of a book reviewer? The goal is to use aesthetic criteria about an art form in a very purposeful context. As an educator who is always thinking about his or her students as readers, your lens is threefold. You should be thinking about the following:

- literary and artistic value of the book as an art form
- the utility of the book as a teaching tool
- the appropriateness of the book for the student reader(s) the teacher has in mind

This is one of the key pivot points in the work that we do with teachers in our college classes. We know educators can converse about children's and young adult literature in the robust way that literary critics and book reviewers do, but then do something entirely different with the conversation: consider the child or teen reader and the many roles the book could play in the classroom.

Over the years, we've developed a shorthand for this work, drawn from an article we read in *The Horn Book Magazine* (Stevenson 2006). In the article, Deborah Stevenson argues that critics of children's literature are "moving away from the notion of a unified, abstract 'good' that all books are trying to achieve for all readers. Now we tend to consider 'good' short for 'good *for*,' to recognize that the word can have a vast range of specific meanings" (2006, 513). Stevenson advocates that reviewers consider the quality of any single book within the context of the genre of literature in which it was written and the purpose that the author had in mind. It is unrealistic to think you can take a stack of very different books in different genres with different purposes and decide that one is better than the others. They are all different.

Instead, Stevenson suggests, you have to "learn reading by reading" (2006, 514) and use the "map of literature" that already exists in your head, based on all the books you have already read. Using knowledge from past reading experiences, evaluation criteria for the literary merits of a book, and your understanding of what the book is trying to do (its purpose, rooted in its genre), you make your best judgment about every new book you read. Stevenson was writing to children's and young adult librarians focusing on collection development. We have appropriated her phrase "good for" and use it as a lens for making selections for the

---

Resources for Evaluating Text

Horning, Kathleen. *From Cover to Cover: Evaluating and Reviewing Children's Books.* New York: Harper Collins, 2010.

Kiefer, Barbara. *Charlotte Huck's Children's Literature. 10th Edition.* Boston: McGraw Hill Higher Education, 2010.

Lukkens, Rebecca J. *A Critical Handbook of Children's Literature. 9th edition.* Boston: Pearson, 2012.

The Horn Book
http://www.hbook.com

School Library Journal
http://www.slj.com

Cooperative Center for Children's Books
http://ccbc.education.wisc.edu

classroom. We ask ourselves, "is this book good?" and "what is it good for?" For the rest of this chapter, we are going to talk about what might make a book "good" for consideration. In chapter three, we'll talk about what it might be "good for" in the classroom.

When evaluating a text, we consider the following general categories: (Horning 2010; Kiefer 2010; Lukens 2012):

- Genre characteristics
- Content
- Text structure
- Language
- Visuals: Illustrations and book design
- Appeal

Of course, considering these categories is a recursive process. We separate these elements of a text, but recognize that they are also interconnected. The visuals are a part of the text structure in a picture book or graphic book; language helps to shape the sense of genre. When we want to deeply consider how a book operates as a whole, we first have to understand how the separate components operate.

To best introduce these categories, we will describe the criteria we consider generally for any text within each category. Following this overview, we dive into genre-specific iterations of the categories and their evaluation criteria, to ground one in the ways in which each separate element works collectively within the different genres.

Genre Characteristics

- How does it meet established criteria?

Genre is the largest category in which we can classify a work. When we refer to genre, we reference the traditional genres of realistic fiction, fantasy and science fiction, historical fiction, poetry, as well as nonfiction. Each of these genres has their own subgenres as well. These will be discussed in greater detail in each of the genre sections. Helping students develop a sense of genre identification is important. Fine-tuning your own understanding of the characteristics of each genre helps you not only teach students those understandings, but helps you select strong examples of these genres for whole-class, small-group, and individual reading experiences, which reinforces those understandings even further.

Content

- What is the book about?

The content of children's and young adult books is as wide and expansive as the human experience. It is impossible to cover the range of what's available in terms of children's and young adult books, but there are important considerations regarding content. Identifying the content helps teachers make connections between national, state, and local standards and the curriculum they develop; and make connections across standards if they are interested in doing interdisciplinary work. For example, selecting books to use in language arts that provide a content match for a social studies unit, or exploring books in science class that help to model and reinforce what the class is learning about nonfiction in language arts. If a book requires research, it is important to know that the author has done that research in order to best craft a character with a particular ethnic background or physical condition, convey information about cutting-edge research, or bring the past to life through setting. We think it is really important to talk about the research process authors and illustrators use with your students. The research they conduct can potentially serve as some of the most meaningful examples of the purpose and process of research. Those who write in developmentally appropriate ways for children and young adults are best suited to model these practices in ways that students can understand.

Text Structure

There are many ways to organize and structure texts. Narrative texts often provide a clear arc that children are pretty familiar with by the end of their primary grade years. However, as they get older, the books they read become more complex, with flashbacks, alternating character narrations, or chapters that alternate first, second, and/or third person narration. Nonfiction presents a whole other range of possible structures that impact how the reader receives information. It is important to be able to identify the text structures an author uses to organize a book, in order to teach those text structures to students. Once students have an understanding of text structures through a wide range of reading and writing experiences, they are more likely to use a range of structures in their own writing and recognize when certain text structures are more appropriate than others. If they don't read with attention to structure, it becomes more difficult to write with attention to structure.

- How is the text organized?
- What is the overall text structure?

Language

It is easy to relegate a discussion of the language of a book to the college English classroom where one discusses literary elements for the fun of it. In truth, we do think it is great fun to analyze and talk about the language of texts. But in the context of selecting books for children and young adults to read, it is also incredibly purposeful. When reading a book, we consider how the author reaches his or her readers in developmentally appropriate ways, specifically, the vocabulary words used and how they are contextualized for readers. We consider the ways in which similes and metaphors support theme and/or characterization in fiction and poetry, and convey conceptual understanding in nonfiction. Language and dialogue establish a sense of characterization in fiction, while direct quotes in nonfiction also establish the character of a subject. We examine sentence length, the ways in which books for younger readers or beginning readers use consistently short sentences or follow a pattern the reader can recognize and anticipate, and the ways in

- How is the language rich and interesting?
- What kind of sentence variation occurs?

which books for older readers vary sentences for stylistic purposes. Identifying the literary elements of language in a text can support students in accessing the text. As developing writers and speakers, students benefit from immersion in rich language experiences, with language modeled in written text as well as the spoken word.

Visuals: Illustrations and Book Design

More and more, we have come to expect high visual appeal in the texts that we encounter. This visual emphasis can probably be attributed to several factors: new technologies that make the creation and reproduction of images easier and more affordable; expectations set by the highly visual nature of the Internet, the appeal of video games, and the interfaces of our portable electronic devices; and the theory of universal design that recognizes how visual cues and reinforcement support a variety of learners. The role of visuals in text varies across genres, playing the strongest role in meaning-making in the picture book (fiction and nonfiction) and graphic fiction and nonfiction. Small illustrations (called spot art) can also enhance the experience of a novel or a collection of poetry. Longer works of nonfiction may incorporate photographs (archival or created to explicate the content of the book), reproductions of primary source documents, charts, diagrams, maps, and/or infographics (highly visual and/or stylized representations of information). When evaluating the visual aspect of the text, we need to consider the aesthetic appeal of the visuals and how they engage and hold the interest of a student reader as well as the relationship between the content of the text and the visual, or how the visuals serve a clear purpose in the text. Do the visuals enhance the reader's understanding of the text?

- How do the visuals engage the reader?
- How do they enhance the content?
- How does the book design reinforce the content?

We also consider the design of the book. By this, we mean the size, layout, and any special features of the book's construction. For example, the overall design of both Lynn Curlee's nonfiction picture book *Skyscraper* (2007) and Deborah Hopkinson and James Ransome's *Sky Boys* (2006) is tall and thin, like the skyscrapers themselves. Layout refers to the arrangement of text and illustration on the pages of the book. Picture books often incorporate double-page spreads with an image that spans two pages. The text accompanying the illustrations might be found anywhere on either of the two pages, or it, too may span both pages. A work of nonfiction may have visuals, such as photographs, diagrams, or maps carefully placed throughout the text, with consideration to how their placement helps to 'chunk' the text for the reader. Pop-ups, lift-the-flaps, and fold-out pages are all special aspects of a book's construction, designed to increase reader interactivity.

Appeal

> ■ How will it appeal to the particularities and preferences of the readers in one's class?

Talking about appeal is a slippery slope, isn't it? All of us have our own preferences for particular genres and storylines, topics, and time periods. For example, Erika loves fantasy fiction, while Mary Ann adores historical fiction. No one book will appeal to all of your students in the exact same way. But knowing and understanding one's students and the developmental range that they encompass allows the teacher to gain an understanding of their likes and dislikes each year. It has been said that "[c]hildren's books are books that have the child's eye at the center" (Kiefer 2010, 7). What books represent the worldview and perspectives of the children and young adults with whom the teacher works? What are common developmental milestones that suggest certain characteristics of students that the teacher can look for when selecting books? Ultimately, it's the teacher who works with them every day, and understands the group dynamics that shift and develop over the course of the year, the combination of personalities that exist in each class, and the ways books will appeal to most, some, or few of them. Cultivating a love of reading is dependent on offering enough consistent choices that appeal to the whole class, small group, and individual students. Teaching is always a delicate balancing act between covering what you must cover and fostering a love of learning and reading in individuals. Text selection mirrors that balancing act between coverage and cultivation; we strive to fuse the two as much as possible.

Figure 2.3 summarizes the general text evaluation considerations we have described. This document can also be found in Appendix E.

Figure 2.3 General Text Evaluation Considerations for Quality Guide

General Text Evaluation Considerations for Quality	Ask yourself:
Genre Characteristics	■ How does it meet established criteria?
Content	■ What is it about?
Text Structure	■ How is the text organized? ■ What is the overall text structure?
Language	■ How is the language rich and interesting? ■ What kind of sentence variation occurs?
Visuals: Illustration and Book Design	■ How do the visuals engage the reader? ■ How do they enhance the content? ■ How does the book design reinforce the content?
Appeal	■ How will it appeal to the particularities and preferences of the readers in one's class?

Genre-Specific Criteria

Contemporary Realistic Fiction

A work of realistic fiction narrates a story set in present times, describing the life events of fictional characters. By definition, everything that happens in a work of contemporary realistic fiction *could* happen in the world in which we live. Often featuring young protagonists grappling with issues and problems similar to those the target audience encounters, this genre has strong appeal to young readers. Ideally, reading in this genre offers students the opportunity to reflect more deeply on their own experiences and/or the opportunity to take on the perspective of someone whose circumstances may be very different than their own. One can find examples of this genre across formats, including picture books, beginning readers, chapter books, graphic fiction, and novels. Teaching with contemporary realistic fiction allows students the opportunity to explore current issues and dilemmas, promoting critical-thinking skills by developing students' abilities to consider multiple perspectives and universal themes in the human experience.

> **Resources for Evaluating Contemporary Realistic Fiction**
>
> If you are interested in exploring this genre more fully, and learning more about ways of teaching with contemporary realistic fiction, we recommend the following resources:
>
> NCTE: Anti-Censorship Center
> http://www.ncte.org/action/anti-censorship
>
> Cooperative Children's Book Center: Multicultural Literature
> http://ccbc.education.wisc.edu/books/multicultural.asp
>
> American Library Association: Schneider Family Book Award
> http://www.ala.org/awardsgrants/schneider-family-book-award

Genre Characteristics: When evaluating a work of contemporary realistic fiction, we consider the elements of literature that you may remember discussing in your high school or college English classes. We consider the *plot* of the book—are the events plausible? What is the main conflict and how is it resolved? We think about the *characters* in the book. Are they authentic to the child experience? Do the characters grow, develop, learn and/or change over the course of the story? We also think about the *setting* of the story. Can readers fully imagine the setting from the level of description that is provided? Is the imagined or real setting a logical match with the characters and events?

Finally, we think about the point of view of the story—the narration of the story. Who is telling the story and whose story is being told? A story may even have multiple narrators, representing different perspectives on the events unfolding. Subgenres of contemporary realistic fiction include mystery, romance, and in young adult literature, the coming-of-age novel, which features a young adult grappling with issues related to understanding his or her identity.

When evaluating the genre, first ask yourself:

- Are the events, conflict, and resolution of the book plausible, engaging and meaningful?

- Will young readers relate to the characters of the book? Do the characters develop over the course of the story?
- Is the setting of the story fully imagined and does it serve to enhance the characters and events?
- Who narrates the story? Whose story is being told and how?

Content: Popular content includes stories about sports, animals, survival, school, and mystery and humorous stories. Stories often explore larger themes such as family, relationships, and growing up, as well as considering problems that humans face in society. Contemporary realistic fiction is a highly challenged/censored genre. Objections to books that fit this genre category are usually connected to how realistic the book actually is. There are differing opinions in our society as to what content is appropriate for children and young adults, and what is not. Ideally violence, 'bad' language, and complex issues, when included, are not included gratuitously. Fiction can offer our students a safe forum to talk about difficult issues and circumstances—while the characters of the story are not real, the issues can be. In evaluating the content, we consider the overall theme of the book, determining whether it is a theme worthy of spending classroom time thinking about and discussing. We also consider how the story presents life experiences—whose perspective is represented in the story? This involves a consideration of how cultural experiences, perspectives, religion, gender, race, social class, and sexuality are portrayed in the story. We want to be sure that stereotyping is avoided and that if writing about a culture, experience, or perspective other than his or her own the author has taken steps to ensure authentic representation.

When evaluating the content of the genre, ask yourself:

- Does the theme of the story prompt critical thinking/ reflection on the realities of life in our world?
- Is the content developmentally appropriate for the age of the students with whom we work?
- Does the theme/content expand students' worldviews by offering them new perspectives on daily life?
- Does the book include an authentic and multifaceted representation of diversity in our society?

Text Structure: Most works of contemporary realistic fiction employ the text structure of a sequential narrative arc. Events are relayed in a time sequence; this is a structure that most students find very familiar. In works meant for older audiences with a more sophisticated understanding of the passage of time, authors may begin to include techniques such as flashbacks or shifts in time, sometimes associated with changes in narrators.

When evaluating the text structure of the genre, ask yourself:

- Does the story follow a sequential narrative arc, or are shifts in time incorporated into the narrative arc?
- Are there changes in point of view or narration that are linked with shifts in time sequence?

Language: Each author brings a unique style to his or her composing process and different readers may prefer different writing styles. At a basic level, style involves word choice and arrangement, but this literal definition belies the abstract nature of style. We can consider the formality of the grammar, the familiarity of the vocabulary used, and even the form of the writing. In recent years there has been a proliferation of contemporary realistic fiction that is written in the form of free verse poetry, a blending of the genres. When evaluating fiction, we consider how the writing style helps to convey a sense of who the characters are and what they are dealing with. Does the author use dialogue to reveal characters' personalities? Are events fully realized in their settings with descriptive passages that are rich with detail and sensory images? How does the writing style work to make the story feel 'real'; to make the characters come alive for readers; or to reinforce the theme and/or conflict of the story?

When evaluating the language of the genre, ask yourself:

- Does the "feel" of the writing, or the writing style, help to convey a sense of the plot, characters, setting, and themes of the book?
- Will the readers in my classroom (or a particular reader) find this writing style engaging?

Visuals (Illustrations and Design): In a picture book or work of graphic fiction, the illustrations by definition play an equal role in conveying the progression of the plot, character development, and in fully realizing the setting. The role of the illustrations in chapter books may be more subtle; spot illustrations illuminate key moments in the text, while their scarcity prompts readers to infer and visualize moments of the narration that have not been illustrated.

When evaluating the illustrations and design, ask yourself:

- How do the illustrations enhance the reader's understanding of the story that is being told?

Figure 2.4 summarizes the text evaluation considerations for contemporary realistic fiction that we have described. This document can also be found in Appendix E.

Figure 2.4 Contemporary Realistic Fiction Text Evaluation Considerations for Quality Guide

Text Evaluation Considerations for Quality	Ask Yourself...
Genre Characteristics	■ Are the events, conflict, and resolution of the book plausible, engaging and meaningful? ■ Will young readers relate to the characters of the book? Do the characters develop over the course of the story? ■ Is the setting of the story fully imagined and does it serve to enhance the characters and events? ■ Who narrates the story? Whose story is being told and how?
Content	■ Does the theme of the story prompt critical thinking/ reflection on the realities of life in our world? ■ Is the content developmentally appropriate for the age of the students with whom we work? ■ Does the theme/content expand students' worldviews by offering them new perspectives on daily life? ■ Does the book include an authentic and multifaceted representation of diversity in our society?
Text Structure	■ Does the story follow a sequential narrative arc, or are shifts in time incorporated into the narrative arc? ■ Are there changes in point of view or narration that are linked with shifts in time sequence?
Language	■ Does the 'feel' of the writing, or the writing style, help to convey a sense of the plot, characters, setting, and themes of the book? ■ Will the readers in my classroom (or a particular reader) find this writing style engaging?
Visuals: Illustration and Design	■ How do the illustrations enhance the reader's understanding of the story that is being told?

Traditional Literature

The label "traditional literature" begs the question: "Whose tradition?" In its broadest definition—the world's! Traditional literature can embody ancient myths; Pourquoi Stories and creation tales; or stories from the Bible, the Koran, and other sacred texts from past cultures and indigenous people around the world. Traditional literature also includes stories that originated in the oral tradition and at some point got written down, such as fables, folktales, fairy tales, legends, and tall tales. Newer works modeled on traditional forms are often considered traditional literature, such as the early 19th century works of Hans Christian Andersen in Denmark and Washington Irving in the United States, each striving to create new texts in the form and mood of tales like those collected and revised by the Brothers Grimm. Retellings of myths, legends, folk tales, and fairy tales have long been a staple in picture books. But children's and young adult literature is enjoying a renaissance of retellings of traditional tales in novel form as well, including graphic fiction. Teaching with traditional literature provides students of all ages with the opportunity to explore cultures and belief systems, ponder moral questions that people have been asking for thousands of years, and compare and contrast elements of the same story over a range of cultures, settings, time periods, and illustrative styles.

> **Resources for Evaluating Traditional Literature**
>
> If you are interested in exploring the genre more fully, and learning more about ways of teaching with traditional literature, we recommend the following resources:
>
> Sur La Lune Webpage
>   http://www.surlalunefairytales.com
>
> The US Library of Congress: The American Folklife Center
>   http://www.loc.gov/folklife/
>
> Maria Tatar, Harvard University's Chair of Folklore & Mythology
>   http://people.fas.harvard.edu/~tatar/Maria_Tatar/About_Me.html

Genre Characteristics: When reading traditional literature it is important to identify whether the story is an authentic retelling or conveying of sacred beliefs, such as creation tales from past cultures or indigenous people today, or literary and fantastical histories from the past, such as *The Odyssey* or *Beowulf*. These texts can and should be explored in the context of other creation stories or histories. But they also have to be read with a respect for and understanding of the people from whose culture the story originates. Looking for identifying characteristics, including whether it was part of a long oral tradition or sacred storytelling tradition helps you to understand the context for the story, as well as its attributes. Most likely the story explains a phenomenon, like the creation of the earth, or articulates characteristics valued and discouraged by the culture, or offers models for behavior or serves as a cautionary tale. Folktales and fairy tales share similar attributes to one another, as they are primarily stories that came from an oral tradition and were written down at some point, most likely during the last five hundred years after the introduction of the Gutenberg printing press in Europe. A range of recurring motifs exist in all of these tales, such as the wicked stepmother, the use of the number three, and magical objects.

When evaluating the genre, first ask yourself:

- What type of traditional literature is this? Is it a myth, legend, history, folktale, fairy tale, tall tale, or fable?

Content: If you are looking for traditional literature in your school or local library, you may be surprised to discover that most books are shelved in the nonfiction section, not the fiction section. Why is that so? As we have pointed out, the content of most of these stories belongs to a culture, religion, or community from the past, and as such, represents prior or current belief systems of a group of people, as well as a reflection of some of the enduring understandings of the human experience. As a snapshot of beliefs and understandings, particularly sacred understandings, the books are considered nonfiction. Because of the many retellings of folktales and fairy tales in picture book, novel, and graphic novel format, one may also find variations on traditional literature in the fiction section of the library as well. The content of these stories, with a new setting and permutation of characters, will parallel a more widely known iteration of a particular tale, which may only become clear to you as you read the book. In all, the content of traditional literature varies widely, representing cultures and belief systems from across the continents over thousands of years. The origins of modern fantasy as a genre lie here.

When evaluating the content of traditional literature, ask yourself:

- How does this story explain a natural phenomenon, human behavior, or imagined history?
- How does this book fuse a particular traditional story within the context of our modern world?
- Does the book say when the story originated orally and/or when it was first written down?

Text Structure: Most traditional tales, because they are narratives, follow the typical narrative story arc that children grow quite familiar with at an early age. In novelized formats for older readers, a more sophisticated narrative may be presented, using flashbacks and alternate narration from different characters' perspectives. Traditional literature originating from indigenous cultures around the world may use the rhythms of the natural world as a part of the story structure.

When evaluating the text structure of traditional literature, ask yourself:

- Does this story follow the same narrative arc as other forms of the story? If not, how does it differ?
- Are there other structures at work that help frame the narrative structure of the story, such as the length of a day, season, month, or year?

Language: In addition to the general criteria about language, it is important to consider the specific vocabulary that traditional literature may contain, such as references to previous time periods and cultures outside those of the students. Such vocabulary may appear in dialogue between the various characters.

When evaluating the language of traditional literature, ask yourself:

- What vocabulary words represent the culture from which this story originates?
- How does the dialogue represent the culture from which the story originates or is set?

Visuals (Illustrations and Design): In the field of children's and young adult literature, a wide array of illustrative styles and media have been used to bring traditional tales to life. When evaluating the illustrations and book design of traditional literature, it is important to once again consider the relationship between the culture of origin and/or the setting of the story and the illustrations. Sometimes the illustrations use an art form or method that originated during the time or culture in which the story is set. Another important component to illustrating traditional literature is conveying the magical and fantastical elements of the story to readers.

When evaluating the illustrations and design of traditional literature, ask yourself:

- What media is used to illustrate this story? Is there any connection between it and the time or culture in which the story is set?
- How does the illustration convey the magical elements, if any, of the story?

Figure 2.5 summarizes the text evaluation considerations for traditional literature that we have described. This document can also be found in Appendix E.

Figure 2.5 Traditional Literature Text Evaluation Considerations for Quality Guide

Text Evaluation Considerations for Quality	Ask Yourself...
Genre Characteristics	■ What type of traditional literature is this? Is it a myth, legend, history, folktale, fairy tale, tall tale, or fable?
Content	■ How does this story explain a natural phenomenon, human behavior, or imagined history? ■ How does this book fuse a particular traditional story within the context of our modern world? ■ Does the book say when the story originated orally and/or when it was first written down?
Text Structure	■ Does this story follow the same narrative arc as other forms of the story? If not, how does it differ? ■ Are there other structures at work that help frame the narrative structure of the story, such as the length of a day, season, month, or year?
Language	■ What vocabulary words represent the culture from which this story originates? ■ How does the dialogue represent the culture from which the story originates or is set?
Visuals: Illustration and Design	■ What media is used to illustrate this story? Is there any connection between it and the time or culture in which the story is set? ■ How does the illustration convey the magical elements, if any, of the story?

Fantasy/Science Fiction

From classic series titles like C.S. Lewis's *The Lion, The Witch and the Wardrobe,* to the contemporary phenomenon of J.K. Rowling's *Harry Potter,* the genre of fantasy invites readers into a fictional world where the impossible is possible, tapping into children's natural abilities to imagine magical and fantastical possibilities. Fantasy, by definition, encompasses any story that includes events or aspects not known to be possible in the physical world as we know it. Books that are examples of this genre can be found across formats, including picture books, beginning readers, chapter books, novels, and graphic fiction. Following the worldwide acclaim for the Harry Potter series, there has been a proliferation of fantasy novels published for middle school and young adult audiences. Teaching with fantasy literature allows students to explore alternate realities, discuss universal experiences, and to foster their own creativity by stepping more deeply into the realms of the imagination.

Genre Characteristics: Fantasy titles may include suspense, horror, or a focus on the supernatural. A great variety of stories comprise the genre of fantasy with several identifiable subgenres:

- Young children frequently find works of *animal fantasy* (also called *anthropomorphic fantasy*) appealing. These stories feature talking animals and often blend animal and human behaviors.

- The classic work of fantasy by A.A. Milne with the beloved character, Winnie the Pooh, is an example of *toy and doll fantasy*, a subgenre that young children readily identify with as it mirrors the play they may engage in with their favorite toys.

- Fantasy novels often immerse the reader in imaginary worlds or alternatively, imbue characters who live in our world with magical powers. You may sometimes hear the term *high fantasy* used. This term usually refers to an elaborately constructed work of fantasy that explores conflict between forces of good and evil.

- In *time-shift fantasy* (also called *time-travel fantasy*), one or more characters are transported to another time period where they will interact with characters and events in the past or future.

- *Science fiction* is a form of fantasy writing that explores the potential of technology and science in our world and in worlds beyond our world. Closely related are the genres of *utopian* and *dystopian fiction*. These genres explore issues of social and political structures, imagining future worlds that are functional or dysfunctional.

- Blurring the line between contemporary realistic fiction and fantasy, is the subgenre of *magical realism*, which introduces some magical happenings or phenomena to an otherwise familiar physical world.

As with contemporary realistic fiction, when evaluating fantasy we consider the literary elements of plot, character, setting, and point of view. Since fantastical elements are involved in the story, the author must work hard to make the setting, events, and characters feel believable to the readers.

When evaluating the genre, first ask yourself:

- What subgenre of fantasy is this?

Resources for Evaluating Fantasy/Science Fiction

If you are interested in exploring the genre more fully, and learning more about teaching with fantasy literature and its subgenres, we recommend the following resources:

Cynthia Leitich Smith: Children's and YA Fantasy Novels http://www.cynthialeitichsmith.com/lit_resources/favorites/by_genre/fantasy.html

Marcus, Leonard S. 2009. *The Wand and the Word: Conversations with Writers of Fantasy.* Somerville, MA: Candlewick Press.

Mythopoeic Society http://www.mythsoc.org

National Public Radio: Children's Fantasy Lit in the Modern World http://www.npr.org/templates/story/story.php?storyId=5039319

- Are the events, conflict, and resolution of the book plausible, engaging, and meaningful?
- Will young readers relate to the characters of the book? Do the characters develop over the course of the story?
- Is the setting of the story fully imagined and does it serve to enhance the characters and events?
- Who narrates the story? Whose story is being told and how?
- Is there consistency in the imaginary world(s) that the author has created for the reader?

Content: Devotees of the fantasy genre claim that the power of the genre is its ability to prompt reflection on everyday life, while imagining alternatives and new possibilities. Reading works of fantasy often allows students to explore overarching themes such as good and evil, heroism, journeys, and changes. These themes can help students consider what kind of a person they would like to be and what kind of a world they would like to live in. Like contemporary realistic fiction, fantasy books can be the target of censorship efforts. The content of fantasy and its subgenres is wide-ranging. By encouraging students to identify familiar elements of fantasy stories such as heroes and villains, familiar plotlines, and motifs, such as magical powers, wishes, or transformations, you can help them to explore deeper meanings, themes, and patterns. Depending on the content of the story, fantasy may also provide an opportunity to engage students in social and political critique. Adolescent students reading Suzanne Collins's *Hunger Games* (2008) might be guided to consider the impact of broad discrepancies of resources across social classes. Students reading Tamora Pierce's novels with their strong female protagonists might question traditional gender stereotypes. Students can engage in debate about cloning research after reading *The House of the Scorpion* by Nancy Farmer (2002).

When evaluating the content of the genre, ask yourself:

- Does the theme of the story prompt critical thinking/reflection on the human experience?
- Is the content developmentally appropriate for the age of the students with whom we work?
- Does the content and/or theme of the story expand students' worldviews by offering them new perspectives on social and political structures?

Text Structure: Fantasy stories, such as contemporary realistic fiction and traditional literature, are usually narratives, a very familiar structure to students. Fantasies written for intermediate grades, middle grades, and young adult audiences, may include more complex narrative arcs, incorporating shifts in the timeline through flashbacks, glimpses into the future, or in the case of time-shift/time-travel fantasy, large leaps in time. Changes in narrators may also bring a disruption in the narrative timeline.

When evaluating the text structure of the genre, ask yourself:

- Does the story follow a sequential narrative arc or are shifts in time incorporated into the narrative arc?
- Are there changes in point of view or narration that are linked with shifts in time in the narrative arc?

Language: When evaluating the language in a work of fantasy, the general criteria for evaluation apply. The writing style should be aesthetically pleasing, clear and accessible to the reader, and well matched to the elements of the story, plot, characters, setting, and theme. In fantasy, however, we add an additional consideration. Elaborate fantasy worlds may require the reader to learn a whole new set of vocabulary terms that may or may not be easily matched to familiar structures and relationships. Writers of fantasy who introduce new vocabulary to populate and enact the world they are creating for readers, need to take care to contextualize and repeat new terminology in order not to overwhelm readers.

When evaluating the language of the genre, ask yourself:

- How does the language of the story contribute to constructing a believable, yet fantastical, narrative?
- Are new vocabulary terms associated with the fantasy elements in the story well-defined and contextualized for readers? Do readers encounter the terms frequently enough to internalize their meanings (to facilitate more fluent reading)?
- Does the feel of the writing, or the writing style, help to convey a sense of the plot, characters, setting, and themes of the book?
- Will the readers in my classroom (or a particular reader) will find this writing style engaging?

Visuals (Illustrations and Design): In works of fantasy, illustrations may play a strong role in supporting readers' visualization and engagement in the fantastical world or events created by the author. In picture book fantasy, they work hand in hand with the text to do an equal share of meaning-making, conveying the plot, setting, and character development while reinforcing theme.

When evaluating the illustrations and design of the genre, ask yourself:

- How does the illustration enhance the reader's understanding of the fantastical events and/or setting of the story?
- What role do the illustrations play in meaning-making in the book?

Figure 2.6 summarizes the text evaluation considerations for fantasy/science fiction that we have described. This document can also be found in Appendix E.

Figure 2.6 Fantasy/Science Fiction Text Evaluation Considerations for Quality Guide

Text Evaluation Considerations for Quality	Ask Yourself...
Genre Characteristics	▪ What subgenre of fantasy is this? ▪ Are the events, conflict, and resolution of the book plausible, engaging, and meaningful? ▪ Will young readers relate to the characters of the book? Do the characters develop over the course of the story? ▪ Is the setting of the story fully imagined and does it serve to enhance the characters and events? ▪ Who narrates the story? Whose story is being told and how? ▪ Is there consistency in the imaginary world(s) that the author has created for the reader?
Content	▪ Does the theme of the story prompt critical thinking/reflection on the human experience? ▪ Is the content developmentally appropriate for the age of the students with whom we work? ▪ Does the content and/or theme of the story expand students' worldviews by offering them new perspectives on social and political structures?
Text Structure	▪ Does the story follow a sequential narrative arc or are shifts in time incorporated into the narrative arc? ▪ Are there changes in point of view or narration that are linked with shifts in time in the narrative arc?
Language	▪ How does the language of the story contribute to constructing a believable, yet fantastical, narrative? ▪ Are new vocabulary terms associated with the fantasy elements in the story well-defined and contextualized for readers? Do readers encounter the terms frequently enough to internalize their meanings (to facilitate more fluent reading)? ▪ Does the feel of the writing, or the writing style, help to convey a sense of the plot, characters, setting, and themes of the book? ▪ Will the readers in my classroom (or a particular reader) will find this writing style engaging?
Visuals: Illustration and Design	▪ How does the illustration enhance the reader's understanding of the fantastical events and/or setting of the story? ▪ What role do the illustrations play in meaning-making in the book?

Historical Fiction

Historical fiction is most typically defined as realistic fiction set in the past. The plot, characters, and conflict have to be representative of the time period in which the story is set. The challenge to the historical novelist is researching and understanding enough about the past to construct a believable and authentic world for the story, and to do so without drowning the reader in extraneous details. Defining what is the past can be challenging. Oftentimes, literary critics of historical fiction have defined the past as a generation, or 25 years. There can be some confusion when fantasy books adopt a medieval motif; that is, when fantasy fiction fuses elements of our understanding of medieval Europe, the belief systems and mores of that time period, and medieval literature within a new fantastical world. It can seem as if the novel is a work of historical fiction when it is not. But there are historical novels that appropriate elements of fantasy fiction as well. Some historical novels use time travel as a plot device, and are a fusion of the two genres. Even those novels that use time travel must responsibly construct a realistic iteration of a past time and place. Historical fiction is one of the literary genres that is published less frequently in the picture book format. Teaching with historical fiction provides students of all ages with an opportunity to time travel, to step inside and walk around in the past, consider multiple perspectives and dilemmas through connections to characters, and develop a sense of historic imagination—their own capability to visualize a past time period—to which they can attach new learning about that time period from a range of sources, including primary and secondary sources.

> **Resources for Evaluating Historical Fiction**
>
> If you are interested in exploring this genre more fully, and learning more about ways of teaching with historical fiction, we recommend the following resources:
>
> Patricia A. Crawford and Vicky Zygouris-Coe. 2008. "Those were the Days: Learning about History through Literature." *Childhood Education* 84(4): 197–203.
>
> Linda Levstik and David Barton. 2010. *Doing History: Investigating with Children in Elementary and Middle School.* New York: Routledge.
>
> Dave Martin and Beth Brooke. 2002. "Getting Personal: Making Effective Use of Historical Fiction in the History Classroom." *Teaching History* 108: 30.
>
> Michael Tunnell and Richard Ammon, eds. 1992. *The Story of Ourselves: Teaching History through Children's Literature.* Portsmouth, NH: Heinemann.

Genre Characteristics: The degree to which a historical novel represents the past varies depending on the choices that the author makes. Some historical novels have a famous figure from the past as a protagonist or key character. In others, a famous person may be referenced, but is not significant to the story. Still others have no famous people. Historical novels sometimes hinge on actual events, large and small. For instance, there may be a historical novel that focuses on a single battle during the American Revolution and another that is set during the duration of the war. Other historical novels use history as a mere backdrop, without mention to any actual events, and are populated with invented characters and events. Many novels for children and young adults mirror the conflict of the historical time period with a conflict experienced by the protagonist. The theme of a historical novel is often one that resonates with its intended readers and their developmental stage, and that focuses on some enduring element of the human condition that exists throughout time.

When evaluating the characteristics of historical fiction, ask yourself:

- What, if any, historical figures are included in this novel? How are they important?
- What events from the novel actually took place and what events are invented?
- How is the protagonist's conflict mirrored by the conflicts within the plot, and vice versa?
- What are the themes of the book and how do they resonate with readers today?

Content: When evaluating historical fiction, setting takes center stage. How authentically has the past been constructed for the reader? How do you *know* that the past is authentic? As a teacher, you can't be expected to be an expert on every time period that you read about. However, there are clues within the text that will guide you. Authors research extensively in order to write a historical novel, and the reader deserves to know what the author learned. Often, historical novels will have an Author's Note at the end that details the research process and the connection between research discoveries, plot, and characterization. Historical novelists often argue that they are not writing the book to teach about the past. Regardless, there is much that students can learn from the historical content of the book. Clarifying what is true and not true in an author's note furthers that learning process. The author's note is usually preceded or followed by a bibliography of sources used. Many manuscripts are vetted by historians and/or historical museum staff, in order to catch errors. Those reviewers are typically thanked somewhere in the manuscript, either before the book starts or somewhere in the back matter, after the conclusion of the narrative.

Another important component of evaluating the content of historical fiction centers on the perspectives represented within it. You want to consider what perspectives from the time period of the book are included and excluded and how those perspectives are represented in the characterization. Even books for the very young should strive to have authentic characterization, not stereotypes. For example, if the book is set during the American Revolution, which characters are Whigs, or Patriots and how are they characterized? Are Tories, those loyal to the King of England, rendered clumsy, selfish, or evil in some way? Look to see that a range of perspectives and characterization is offered. You also want to consider the gender and social class of the protagonist and the other characters that play important roles in the book. For example, in keeping with our focus on the American Revolution, consider characters' status as free, enslaved, or indentured.

When evaluating the content of historical fiction, ask yourself:

- What sources did the author use to research the book?
- Has the manuscript been vetted by an authority on this time period?
- What characters really existed and what characters are invented?
- What parts of the plotline are invented and what parts are real?

- What do I learn about everyday life during this time period? About political or social conflicts? Specific events?
- What do I learn about the different perspectives of this time period?
- What do I learn about gender roles in this time period?
- What do I learn about social class during this time period?

Text Structure: Historical fiction in picture book and novel format typically follows the traditional narrative arc. Middle grade and young adult books might make use of more sophisticated plot shifts or temporal sequencing, particularly if time travel is involved. Sometimes, the narrative parallels a known series of events during a historical time period, which reinforces the structure of the story and the sequence of events. But this is not always the case.

When evaluating the text structure of historical fiction, ask yourself:

- What relationship exists between the plot structure and actual historic events that I know of from this time period?
- To what extent does the plot progress chronologically and to what extent does the timeline shift over the course of the narrative?

Language: Perhaps the most difficult part of writing historical fiction is the dialogue. Historical novels can be set during time periods for which we have few written records, let alone documented spoken words or evidence of how the "average" person spoke. They can also be written about time periods from which a great deal of written evidence exists, but the written evidence is comprised of legal or religious information, or the lives of the educated and wealthy who were literate, but not the "average" person. While there is much we can learn about people from census records, government rolls, etc., they provide little evidence of how people spoke to one another. Therefore, historical novelists make choices about language, based on what they have learned through primary source documents from the time period, and secondary sources that interpret historical evidence. Essentially, they make a judgment call. If you read two historical novels set during the American Revolution, one written in the 1950s and one written today, you will hear the difference in the dialogue, moving from more formal language to more informal. Whether or not either approximates the reality is something we are unlikely to learn. Social class and levels of education can oftentimes impact how people speak to one another, and books with characters from varying social classes might exhibit a range of speech within a time period.

Additionally, the book will have vocabulary from the time period that references items that no longer exist. Some vocabulary may be specific to political or social events, others, to everyday life. For example, up until the early 20th century, men and women used to wear pattens, which got tied to the bottom of one's shoes to raise you off the ground when conditions were icy, muddy, or wet. Pattens are no longer used. We still have bedrooms, but in colonial times they were called bedchambers. People and circumstances specific to the time period, but possibly unfamiliar to the reader, will also surface. Unless a pivotal scene in the story involves the protagonist wearing pattens, it may not be important for students to understand the meaning of every label. However, key concepts and events in the story, and the vocabulary around these, may be central to understanding the novel's plot, conflict, and themes, and you will want to ensure that students understand those words.

When evaluating the language of historical fiction, ask yourself:

- In what ways does the language sound realistic to you? Does it sound too modern? Too stilted?
- Does everyone speak the same way or do people of different social classes have different dialects?
- To what extent is period-specific vocabulary described in context clues to support the reader?

Visuals (Illustrations and Design): What is most important to consider when evaluating illustrations within a historical fiction picture book or novel is the attention to historic detail. Consider how the illustrator makes a match between the time period and the story, and details evidence of the past in the illustrations. Sometimes, illustrators will use the art from the time period to illustrate the story, adopting a medium that immerses the reader in the art of the time period. Increasingly, illustrators of historical fiction picture books and chapter books may provide readers with their own illustrator's note to complement the author's note, articulating how they learned what they needed to learn in order to illustrate the book as authentically as possible.

When evaluating the illustrations and design of historical fiction, ask yourself:

- What, if any, match exists between the illustration style and the time period?
- What evidence of the past is detailed in the illustrations?
- Who is in the foreground of the illustrations? Who is in the background? Who is left out?
- What does the illustrator reveal about his or her research process in the illustrator's note? How does that inform how you approach the book with your students?

Figure 2.7 summarizes the text evaluation considerations for historical fiction that we have described. This document can also be found in Appendix E.

Figure 2.7 Historical Fiction Text Evaluation Considerations for Quality Guide

Text Evaluation Considerations for Quality	Ask Yourself...
Genre Characteristics	- What, if any, historical figures are included in this novel? How are they important? - What events from the novel actually took place and what events are invented? - How is the protagonist's conflict mirrored by the conflicts within the plot, and vice versa? - What are the themes of the book and how do they resonate with readers today?
Content	- What sources did the author use to research the book? - Has the manuscript been vetted by an authority on this time period? - What characters really existed and what characters are invented? - What parts of the plotline are invented and what parts are real? - What do I learn about everyday life during this time period? About political or social conflicts? Specific events? - What do I learn about the different perspectives of this time period? - What do I learn about gender roles in this time period? - What do I learn about social class during this time period?
Text Structure	- What relationship exists between the plot structure and actual historic events that I know of from this time period? - To what extent does the plot progress chronologically and to what extent does the timeline shift over the course of the narrative?
Language	- In what ways does the language sound realistic to you? Does it sound too modern? Too stilted? - Does everyone speak the same way or do people of different social classes have different dialects? - To what extent is period-specific vocabulary described in context clues to support the reader?
Visuals: Illustration and Design	- What, if any, match exists between the illustration style and the time period? - What evidence of the past is detailed in the illustrations? - Who is in the foreground of the illustrations? Who is in the background? Who is left out? - What does the illustrator reveal about his or her research process in the illustrator's note? How does that inform how you approach the book with your students?

Poetry

Journalist Bill Moyers has described poetry as "The Language of Life." While poetry, with its infinite variety of forms and purposes is difficult to define, we, like Moyers, view poetry as an expressive and highly aesthetic form of writing in which the author offers insight to life experiences. Poets employ language in its most concentrated form, seeking to express layers of meaning with precise and creative word choices. By its nature, poetry is a wonderful teaching tool, offering many possibilities across the curriculum. Because poems are often shorter texts tightly packed with meaning, and often open to multiple interpretations, they provide a quick and effective way to prompt critical thinking and discussion. The range of poetry available for children and young adults is really quite astonishing. Whether studying space travel, family, the rainforest, or force and motion, you are very likely to be able to find a poem that you can use to enhance your curriculum.

Characteristics: Poets use language in unexpected ways, inspiring us to view our world from new angles. To accomplish this wonderful feat, they play with language. Georgia Heard (1998) encourages us to use the metaphor of a toolkit to describe how poets go about constructing a poem. One of the hallmarks of good poetry is that it contains multiple layers of meaning. To create this depth of interpretive possibilities, a poet often uses figurative language, employing similes and metaphors, or comparison and contrast. Also in the poet's toolkit are words to create aural effects. As a genre that begs to be read aloud, poems often have a musical or rhythmic quality to them. Pacing, word and sentence length, and line breaks determine how a poem will sound read aloud or in the reader's head. The sound of a poem should be well matched to the poem's content. Poets also use imagery as tools to create meaning and emotional responses. Powerful imagery and sensory descriptions draw readers into the experiences described in the poem. Students are quick to notice that poems differ visually than other forms of writing. Another one of the poet's tools is shape. Poets carefully consider where and how their words will be placed on the blank page, as line breaks and position can greatly enhance the meaning that is being conveyed by the words on the page.

Resources for Evaluating Poetry

If you are interested in exploring the genre more fully, and learning more about ways of teaching with poetry, we recommend the following resources:

Barbara Chatton. 2010. *Using Poetry across the Curriculum: Learning to Love Language*, 2nd ed. Santa Barbara, CA: Libraries Unlimited.

Georgia Heard. 1998. *Awakening the Heart: Exploring Poetry In Elementary and Middle School.* Portsmouth, NH: Heinemann.

Sara Holbrook. 2005. *Practical Poetry: A Nonstandard Approach to Meeting Content-Area Standards.* Portsmouth, NH: Heinemann.

Bill Moyers. 1995. *The Language of Life: A Festival of Poets.* New York: Bantam Doubleday Dell.

The Poetry Foundation
http://www.poetryfoundation.org

Favorite Poem Project
http://www.favoritepoem.org

Library of Congress: Poetry 180: A Poem a Day for American High Schools
http://www.loc.gov/poetry/180/

"Purposeful Poetry" by Susan Dove Lemke
http://archive.hbook.com/magazine/articles/2005/may05_lempke.asp

NCTE Award for Excellence in Children's Poetry
http://www.ncte.org/awards/poetry

When evaluating the characteristics of poetry, ask yourself:

- How does the author use sound (rhythm, rhyme, and musical qualities) to convey meaning in the poem?
- How does the author create imagery and a sensory experience for the reader of the poem?
- Does the poem have multiple layers of meaning, prompting discussion and offering space for multiple interpretations?
- How does the shape/ physical appearance (pacing and spacing) of the poem serve to convey, reinforce, or enhance the meaning of the poem?

Content: As we said previously, you can find a poem that addresses just about any topic. When Erika teaches the survey course in children's literature that we offer at our university, a favorite class activity is a scavenger hunt through a collection of children's poetry books. She gives her students a long list of classroom scenarios and curriculum topics and asks the students to browse through the books to locate a poem that could be used for each item on the list. For example, they look for a poem that could be used to celebrate the loss of a tooth, during a study of the solar system, in a math lesson on addition, or on the occasion of the first snow of the season. Each time Erika leads this activity with her students they are amazed by the range of content in this sampling of poetry books—and it is truly just a small sampling!

Poetry for children can be found across the book formats. There are wonderful poetry offerings in picture book format. These include picture book versions of a single poem; for example, several picture book versions of the now classic poem "Casey at the Bat" by Ernest Lawrence Thayer are available. Poetry collections may be authored by a single person or may be the work of multiple authors. Poetry collections by single authors might be thematically or topically related, or they might be a collection of unrelated poems that represent the poet's body of work over a particular time period. When collections of poems are by multiple authors, they are usually edited collections; the poems in the collection have been gathered and compiled by an editor for a particular reason—perhaps they all relate to the same broad theme, such as early childhood experiences (for example, *Here's A Little Poem: A Very First Book of Poetry* collected by Jane

Yolen and Andrew Fusek Peters 2007), or they may all address a specific topic (for example, *Nasty Bugs,* collected by Lee Bennett Hopkins 2012).

Poetry collections, both edited and by a single author, are also available in a novel format, although they may or may not be organized in chapters. Recently, though, there have been many narratives in verse that are novels, such as *Love That Dog* by Sharon Creech (2001) for intermediate grade readers, *Words with Wings* by Nikki Grimes (2013) for middle grade readers, and more complex works like *October Mourning: A Song for Matthew Shepherd* by Leslea Newman (2012) for a young adult audience. Poetry can even be found in graphic novel format, for example Gareth Hinds' version of the epic poem *Beowulf* (2007).

When evaluating the content of the genre of poetry we also consider the intention or purpose of the author. Much poetry for children has been written with the purpose of entertainment. Humorous poetry for children, exemplified in collections by well-known authors such as Shel Silverstein and Jack Prelutsky, is immensely popular. Poetry for children is also often written to prompt reflection, observation, or critical thinking. The beautifully illustrated collection *Outside Your Window: A First Book of Nature* written by scientist and author Nicola Davies (2012) inspires children to find and appreciate diversity, beauty, and patterns in the natural world. Marilyn Nelson's (2004) *Fortune's Bones: The Manumission Requiem* compels young adult readers to consider the pervasive impact of slavery and the concept of ownership and self-agency. Recently there have been many wonderful collections of nonfiction poems, written with the purpose of conveying information to readers. Douglas Florian's engaging nonfiction collections, including *Poetrees* (2010), and works by Joyce Sidman, such as *Ubiquitous: Celebrating Nature's Survivors* (2010), demonstrate how nonfiction content can be conveyed in poetic form.

When evaluating the content of poetry, ask yourself:

- What is the content of the book and how is the content organized? Is it a single poem or a collection of poems? If it is a collection, how do the poems in the collection relate to one another?
- What is the author's or authors' intent for the poem, poetry collection, or edited collection?
- Is the content of the poem developmentally appropriate and of interest to the reader(s) you have in mind?

Text Structure: When you think of poetry forms, you may be transported back in time to your high school or college English class. Poetry for children incorporates the traditional forms of poetry you may have studied in these classes, but leaves the door open for experimentation. Across single-poem works and in collections of poetry for young people, you will most commonly find examples of the following (Kiefer 2010):

- Narrative poems: poems that tell a story
- Lyrical poems: poetry that "sings its way into the minds and memories of its listeners" (Kiefer 2010); usually descriptive poetry without formal length or structure

- Free verse poems: poetry that does not rhyme, but is structured by some pattern in rhythm, pacing, or format
- Haiku poems: traditional Japanese poetic form of three lines and seventeen syllables, distributed as follows: the first and third line have five syllables and the second line has seven
- Concrete poems: poems for which the placement of the written poem on the page creates a visual image related to the content of the poem

While these formats are those you are most likely to encounter in poetry written for children and young adults, there are many other poetic forms in use. You may enjoy reviewing the definitions and examples of poetic forms found in *A Kick in the Head: An Everyday Guide to Poetic Forms* edited by Paul B. Janeczko and illustrated by Chris Raschka (2005).

When evaluating the text structure of poetry, ask yourself:

- What form or forms of poetry are used in the book?
- Is the form of the poem well matched with the content of the poem?

Language: The poet is a master wielder of language, selecting and arranging words precisely to construct meaning while creating an aesthetic experience. Reading poetry with students offers wonderful opportunities to talk about language use. Perhaps most importantly, poets use figurative language as a tool to convey meaning creatively. Using simile, metaphor, and allusion, the poet leaves the reader to infer meaning, offering room for multiple interpretations. Poets also attend to the sound and musicality of the language, choosing to use techniques such as rhyme, rhythm, alliteration, assonance, consonance, and onomatopoeia. Word choice and arrangement are essential to the poetry writing process.

When evaluating the language of poetry ask yourself:

- Do the words chosen by the author effectively convey the content and meaning of the poem?
- How does the author use figurative language to convey meaning in the poem? Will children be able to relate the figurative language to their life experience, thus being able to understand multiple layers of meaning?
- How does the rhythm and pacing of the poem create and enhance the meaning? What aural devices are used by the author?
- If it is a rhyming poem, do the rhymes feel forced or contrived?

Visuals (Illustrations and Design): The general criteria for evaluating illustrations and design can be applied to the genre of poetry. Special consideration might be given to how illustrations help readers to access multiple layers of meaning in poetry or to more fully understand figurative language used by the author. In picture book versions of single poems, the illustrations play a strong role in conveying the meaning of the poem. When multiple illustrated versions of the same poem exist (for example, Robert Louis Stevenson's "My

Shadow," Clement Moore's "T'was the Night Before Christmas," Ernest Lawrence Thayer's "Casey at the Bat," and Longfellow's "The Midnight Ride of Paul Revere") engaging students in a comparison of the illustrative interpretations can help them to consider multiple perspectives on the poem's content.

When evaluating the illustrations and layout of poetry, ask yourself:

- How do the illustrations convey and enhance the content and meaning of the poems?

Figure 2.8 summarizes the text evaluation considerations for poetry that we have described. This document can also be found in Appendix E.

Figure 2.8 Poetry Text Evaluation Considerations for Quality Guide

Text Evaluation Considerations for Quality	Ask Yourself...
Genre Characteristics	■ How does the author use sound (rhythm, rhyme, and musical qualities) to convey meaning in the poem? ■ How does the author create imagery and a sensory experience for the reader of the poem? ■ Does the poem have multiple layers of meaning, prompting discussion and offering space for multiple interpretations? ■ How does the shape/ physical appearance (pacing and spacing) of the poem serve to convey, reinforce, or enhance the meaning of the poem?
Content	■ What is the content of the book and how is the content organized? Is it a single poem or a collection of poems? If it is a collection, how do the poems in the collection relate to one another? ■ What is the author's or authors' intent for the poem, poetry collection, or edited collection? ■ Is the content of the poem developmentally appropriate and of interest to the reader(s) you have in mind?
Text Structure	■ What form or forms of poetry are used in the book? ■ Is the form of the poem well matched with the content of the poem?
Language	■ Do the words chosen by the author effectively convey the content and meaning of the poem? ■ How does the author use figurative language to convey meaning in the poem? Will children be able to relate the figurative language to their life experience, thus being able to understand multiple layers of meaning? ■ How does the rhythm and pacing of the poem create and enhance the meaning? What aural devices are used by the author? ■ If it is a rhyming poem, do the rhymes feel forced or contrived?
Visuals: Illustration and Design	■ How do the illustrations convey and enhance the content and meaning of the poems?

Nonfiction

Nonfiction literature for children and young adults has often been missed as an opportunity to cultivate excitement over reading, provide access to important content information required in curriculum standards or of particular interest to students, and model excellent writing. First, let's admit that nonfiction is oddly named. No other literary genre that we discuss in this section is named in opposition to something else. What is nonfiction besides "not fiction"? Nonfiction books are books that are true; the information they contain can be verified by other sources, with nothing made up. But this does not mean that they are dry or dull or serve only as books for research. Nonfiction books can provide information on just about any topic, snapshots of theories, procedural steps for completing a task, and stories of people's lives using language and formats that are interesting, engaging, relevant, and developmentally appropriate reading for their audience.

Many teachers that we work with are surprised to learn of the range of nonfiction books available today. Most remember reading encyclopedias, atlases, and textbooks when they were in school and they think that most nonfiction books are like those reference books. This can't be further from the truth. Just as literary nonfiction exists in the world of adult reading, so it exists in the world of children's and young adult literature. Over the past 15 years, the genre has shifted dramatically with increasing attention, thanks to technology, to the visual components of nonfiction and artful design. With the rise of the nonfiction picture books, there is a range of literary nonfiction for all audiences, from primary grades to young adult. Many young people actually prefer to read nonfiction, but do not have the opportunity to do so during independent, small group, or whole-class reading. Teaching with a wide range of nonfiction literature allows students to explore topics of their own choosing so students may improve their reading or change their disposition toward reading; consider a topic in-depth in science, social studies, math or the arts; and examine mentor texts for writing that presents a range of ways of writing about the world beyond the "essay," "composition," or deadly dull "constructed response" that only exists in the world of testing.

Resources for Evaluating Nonfiction

If you are interested in exploring the genre more fully, and learning more about ways of teaching with nonfiction, we recommend the following resources:

Rosemary Bamford and Jan Kristo. 2002. *Making Facts Come Alive: Choosing and Using Nonfiction Literature K–8*, 2nd ed. Norwood, MA: Christopher Gordon Publishers.

Stephanie Harvey. 1998. *Nonfiction Matters: Reading, Writing, and Researching in Grades 3–8*. Portland, ME: Stenhouse Publishing.

Kathleen T. Issacs. 2013. *Picturing the World: Informational Picture Books for Children*. Chicago: American Library Association.

Barbara Moss. 2002. *Exploring the Literature of Fact: Children's Nonfiction Trade Books in the Elementary Classroom*. New York: Guilford Press.

Myra Zarnowski. 2003. *History Makers: A Questioning Approach to Reading and Writing Biography*. Portsmouth, NH: Heinemann.

The Uncommon Corps http://www.nonfictionandthecommoncore.blogspot.com

Genre Characteristics: Many teachers are also surprised to learn of the range of subgenres of nonfiction that exist beyond biography and autobiography. Helping students to understand and identify the types of nonfiction books on the library shelves will help them become stronger readers and writers of the genre. By identifying the subgenre of nonfiction, students can better understand the author's purpose in writing the book from the beginning, allowing them to anticipate not only the type of information they will be reading about, but some of the possible text structures through which the information will be delivered.

Here is a sampling of some of these subgenres and what makes them different from one another.

Survey Book: Survey books are the most common form of nonfiction book published and, most likely, the greatest number of titles in your school library. Survey books tend to focus on one broad topic and break it down into a variety of subtopics. They do not go too in-depth with any of these topics, but they give the reader a general introduction. Survey books often have a noun as the title (e.g., *Sharks* or *The Renaissance*). Think of the survey book as a pair of binoculars. Binoculars help you see a range of things at a distance more closely. Survey books bring a broad topic a little closer to your students. Within your curriculum, a survey book can be used in small groups or whole-class instruction to introduce a topic that you will study in depth. It is rare, but not out of the question, for a survey book to lend itself to literature circles or read alouds. Most, but not all survey books do not have to be read from cover to cover, so they are useful for doing research. Avid nonfiction readers often love to read survey books. But if the teacher is looking to hook students on nonfiction who are unaccustomed to it, a specialized book might be more appealing.

Concept Book: Concept books can sometimes be confused with survey books, because they too, can serve as an introduction to a topic. However, a concept book goes more deeply into one concept, abstract idea, or explanation of a particular category. For instance, life cycle books are concept books, as are nonfiction ABC and counting books that focus on teaching the concepts of letters and numbers. There are some nonfiction survey books that adopt the structure of an alphabet book or a counting book as a way to convey information within a structure. How do you tell the difference between a survey book and a concept book? Sometimes it's tricky. If a book focuses on explaining a system of classification and why, it is more likely a concept book. If it is to give you a little bit of information about the subtopics within a larger category of information, then it's a survey book. This isn't an exact science, and the conversation around the books, amongst your teaching team and your students, is more important than the label. Concept books are more frequently written for babies, preschoolers, and elementary grade students. For example, there are many board books for babies and toddlers that focus on introducing certain concepts or processes, like eating or going on a trip. There are science-related concept books for preschool and primary grade students. Concept books are a bit like microscopes or magnifying glasses. They magnify something very particular for specific exploration and study. They explore in depth a single concept (or sometimes two or three), going deep rather than broad. Within one's curriculum, concept books can be at the heart of exploration in science and sometimes social studies as well. While there are some chapter-length concept books, the majority seem to be published as picture books.

Biography, Memoir, Autobiography: Biography is the subgenre of nonfiction with which many teachers and students are most familiar. The range of biographies published today is quite exciting, from picture books to chapter books, photo essays to graphic nonfiction. Some biographies are specific, and focus on one particular event in someone's life, or one particular theme that resonates through a life. Others are complete ("cradle-to-grave") and cover the entirety of someone's life. Biographies are ideal for genre study in language arts or for individual or small-group research on a historic or contemporary figure. Picture book biographies in the intermediate and middle grades also serve as wonderful introductions to a time period or scientific concept, particularly as read alouds.

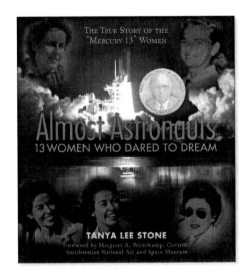

Specialized Nonfiction: Specialized nonfiction, as the name suggests, focuses deeply on a specific event, situation, or problem, etc. Teachers and students are likely least familiar with this genre because there is so much nonfiction published today on topics never before represented for children or young adults. For instance, Tonya Lee Stone's (2009) Sibert Award-winning middle grade nonfiction *Almost Astronauts* examines the evaluation process for female candidates for the U.S. space program in the 1960s. Many authors are also making their own research, or the research process of their subjects, more visible using the format of specialized books. For example, *The Scientists in the Field* series of middle-grade nonfiction highlights cutting-edge scientific research being done under the sea, in the polar regions, in remote tropical jungles, and in caves beneath our feet. Within the classroom, specialized books make marvelous choices for independent reading, if students can select the books most interesting to them. Specialized nonfiction is ideal for student research, and also for small and whole class exploration within units of study in science, social studies, the arts, and language arts. Specialized nonfiction also makes for wonderful read alouds as part of content-based units of study, as a mentor text for student research and writing, and for community-building within the classroom. We also encourage parents and children to read specialized nonfiction aloud together, to explore topics of interest to the whole family.

In addition to this range of subgenres, there are also a range of subgenres of reference books for children and young adults, such as how-to books, field guides, atlases, and dictionaries.

When evaluating the characteristics of nonfiction, ask yourself:

- What subgenre of nonfiction is this book?
- How does the choice of subgenre influence how the content is conveyed to the reader?

Content: The content of nonfiction books is as wide and vast as the history of our world and beyond. There are few topics that are not covered in nonfiction books for children and young adults. As mentioned in the section above, the subgenre of nonfiction will determine the range of content discussed in each book. A survey book will provide more general information on a topic, whereas a specialized book will go into greater detail on one aspect of that topic. For example, there are many survey books about dolphins, but the Scientists in the Field book *The Dolphins of Shark Bay* (Turner 2013), a specialized nonfiction book, provides an examination of specific dolphins in a specific time and place, as well as the researchers who study them. Similarly, a partial biography will provide only a portion of someone's life, where a complete cradle-to-grave biography will provide more information, although the sheer amount of information within any text will also be dependent on the age range of its intended audience. A partial biography may be a great introduction book before reading a complete biography on someone; just as a short survey book on dolphins may provide the prior knowledge middle-grade readers may need to tackle *The Dolphins of Shark Bay*. Moreover, the content of nonfiction books on the exact same topic can vary. When considering different picture book biographies of someone, each book might highlight a different aspect of the figure's life. Each might have a different theme. By having students read a range of nonfiction books on a topic, perhaps presented via different subgenres, students begin to see that nonfiction authors make choices about what to include and exclude, and readers have a command of that content by approaching each book as a source of "some" information on a topic but not "the" information on that topic.

Key to evaluating the content of any nonfiction book is examining the author's process. You want to be sure that the book is well researched and has been vetted by experts in the field. More and more nonfiction authors not only share select source materials or their full bibliography; many, including nonfiction picture book authors, discuss their research process in a lengthy author's note. Always be sure to read the author's note and back matter in a nonfiction book. There can be important details in those sections that frame and contextualize the book in an entirely new way, sharpening one's focus and helping shape instruction or frame the book in connection to others on the topic. Author's notes can also be mined as models for the research process itself, something we will discuss more specifically when we discuss instructional practices.

Authors will often bring in multiple perspectives on the content, drawing from a range of resources researched to convey to readers that not everyone thinks or has always thought what we think today about a topic. For instance, books on dinosaurs may demonstrate our changing thinking over time about these prehistoric creatures, moving from what we used to know to what we know now. Books that focus on historical events may articulate the differing ways in which that event, or the figures involved in it, have been represented over time.

On a final note about content, many authors writing today are writing about more diverse topics than ever before, and topics that are more precise. The field has gotten wider and more expansive, as well as "deeper" into the topics young people may be interested in. This is particularly true in the field of biography. While many famous and previously well-represented historic figures continue to get written about in new ways, there are more and more books published about lesser-known figures, women in particular, and men and women from diverse nations, backgrounds, and time periods.

When evaluating the content of nonfiction, ask yourself:

- What content is conveyed in this book?
- How do I know the author has done an appropriate level of research? What can I learn from the bibliography? Has the book been vetted by an authority on the topic?
- What does the author's note tell me about the research process and content?
- How does this slice of content compare to how other books on this topic convey the content? Are important details missing, or does the book cover various elements of the topic?
- Is the subject of this book a fairly new subject for children's or young adult nonfiction? In what ways?

Text Structure: There is a range of text structures used in nonfiction works, and having students read a wide range of nonfiction allows them to become adept at identifying these structures. Understanding and knowing these structures as readers and writers reinforces student expectations of each new text. For example, if a student can identify the difference between a compare and contrast structure versus cause and effect, he or she can better access the content of the text, because the content is articulated through the relationships around which the text structures are organized. All nonfiction texts have a general text structure that they adopt including narrative, expository, chronological, cause and effect, problem/solution, and question and answer. However, within any one of these text structures, the other text structures may be used within it, through inserted sidebars, separated sections from the main text, or even at the paragraph level.

It sometimes surprises teachers and young readers to discover that nonfiction books can adopt a narrative structure. Many readers expect nonfiction books to look like encyclopedia entries or the survey books made famous by the D.K. Eyewitness series, with lots of text features, charts, and diagrams. Certainly, there are many works of nonfiction that provide readers with an array of text or access features. But there are many nonfiction books, particularly those for middle grade and young adult readers, that rely on a strong narrative structure to convey the information. These books may still have a strong visual component to their design, using pictures and illustrations to create a parallel narrative and expand the information in the text; but they do not rely on other organizational structures or access features to do so. Sometimes, nonfiction simply tells a good story in the same way that fiction does. While readers may have their preferences for certain nonfiction text structures over others, there is no single or right way to write nonfiction.

When evaluating the text structure of nonfiction, ask yourself:

- What is the primary text structure used by the author?
- What are some of the other text structures used within the larger structure?
- What text features are used to help readers access the information and how well are they matched with the text structure?

Language: The language of nonfiction can be as varied and rich as the language of fiction or poetry. In fact, there are full-length nonfiction books in verse that convey factual information through poetry rather than prose. Specialized literary nonfiction that adopts a narrative text structure often exhibits a strong sense of voice. While students are often taught in school that first person narration should not be used when writing reports or compositions, there are many nonfiction authors today who insert themselves into the text. This happens most frequently when the author is passionately connected to his or her subject and/or actively engaged in the research process, trailing or working alongside actual researchers. Not only does this foster a sense of connection and engagement between the reader and the text, but it also models the research process. Books that provide the reader with a ringside seat to the research process have been called "the literature of inquiry" (Zarnowski and Turkel 2010). This is not to say that books that don't do this are not as good. Different writers write for different purposes and convey the research process in different ways, within the structure of the text or outside of the primary text in the author's note.

There are particular attributes to look for when evaluating the language of nonfiction. Not only should the language be interesting and engaging, it ideally cultivates questions. Well-written nonfiction provides references and comparisons on new information, adding to what the reader may already know and understand. For instance, in nonfiction, similes and metaphors aren't simply beautiful, flowery language. They are purposeful connections between the known and unknown that convey important concepts to readers. Additionally, well-written nonfiction often provides direct quotes from source material, drawing from documents, letters, primary sources, interviews, etc., bringing in multiple voices.

When evaluating the language of nonfiction, ask yourself:

- To what extent is the author's voice included in the work?
- To what extent does the language model inquiry?
- How are similes and metaphors used to convey conceptual information?
- How is source material brought into the language of the text?

Visuals (Illustrations and Design): Increasingly, visuals have become a very important component of nonfiction literature. Gone are the days of nonfiction books with pages and pages of text and no visuals. Gone are the days of black and white sketches or photographs alone as the primary visuals. Thanks to digital technology, the range of media used to illustrate nonfiction books appears to be infinite. Like historical fiction and traditional literature, nonfiction books about particular time periods or cultures may adopt the art forms from that time or culture as a means of illustrating, particularly in picture book format. D.K. Publishing harnessed the power of photography when it developed its popular Eyewitness series in the 1980s, and many nonfiction books now use photography to capture primary source documents and artifacts, microscopic cells, and the natural world. Nonfiction books may blend a range of media in collage format as well, such as Melissa Sweet's award-winning picture book biography *Balloons Over Broadway: The True Story of the Puppeteer of the Macy's Parade* (2011). Regardless of what media is used, the illustration and book design for nonfiction books constructs a visual narrative for readers and extends and expands upon the information gleaned from the written word.

The illustrated nonfiction picture storybook is a relative newcomer to the field of nonfiction that has seen increasing popularity over the past decade. A nonfiction picture storybook reads just like its fictional sibling, with a narrative arc that builds, climaxes, and resolves itself. Students who are used to reading fiction picture books will be very comfortable reading nonfiction picture storybooks, and these texts provide a fertile starting point with primary grade readers for discussing the attributes of fiction and nonfiction.

Most illustrators are as meticulous about their research process as the authors are, and they choose to write about their illustration process in an illustrator's note and/or on their webpage. There are also author-illustrators who research, write, and illustrate their own nonfiction books. But whether or not the author illustrated the book or the work was done by a separate author and illustrator, chances are the illustrator has information to share about capturing research in a visual format, and that is valuable for the teacher to harness.

When evaluating the visuals of nonfiction, ask yourself:

- What media was used to illustrate the text? Does the media feel appropriate for the subject of the book?
- If I just read the illustrations, and not the text, what kind of visual narrative is constructed?
- What does the illustrator have to say about his or her research process? How did the content of the book shape the creation of the illustrations?
- How do the illustrations shape perspectives and point of view within the book?

Figure 2.9 summarizes the text evaluation considerations for nonfiction that we have described. This document can also be found in Appendix E.

Figure 2.9 Nonfiction Text Evaluation Considerations for Quality Guide

Text Evaluation Considerations for Quality	Ask Yourself...
Genre Characteristics	▪ What subgenre of nonfiction is this book? ▪ How does the choice of subgenre influence how the content is conveyed to the reader?
Content	▪ What content is conveyed in this book? ▪ How do I know the author has done an appropriate level of research? What can I learn from the bibliography? Has the book been vetted by an authority on the topic? ▪ What does the author's note tell me about the research process and content? ▪ How does this slice of content compare to how other books on this topic convey the content? Are important details missing, or does the book cover various elements of the topic? ▪ Is the subject of this book a fairly new subject for children's or young adult nonfiction? In what ways?
Text Structure	▪ What is the primary text structure used by the author? ▪ What are some of the other text structures used within the larger structure? ▪ What text features are used to help readers access the information and how well are they matched with the text structure?
Language	▪ To what extent is the author's voice included in the work? ▪ To what extent does the language model inquiry? ▪ How are similes and metaphors used to convey conceptual information? ▪ How is source material brought into the language of the text?
Visuals: Illustration and Design	▪ What media was used to illustrate the text? Does the media feel appropriate for the subject of the book? ▪ If I just read the illustrations, and not the text, what kind of visual narrative is constructed? ▪ What does the illustrator have to say about his or her research process? How did the content of the book shape the creation of the illustrations? ▪ How do the illustrations shape perspectives and point of view within the book?

Considering Quality: Using the Quality, Utility, and Complexity Chart

Earlier in this chapter, we shared a blank version of the template that we created as a helpful note-taking tool when evaluating a text for its potential uses in your curriculum. This chart captures the three essential elements of our selection process. Now that we have reviewed both general and genre-specific considerations for evaluating the *quality* of the book, let's take a look at the *Quality* section of the chart in the left-hand column, which focuses on the question: *Is it good*?

Let's walk through this initial part of the evaluation process with an example: Mary Ann and Erika are working with a fifth grade teacher, and we know that there are a range of social studies state standards and Common Core English Language Arts and Content Literacy standards that will need to be covered throughout the year. Knowing that the American Revolution is a foundational part of fifth grade social studies, we researched books about the American Revolution intended for grades 4 to 6. *Those Rebels, John and Tom* written by Barbara Kerley and illustrated by Edwin Fotheringham (2012) is one of our discoveries. To take a closer look, we look up reviews for the book and find that this particular title has been reviewed by a number of sources, and that the reviews are overwhelmingly positive. The book reviews even point us to another text on this very same political friendship, published just one year before this one.

Browsing through the book, we are impressed by its appealing layout and focused comparison and contrast of these two historical figures. While the focus of the book is on the lives of these two individual men, there is also a great deal of content about the time period, specifically the process of writing the Declaration of Independence. We take notes from the book reviews, and then we evaluate the quality of the book, and the strengths we note as we read the book. Ultimately, we complete the first two sections of our Quality, Utility, and Complexity chart, to capture our thinking. But before you look at the chart below, we want to describe our reaction to this particular book in narrative format first. We think this will help you better understand the shorthand of the language written in the chart.

We are both big fans of Barbara Kerley, the award-winning author of multiple picture book biographies. When she has a new title we seek it out to read it. Because of our prior experiences with her work, we have high expectations for this book, and are not disappointed. The story begins at the beginning, like so many biographies do, with the childhoods of John Adams and Thomas Jefferson, two men who went on to become both members of the Continental Congress and presidents of the newly-formed United States.

Immediately, we are struck by the visual composition of the book. The whole format works to support meaning-making for the reader. The color palette consists of red, white, and blue, the colors of the American flag. Consciously or unconsciously, these colors reinforce the singular identity of our nation. Dark navy and white are used to create contrasts, reinforcing the ways in which the book initially contrasts the differences between Thomas Jefferson and John Adams, from their childhood experiences to their personalities as grown men. This comparison and contrast solidly introduces the notion that the members of the Continental Congress were as different from one another as members of Congress can be today. They came from different parts of the east coast of what is now America, with different customs, belief systems, and political ideas during a time of great change and uncertainty.

Kerley uses parallel structure in her writing to make this contrast between the two men clear and effective, as does Fotheringham with his illustrations. Take a look at the two-page spread above, and you can see how this is accomplished. Notice how Kerley uses a transitional phrase and italics to support the reader from one page to the next? "When JOHN and TOM grew up, they were even *more* different." Next, she describes each man's particular behavior in a single paragraph, summarizing the behavior in a final concluding sentence. The font of that final sentence is larger than the others, providing readers with easy access to the main idea of the paragraph. In addition, the visuals for each support readers' developing understandings of each man. Adams's body language and the response from the jury demonstrates that he was often aggressive in the courtroom, enjoying verbal arguments. In contrast, the illustration of Jefferson shows a quiet, reserved man, writing in the corner.

The jury watches with confusion, not knowing what Jefferson thinks. Despite the contrasts between the two, we also learn of a similarity: both men were lawyers. We learn so much from this one spread.

Kerley deftly shows how the two men come together despite their differences to write the Declaration of Independence. In her author's note, she writes about the ups and downs of their lifelong friendship, including the many years in which they did not speak or correspond with one another out of anger. As such, she balances the specifics of a particular point in time in the narrative, while giving readers a fuller sense of the intersecting lives of these two men beyond the narrative, in the back matter. Generally speaking, this book is an excellent example of nonfiction at work. It's interesting, engaging, and informative.

Now that you have learned a bit more about this book, you can better understand our notes in the chart below (Figure 2.10), and what yours might look like when you try it out.

Figure 2.10 Example of a Partially Completed *Quality, Utility, and Complexity Chart* for *Those Rebels, John and Tom*

Title: *Those Rebels, John and Tom*

Author: Barbara Kerley

Year of Publication: 2012

Notes from the Book Reviews
Booklist calls it a "double portrait," (2011) which is a good name to use in teaching with the book. Booklist also gave it a starred review and said, it "... is a terrific book to lead the charge in learning about the Revolution, as well as a lesson in how dedicated cooperation can achieve great ends. An obvious choice to pair with *Worst of Friends*." (Booklist 2011).
All reviews focus on how the book addresses the issue of class differences between them and the issue of slavery, since Jefferson was a slave owner.
All reviews address the focus on the two men and the story of the writing of the Declaration of Independence.
The *School Library Journal* review talks about the content of the author's note and their presidential years and changing relationship and an "authoritative" but "child-friendly" approach to history (Whitehurst 2012).

Genre Characteristics: Literary and Artistic Value	Genre Characteristics: Complexity and Accessibility
How does it meet established criteria? As a "double portrait" it is a biography of two people, but a partial biography of each. As a double biography it shows parallel events in each of their lives chronologically, as one would expect. There is no invented dialogue (which would be problematic), but Kerley does use direct quotes from each man's writings to create a sense of immediacy with the reader. We get to "hear" each of them through her selective quotes. Research is well documented in the back matter, with citations for different source material and an author's note that explains the origins of the book and the relationship between the two after the Declaration of Independence was written.	*How does the book meet and/or differ from genre characteristics? How does this impact accessibility?*

Content: Literary and Artistic Value	Content: Complexity and Accessibility
What is the book about? It is a partial picture book biography about Thomas Jefferson and John Adams. It covers their childhood and early years, leading up to the writing and signing of the Declaration of Independence. The book focuses on how different they were and how they worked together as a team to get the Declaration both written and then approved by the Continental Congress.	*How complex is the content for the intended audience? How does this impact accessibility?*

Text Structure: Literary and Artistic Value	Text Structure: Complexity and Accessibility
How is the book organized? What is the overall text structure? It is a chronological narrative. At the start, there is a page about John, then a page about Tom, and then a page about the two together. Sometimes the book talks about each separately on different sides of the two-page spread; when talking about events they were both involved in, it talks about them together.	*Is the text structure simple or more complex? How does this impact accessibility?*

Language: Literary and Artistic Value	Language: Complexity and Accessibility
How is the language rich and interesting? What kind of sentence variation occurs? It starts off with a great hook that frames the whole narrative ("formed a surprising alliance, committed treason, and helped launch a new nation.") The book is filled with rich adjectives and parallel structure within paragraphs and pages. Direct quotes from each, taken from primary source materials, are included in quotation marks throughout. There is a jovial mood to the text in general.	*How challenging is the language? How does this impact accessibility?*

Visuals: Literary and Artistic Value	Visuals: Complexity and Accessibility
How do the visuals engage the reader? How do they enhance the content? *How does the book design reinforce the content?* The book is illustrated with a palette of red, white, and blue, which reinforces the identity of the United States of America. The cover illustration and the final illustration are both allusions to famous images associated with the American Revolution. The cartoon drawings of Adams & Jefferson reinforce the comparisons and contrasts within the text. Background colors of white and navy also set up contrasts just as the book contrasts the two men. John and Tom are always mentioned in capital letters. Some sentences are in a larger bold font to emphasize their importance.	*How do the visuals and design impact accessibility?*

As we read the book, teaching ideas are also popping into our head. We find that when we discover really well written, artfully designed books, we can't stop these brainstorms, so we try to write them down as quickly as possible to capture them. In the next chapter, we explore teaching possibilities and instructional purposes to include as part of our evaluation process.

Conclusion

This chapter explored a wide range of text types and genres and provided you with evaluation criteria to use as a tool for selecting texts in the classroom. We know that this is a lot to digest! As you use the criteria, it will become automated and you'll use it without being conscious of the intricacies of the criteria. It becomes a part of you—internalized, part of your "map of reading" (Stevenson 2006). At the heart of this work, we want to empower you. We want you to understand how texts operate so that you can make optimal choices for your teaching. In the next chapter, we will map out the process for considering a text for a wide range of instructional purposes and practices. In other words, "what is it good for?"

Questions for Reflection

1. When did you first learn to analyze children's and young adult books? How has that process shaped your thinking about text selection?

2. What kinds of texts do you feel you know the least about? Which sections in this chapter were most helpful in filling in those gaps?

3. How does this process of talking about texts as teachers mirror the ways that you talk about texts with students?

Chapter 3

Evaluating for Instructional Purpose and Practice

Now that you are equipped with the tools to consider and evaluate different books of different genres for their quality—comparing and contrasting your new reading experiences with the "map of literature" (Stevenson 2006) already in your head—it is time to consider the utility of these books for the classroom. If you have determined they are "good," what are they "good for"? What do you want to do with them in the classroom? The second step in our process of evaluating texts for the classroom focuses on instructional purposes, or the "Task" component of the reading process outlined in Chapter One and shown in Figure 3.1.

Figure 3.1 Considerations for Text Complexity

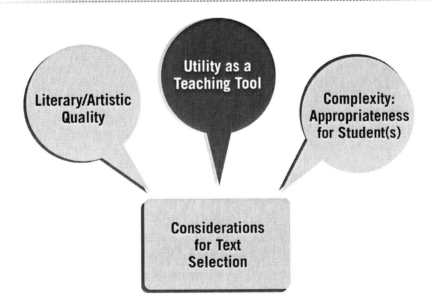

As teachers, we're a bit like sharks—we never stop moving, always on the hunt for new materials. When we pick up a book and evaluate the quality of that book using the criteria that we have outlined in Chapter Two, we are at the same time engaged in a process of evaluating the text for other reasons. When we make choices about which texts we will use in our classroom, there are many factors to consider.

When evaluating a text for classroom use, we consider it:

- In relation to our curriculum goals: How does it help us meet state and local standards for science, social studies, mathematics, and the arts?
- In relation to our instructional goals for literacy: How can reading the text support student growth as readers, writers, speakers, and listeners?
- In relation to other texts that we have available: How does it connect to, compare with, and contrast with the content, perspectives, and language that they offer?
- In relation to our students, their interests, and their literacy needs: How will it support the class as a whole, groups of students, and individuals?

Considering Quality and Instructional Purpose

In our teaching lives, we plan instruction and gather materials in a range of different and ongoing ways. There is the thrill of discovery that comes from creating something new from scratch, filling in some missing piece in the school year. There is the joy in finding a particular book that you know will delight one particular reader. There are also certain "golden" units at every grade level—units that are taught every year because they are tried and true. The resources for these units are extensive from years of cumulative planning—the materials, curriculum, and assessments are well matched to the national, state, or local curriculum standards; there is consistent demonstrated student learning in a range of ways; and the students eagerly participate.

For example, you teach fifth grade, and there is a unit on the American Revolution that has existed in different permutations for years. You know you are teaching it every year, and because you have a lot of experience with it, you are comfortable changing it in slightly different ways to meet the needs and interests of students or take students to a deeper level of learning about the content. In this case, given the emphasis on comparing and contrasting perspectives, and author's purpose, in the Common Core, you might look for a new historical novel that represents a new perspective, such as the war in the southern colonies or the roles of free or enslaved Africans and African Americans. Or, because of the Common Core's emphasis on reading informational text at the elementary level, you decide that you want to pair historical novels and nonfiction texts to deepen students' understanding of the content and expand their reading experiences. In doing so, you know that you are going to be meeting both literacy and social studies standards, and emphasizing important critical thinking skills, all within the same unit.

Or perhaps you teach second grade, and your team is trying to merge genre study in writing instruction with your reading instruction. You are not only looking for a wider range of books for the varying range of readers in your classroom within one particular genre, but also looking for great picture books and perhaps a short chapter book to read aloud for whole-class modeling and exploration of that genre. For guided reading, you are searching for books that are at the students' varying capacities, and a few that are a stretch, but filled with rich examples to serve as mentor texts for critical thinking about the genre and possibly student writing in the genre.

Or, maybe you teach seventh grade science, and with the transition to the Common Core Standards for Content Literacy Grades 6–12, and the advent of the Next Generation Science Standards, you realize that you could be using a much wider range of texts to introduce students to the topic of human impact on Earth. You are looking for a range of print and digital texts that students can read to further explore the content and inform hands-on experimentation with, and design of, systems for minimizing human impact. Because this is a brand new unit, based on the new science standards for middle school, you are starting from scratch, and your team needs to identify a whole new range of materials. The science content will be the driving force behind the selection.

Further still, sometimes you simply stumble upon a book, find it fascinating, and want to consider all the different ways that you can use it in the classroom and integrate it in a range of contexts.

Many teachers we work with are realizing that the implementation of new standards does not necessitate brand new materials. Rather, they necessitate a "pivot," a way of teaching with materials in a different way. Sometimes that means adding new texts to meet the "pivot," such as building in more small-group work to explore different perspectives through novels, nonfiction books, or both. Sometimes it means transitioning from teaching with a single text to teaching with a text set (Cappiello and Dawes 2012).

So we can see that teachers, teams, and school districts have a range of ways they are addressing the standards and looking for new texts or looking at the texts they have in new ways. *Is it good? What is it good for?* There is the purposeful hunt for a text that does *X*, the more expansive search for materials for a brand new unit, the ah-ha moment when you see how you can use a text you have taught with for years in a new way, and the serendipitous "find."

There is also the synergy between the different purposes we have for using texts and how they complement one another. In Chapter One, we reviewed the different instructional purposes for reading at school (see Figure 3.2). As shared previously, we see fostering a love of reading and healthy reading habits as a component of each of these different purposes.

Figure 3.2 Instructional Purposes for Text Selection

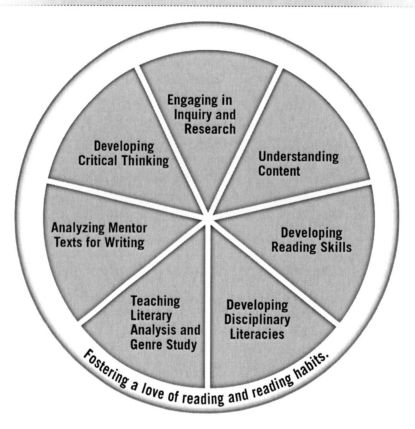

One or more of these different purposes may be a driving force for text selection at any one time. One purpose may be primary in the decision-making, the others secondary. These are considerations that teachers will be making while they are reading the book, and after, as they consider the relationship between the literary and artistic merit of the text and the utility of the text. Depending on whether the primary focus is on instruction in the language arts or on content-area instruction, the initial assessment of the teaching potential may vary.

If we are selecting a text for content-area instruction, such as math, science, or social studies, our primary focus will likely be on whether the content of the text is a good match for our topic of study. After this initial determination, we would then consider what the text offers to support students in their growth as readers and writers. For example, when studying the American Revolution we might select *Hope's Crossing* (Goodman) or *War Comes to Willy Freeman* (Collier and Collier) for a literature circle in a fifth grade classroom because of the opportunity these works of historical fiction provides readers to vicariously engage with the time period. We might have multiple ongoing literature circles, with each group reading a different historical novel. Then, switching gears slightly, to focus more on literary analysis and genre study, we might consider how these novels could be used to help students examine character development across the span of a book. We would strive to connect our exploration of characterization and character development with the actual perspectives and points of view that different groups of people had during the war.

If we are focusing on selecting texts for language arts instruction—perhaps doing a genre study of procedural texts with a first grade class—we would first consider whether the "how-to" text that we have located models key features of the genre, such as transitional words that highlight sequence (e.g., first, next, then, finally). Considering the content of the "how-to" text, we would also want to be sure that the procedure being described is appropriate for, and interesting to, our student audience. For example, as we write this book, the Rainbow Loom craze has our own children and many others we know poring over procedural texts. By the time you read this, there will be another craze, and another set of texts for which children or teens are scrambling.

To better support your evaluation of texts, we will discuss each of the instructional purposes identified in Figure 3.2 and the stand out qualities that a text of any genre or modality may have for each specific instructional purpose.

Understanding Content

With the ever-increasing range of nonfiction books being published today, it is an exciting time to consider using trade books as well as digital texts to explore content knowledge in the areas of science, social studies, mathematics, and the arts. When evaluating a new text with a specific instructional purpose in the content areas, the content of the standards for that particular unit will be an important consideration.

If using the text as a stand alone or as part of a text set, you will want to consider the ways in which the content that must be taught, as dictated by state and local curriculum standards, is robust within each text. If looking at a collection of texts on a topic, you will want to consider how the content is represented across those texts and how, collectively or in different groupings of texts, the content can be conveyed to students. Of course, we know that educators have to teach certain standards to mastery. But there is no reason that teachers can't present more content to the students, particularly if they know it is going to help shape and frame what it is they have to learn or fill in gaps in prior knowledge that will enable them to learn the new information. Sometimes, the extra information serves as the catalyst or the hook that grabs attention. Sometimes "less is more," and sometimes "more" allows students to see what you must teach in a clearer context.

When evaluating a text for the instructional purpose of teaching content and/or content standards, ask yourself:

- What is the match between my content standards and the text?
- What is the match between my content standards and this text in relation to other texts on the topic?
- Is information presented in a way that will hook my students and get them even more interested in the unit topic?
- Does the information in this text go beyond the standards? How will that impact how my students read it?

Developing Disciplinary Literacies

Our goal in literacy instruction is to help our students develop as readers, writers, speakers, thinkers, and listeners across the discipline areas. We want to support students to begin to use language in the ways of scientists, historians, mathematicians, and artists. From the earliest grade, as students engage with texts, 'reading' texts with the support of parents and teachers, and 'writing' their own texts using approximate spellings with the intent of expressing their experiences and their evolving understandings (Lindfors 2008), they work to develop their decoding, comprehension, and fluency skills in the context of literacy activities that feel meaningful to them and that approximate and mirror the ways that they see adults using reading, writing, speaking, and listening to make things happen in the world. We continue this apprenticeship in disciplinary literacy across the grade levels (Gee 1990; Buehl 2011) engaging students in reading and writing increasingly sophisticated texts with an explicit focus on how language is used within the context of these areas of study.

When evaluating a text for the instructional purpose of fostering and teaching disciplinary literacy skills, ask yourself:

- Is the vocabulary used in the text authentic to the discipline, but contextually defined in a manner that makes it accessible to my students?
- Does the text model the inquiry and/or critical-thinking processes of the discipline either implicitly (for example in an author's note) or explicitly (through direct description in the text)?

Developing Reading Skills

There are many literacy practices that foster developing literacy skills: reading aloud, shared reading, guided reading, and independent reading. When evaluating a text for use in reading instruction, the match between the text and the developing literacy skills of the students within that pair or group will be central. The richness and complexity of the vocabulary should be considered. Where do the majority of the words fall on a continuum from sight words to polysyllabic? How well are less-familiar words contextually defined so that students can employ a range of strategies for decoding? It is also important to consider the content of the book and whether or not it will be of interest to students and worth the work required to read it. Moreover, teachers will need to know whether students have enough background knowledge to be able to comprehend the book as they work on their decoding.

When evaluating a text for the instructional purpose for developing literacy skills, ask yourself:

- Does this book appeal to students? Will it be worth working on?
- How much background knowledge does the book require? Will students be able to comprehend as they decode?
- What kinds of words does it contain? What is the balance of sight words, monosyllabic, and polysyllabic words?

- How long are the sentences? Too long? Too short? Just right?

Teaching Literary Analysis/Genre Study

When evaluating a text for the instructional purpose of teaching literary analysis and genre study, one will read with a literary lens. Using the evaluation criteria for quality, one will be examining the book for its strength and its novelty as an expression of a particular genre. Keep a running list of notable aspects of the different literary elements at work in the book, such as characterization, plot, theme, setting, and figurative language, all of which can be at work in fiction, nonfiction, and poetry. Also consider the match between the literary elements within the text and the literary elements students should identify in texts and begin to use in their own writing. Consider what students can learn about the genre from reading this text as compared to another, what genre understandings they can develop from reading this single text, and what genre understandings they can develop by reading this text in relationship to other books in the genre or on the same topic but in a different genre. Sometimes, we see things more clearly when we look at them in a different context. Genre study can be an ideal way to explore the conventions of genre. But so can studying a theme, a topic, or an essential question. Sometimes, it's when we use a different set of lenses that we see most clearly. This is why we love the flexibility of teaching with multigenre, multimodal text sets.

When evaluating a text for the instructional purpose of teaching literary analysis and/or genre study, ask yourself:

- How does this book represent the genre we are studying?
- How does the book represent the genre on its own and how does it accomplish this understanding in the context of other books of the same genre or of different genres that focus on the same topic?
- What literary elements are at work in the book? Does the author do anything unique with one or two in particular that stand out as very effective examples to use in instruction?
- What is the match between the literary elements that are required to be taught according to your school's scope and sequence, and national, state, and district standards?

Analyzing Mentor Text for Student Writing

Students write to share what they think and how they feel. They write to convey experiences and craft personal and fictional narratives. They compose poems; they write lyrics to songs. Students write to show what they have learned about the world; sometimes they turn that knowledge to advocacy, and they write to work for change in the world, using their newfound knowledge as a tool to help make it happen. With this range of purposes, and with the diverse array of texts available today in increasingly creative and blended formats, it seems that every text can serve as a mentor text one way or another. In our own teaching lives, we find it rare to be looking at a text in isolation, for the sole purpose of serving as a mentor text for student writing. It seems that students are always writing in the service of something else, either within a particular genre and/or within a range of text types or formats for the purposes of demonstrating what they have learned about a topic of study. Or, students are writing in test-based and school-based genres like "open response" or "constructed response," which are limited to the world of standardized testing. Student writing can be highly creative and carefully constructed; it can also be highly academic and carefully constructed. Their construction and composition of texts is dependent on their understanding of the expectations through the careful study of craft and a wide reading of mentor texts.

When evaluating a text for the instructional purpose of teaching writing, ask yourself:

- If students are reading "like a writer," what do they learn about genre through this text?
- How does this particular text model a particular quality of good writing (for example, varied sentence length) for targeted practice of that skill?
- How does this particular text model the ways in which writing can be used to communicate knowledge to the world, by informing readers or informing and persuading readers simultaneously?

Developing Critical Thinking

As we mentioned in Chapter One, critical-thinking skills, like writing instruction, are often focused on in the context of other instructional purposes. Learning doesn't happen in a vacuum. You need substance. Therefore, texts that are selected for the purpose of cultivating critical thinking are often selected within another context as well, perhaps providing required content information, serving as a mentor text, or representing a genre. When selecting texts to foster critical-thinking skills such as comparison, synthesis, analysis, and critique, you need to pay attention to the content, the perspective, and the point of view not just of each single text, but how the texts speak to one another and offer students a range of positions on a topic, time period, or genre.

When evaluating a text for the instructional purpose of cultivating critical thinking, ask yourself:

- What are the key ideas and details in this text?
- What perspectives and points-of-view are offered within this text? Which are left out?
- What can a student learn by reading just this text? What does the student learn by reading this text in the context of other texts within a text set?

Engaging in Inquiry and Research

When fostering inquiry as an approach to the overall learning in your classroom, specifically, when the teacher is having students do individual, paired, or small-group research, the teacher is not only choosing a wide range of texts to have available in the classroom, he or she is choosing texts that serve as models of appropriate resources that the students can then use as part of their research. Part of a teacher's planning process is finding texts that are ideally suited to the content in which he or she is doing inquiry and research. Another part of the planning process is finding texts that are great examples of quality and informed research. Yet another part is finding examples of texts that model the kind of writing and composing—whether print, digital, visual, or multimodal—that you want your students doing. Some of the texts that you choose are ideally nonfiction books that represent the "literature of inquiry" (Zarnowski and Turkel 2011), wherein the author models inquiry and the research process. Research is in many ways an apprentice's task. It is best done in the company of someone who can model strong questions, and the ability to make connections across texts. As a teacher, using the right set of texts, you can serve as a mentor researcher as well. Of course, you will also be selecting a wide range of texts that you want your students to use for research, ideally taking on the role of vetting them on their own. Teachers should also encourage students to find new texts independently. The databases paid for by so many state library systems, particularly those created by EBSCO and Gale, have a variety of platforms, that even the youngest of students can learn to use.

When evaluating a text for the instructional purpose of teaching and modeling inquiry and research, ask yourself:

- What is the match between the text and the content we are learning about, either individually, in pairs, small groups, or as a class?
- Is this text well researched? Does the back matter and bibliography demonstrate to my students how someone does thorough research using quality sources?
- Does this text represent "the literature of inquiry"? Does it model the inquiry process, the having of questions, and the ways around stumbling blocks and dead ends?
- Will this text help my students persevere through their own research?
- Is this text going to help me model how I do research? Or is it one that I will have my students explore? Or both?
- How does this text compare to other texts on the topic in terms of all of the above questions?

Fostering a Love of Reading and Reading Habits

To cultivate a love of reading in our students, teachers need to make sure that students are provided with access to texts that capture their interest. This is as true of the high school biology teacher, who might maintain a blog for his or her students in order to curate related content online, as it is of the first grade teacher who immerses his or her students in a print-rich environment. But what interests Erika is not necessarily what interests Mary Ann. Or you. And so it is with our students. What we love isn't always what they love, and when it comes to fostering their reading identities, we need to think of what our students are interested in more than what we like or dislike.

Many times, the classroom library is filled with any and all books that a teacher can find. But targeting your collection development, like a librarian, to meet the varied needs of your current and future students, is an important goal. This is perhaps the simplest instructional purpose to consider, as it becomes automatic. Moreover, when fostering literacy skills and helping students become more adept readers, reading widely is invaluable (Allington 2009). Students need to be able to determine whether texts are both appropriate for their reading level and of sufficient interest to them to be worth reading. Stocking your classroom with books that can meet this wide range of interests will go far in cultivating a love of reading that is combined with growth in reading (Guthrie and Wigfield 2000).

When selecting books to develop a love of reading, ask yourself:

- Who is the audience for this text?
- What about this book reflects my students' interests, passions, worries, or senses of humor?
- Who in my class this year, last year, or maybe in future years, might find this of interest?
- If the book is going to be a challenging read, is there enough interesting content to make students stick with it?

Figure 3.3 provides a guide of the considerations for evaluating a text for instructional purposes. This resource can also be found in Appendix E.

Figure 3.3 Evaluating Text for Instructional Purposes Guide

Instructional Purpose	Ask Yourself...
Understanding Content	- What is the match between my content standards and the text? - What is the match between my content standards and this text in relation to other texts on the topic? - Is information presented in a way that will hook my students and get them even more interested in the unit topic? - Does the information in this text go beyond the standards? How will that impact how my students read it?
Developing Disciplinary Literacies	- Is the vocabulary used in the text authentic to the discipline, but contextually defined in a manner that makes it accessible to my students? - Does the text model the inquiry and/or critical-thinking processes of the discipline either implicitly (for example in an author's note) or explicitly (through direct description in the text)?

Instructional Purpose	Ask Yourself...
Developing Reading Skills	▪ Does this book appeal to students? Will it be worth working on? ▪ How much background knowledge does the book require? Will students be able to comprehend as they decode? ▪ What kinds of words does it contain? What is the balance of sight words, monosyllabic, and polysyllabic words? ▪ How long are the sentences? Too long? Too short? Just right?
Teaching Literacy Analysis/Genre Study	▪ How does this book represent the genre we are studying? ▪ How does the book represent the genre on its own and how does it accomplish this understanding in the context of other books of the same genre or of different genres that focus on the same topic? ▪ What literary elements are at work in the book? Does the author do anything unique with one or two in particular that stand out as very effective examples to use in instruction? ▪ What is the match between the literary elements that are required to be taught according to your school's scope and sequence or state and district standards?
Analyzing Mentor Text for Student Writing	▪ If students are reading "like a writer," what do they learn about genre through this text? ▪ How does this particular text model a particular quality of good writing (for example, varied sentence length) for targeted practice of that skill? ▪ How does this particular text model the ways in which writing can be used to communicate knowledge to the world, by informing readers or informing and persuading readers simultaneously?
Developing Critical Thinking	▪ What are the key ideas and details in this text? ▪ What perspectives and points of view are offered within this text? Which are left out? ▪ What can a student learn by reading just this text? What does the student learn by reading this text in the context of other texts within a text set?
Engaging in Inquiry and Research	▪ Does this text represent "the literature of inquiry"? Does it model the inquiry process, the having of questions, and the ways around stumbling blocks and dead ends? ▪ Will this text help my students persevere through their own research? ▪ Is this text going to help me model how I do research? Or is it one that I will have my students explore? Or both? ▪ How does this text compare to other texts on the topic in terms of all of the above questions?
Developing Reading Habits and Love of Reading	▪ Who is the audience for this text? ▪ What about this book reflects my students' interests, passions, worries, or senses of humor? ▪ Who in my class this year, last year, or maybe in future years, might find this of interest? ▪ If the book is going to be a challenging read, is there enough interesting content to make students stick with it?

Evaluating for Instructional Practices

Our intentions for using a book—our purposes and goals for instruction—influence how we evaluate that book. We have just discussed varying instructional goals in relation to the texts that we select for classroom use. As part of our daily teaching, we employ a variety of classroom practices to help us meet those goals. Sometimes we read a book aloud to our students for whole-group discussion and response. At other times, we select texts for literature circles, engaging a small group of students with the same text and asking them to interpret and respond to the text, or for guided reading groups or teacher-led small group work. We also select books for students to read independently, closely matching the book to a particular reader. Starting in the intermediate grades and continuing through high school, teachers may ask the whole class to read the same book at the same time.

In the sections that follow, we'll share guidelines for how to select texts for use in each of these practices, considering their potential for both literacy and content-area instruction. One's decisions will always be shaped by one's curriculum focus, instructional purposes and goals, and students.

What Makes a Good Read Aloud?

One of our chief pleasures in teaching is the opportunity to read aloud to a whole class or small group of students. At times, teaching is a lot like performing and reading aloud is a wonderful opportunity to interact with a receptive audience. We love the give and take that happens as we share a book with students, especially the responses that surprise us and prompt all of us to think more deeply about the content of the book. We are strong advocates for reading aloud to students at *all* grade levels; we frequently read aloud to even our adult graduate students. We know from our experiences that being read to has almost universal appeal, and we know that when we read aloud we model a love of language and information, fluent expressive reading, and our own engagement with and responses to well-written text.

Our colleagues at Lesley University are probably no longer surprised when they walk by our office to find one of us holding a children's or young adult book and reading a section out loud to the other. When we come across beautiful language or fascinating information, we can't help but share it. Considering the potential of a book, or section of a book, as material for reading aloud, the first question that we ask ourselves is whether we think the text will hold the interest of our audience. Is the language engaging—does it flow well with strong pacing, have interesting word choices, and opportunities for expressive reading/ performance? Of course, we also consider the information that the text contains. Does the book convey information that we want all of our students to consider? Is it a good match to the standards for this particular area of study? We also think about whether the book will generate productive discussion around this information, allowing us to meet a literacy instructional goal of enhancing students' speaking and listening skills, while simultaneously meeting a content learning goal. Often the text that we read aloud is a more complex text, one that students would not be able to read on their own. Reading it to students allows us to engage with the text together and students are supported in understanding vocabulary and concepts that they might not be able to understand on their own. We also find it an added bonus when we think the reading of the book will foster inquiry, either by prompting students to ask questions about the information or when the text itself models the inquiry process. When evaluating a text for use as a read aloud to model various aspects of reading fluency, the effectiveness of the text at highlighting certain language conventions is important. For example, a text may have rich language, varied sentences, and the repetition of a question, all of which can be modeled with inflection and voice.

When evaluating a text for the instructional practice of reading aloud, ask yourself:

- Is there a flow to the language that makes it enjoyable to read aloud?
- Will the content engage the interest of the whole class?
- Is there potential for the text to generate discussion?
- Does it contain information that is critical for your unit of study?
- Does the book inspire inquiry by prompting students to ask questions?

What Makes a Good Literature Circle Book?

Harvey Daniels describes literature circles as student-led book discussion groups (2002). In this structure, groups of students read the same text independently and then come together to discuss the book. The teacher serves as a facilitator, making sure that groups operate smoothly, while students are responsible for navigating the content of the text together. This practice has several benefits: students hone their reading, speaking, and listening skills (and their writing skills if we ask students to prepare for their discussion groups with written notes) and we are also providing students time and space to offer their own questions and understandings around a topic of study. The length of a text for literature circles can vary, depending on the reading abilities of your students and whether the group will meet for multiple sessions together or for a single discussion meeting.

Daniels and Harvey (2009) explore the potential of literature circles for content-area learning in their book, *Comprehension and Collaboration: Inquiry Circles in Action*. When considering a text for literature circles in the context of a unit of study, we first consider the information contained in the text. Typically, we use this practice as an opportunity for small groups of students to either review or explore more deeply the information that has been previously discussed in a whole-class activity. Then using our lens of evaluating for quality, we consider whether the text will generate productive discussion among students. Will students benefit from the chance to explore their understandings of the ideas and concepts in the book with their classmates? Finally, we think about how the students will read the book. Is the text at a level of complexity that students will be able to access independently (remember, we will be discussing the definition of text complexity in more detail in the next chapter)? We might also consider whether we can provide support for some students to access the text, either through reading the text with the direct support of a parent, teacher, or classroom assistant or by listening to an audio version of the text.

When evaluating a text for the instructional practice of literature circles, ask yourself:

- Will the text generate student discussion?
- Will students benefit from the opportunity to discuss/extend their understanding of the content with peers?
- Does the text provide a review of important content information or does the text provide an expansion of information that is well matched to the readers in the group?

What Makes a Good Guided Reading Book?

Working with a small group of students allows the teacher to provide more targeted support for students. Our colleagues at Lesley University in the Literacy Collaborative provide wonderful guidance for thinking about how to use flexible guided reading groups to tailor your instruction to student needs (Fountas and Pinnell 1996; Fountas and Pinnell 2001). As described by Fountas and Pinnell this practice offers a forum for precision reading instruction: "[Guided reading] is an instructional context within which the precise teaching moves and language choices are related to the behaviors observed, moment by moment, and which guide the reader to engage in problem solving that expands his or her reading power" (2013, 279). Teachers may be very familiar with using this structure in their literacy instruction, but we see this structure as having tremendous potential for content-area instruction as well. Generally, guided reading sessions with a small group run around 15–30 minutes long, so when we select a text for use in this structure, it is usually a shorter text or a selection from a longer text. Students will read the text during the session, receiving guidance from the teacher.

When considering a book for use in a guided reading lesson with a small group of students, we consider the potential of the book from several angles. First, since students will be working toward reading this text independently, we consider the complexity of the text (we will be offering you more guidance on how to do this in Chapter Four). Will the text offer students the right level of challenge to help them grow as readers? Can students read and comprehend the text with some adult support? At the same time, since we use the practice of guided reading as a coaching structure, we also consider the potential of the text for reading strategy/ comprehension instruction (for more support with this, please see our list of favorite resources in the sidebar). Can we use the text to model a comprehension strategy for students that can be followed by an opportunity for students to practice this strategy themselves? We also consider the informational content of the text in relation to the curriculum goals. Does the text offer an opportunity to review key information? Or alternatively, does the text offer a chance for interested students to expand upon, or explore more deeply, information that was previously learned?

When evaluating a text for the instructional practice of guided reading, ask yourself:

- Is the text at a level that students can read and comprehend with some support?
- Does the text offer an opportunity for strategy instruction to help students grow as readers?
- Does the text provide a review of content study information previously discussed in a whole-group setting, or does it provide an opportunity to expand on content information that is well matched to the readers in the group?

What Makes a Good Independent Read?

In the context of a unit of study, the structure of independent reading offers several opportunities. One might provide a student with a text that reviews content from the unit, providing reinforcement for key concepts that he or she may be having difficulty with. An English language learner may also benefit from an independent read with a text that reviews key vocabulary from the unit. Independent reading may also offer students an opportunity to pursue an area of personal interest further. When we provide, or guide a student to select, a text for independent reading, we consider the complexity of the text (we will be offering you more guidance on how to do this in Chapter Four). We want to make sure that the student can read and understand the text independently and that the text is neither too hard nor too easy, but offers students a chance to practice their decoding and comprehension skills and grow as a reader.

When evaluating a text for the instructional practice of independent reading, ask yourself:

- Is the text neither too hard nor too easy, offering the reader a chance to develop his or her reading abilities?
- Does the text provide either a review of information previously learned or an expansion of content study information that is well matched to the reader's particular interests?

> Kylene Beers. 2002. *When Kids Can't Read: What Teachers Can Do*. Heinemann.
>
> Nancy Frey and Douglas Fisher. 2007. *Reading for Information in Elementary School: Content Literacy Strategies to Build Comprehension*. Pearson/Merrill Prentice Hall.
>
> Nancy Frey and Douglas Fisher. 2011. *Improving Adolescent Literacy: Content Area Strategies at Work*, 3rd ed. Pearson/Merrill Prentice Hall.
>
> Irene C. Fountas and Gay Su Pinnell. 1996 *Guided Reading: Good First Teaching for All Children*. Heinemann.
>
> Irene C. Fountas and Gay Su Pinnell. 2001. *Guiding Readers and Writers, Grades 3-6: Teaching Comprehension, Genre, and Content Literacy*. Heinemann.
>
> Stephanie Harvey and Anne Goudvis. 2007. *Strategies that Work: Teaching Comprehension for Understanding and Engagement*, 2nd ed. Stenhouse Publishers.
>
> Chris Tovani. 2000. *I Read It, But I Don't Get It: Comprehension Strategies for Adolescent Readers*. Stenhouse Publishers.

What Makes a Good Whole-Class Read?

There are a range of reasons why a teacher in upper elementary, middle, or high school might assign the same book for all students to read, knowing that a wide range of reading abilities and dispositions are represented in the class. When we refer to a "whole class read," we mean that everyone is reading the book independently in some fashion. The decision to do a whole text read is informed by one's instructional purpose(s). What match exists between the instructional purpose and the content of the book? But the decision also hinges on the balance between the complexity of that text and the varied needs, interests, and abilities of one's readers.

As we have said often in this book, instructional purposes for reading in school vary a great deal. Sometimes the content that must be covered drives the instructional purpose. Students may read the same book in order to tackle the content that it contains, whether that be genre, theme, and literary elements in English language arts, or content information and disciplinary understandings in science and social studies. When integrating curriculum, the content could be both. Sometimes, a whole-class read is selected because you want to create a classroom community, much like many towns and cities have begun to create a One Book program in which hundreds or even thousands of people choose to read the same book at the same time. Conversation brings people together. A single book can both create and challenge the sense of community in your classroom; having everyone read the same text allows everyone to be a part of the same conversation.

A book that is ideal for a whole-class read therefore is one that matches the instructional purpose. In terms of content, an English language arts class might focus on a genre or theme, and the collective reading of the text serves as a core text or anchor for the other kinds of reading and multimodal experiences the students might have. As such, the book selected should be one that best demonstrates particular attributes of a genre, or disrupts students' preconceived notions of the genre. Sometimes a book is selected for required whole-class reading in language arts because it captures an intended theme or raises important and interesting questions that your students will dig in to with passionate written responses, class discussions, and debates. In social studies, science, the arts, or even in mathematics, a book might be selected as a whole-class read because it conveys content dictated by state curriculum standards, and the book will serve as one of the vehicles through which students access that content. There are also books that can serve as milestone experiences for readers—books that raise the kinds of questions and concerns that match the developmental stage of the reader. For example, we know many seventh and eighth grade teachers who teach with *The Giver* by Lois Lowry (1994), precisely because the range of issues the book raises and the age of the protagonist greatly resonates with the young adolescents in their classrooms, giving them rich content to explore and discuss.

While we will discuss complexity in great detail in the next chapter, it is important to address it briefly here, in the context of whole-class reads, that the complexity matters. Not all students in a class can read all texts, and they can't all read them in the same way. So when selecting a book as a whole-class read, the interests and the abilities of all of the students have to be considered. Who might struggle with the book? What supports are in place to scaffold that experience? How will class explorations help students access the text in ways that further support understanding? This is where differentiated instruction is essential, and through the use of small and large group discussions, audio books, e-readers, and other methods, students are given the opportunity to access the text and participate in shared conversations. Another important consideration is the length of the book, and how long it will take students to read it cover to cover, and if they are expected to read it at the same pace as one another.

When evaluating a text for the instructional practice of whole-class reading, ask yourself:

- Is the text a good match for your instructional purpose and content learning goals?
- Can enough of the students in the class read and interpret the content independently?
- Will the text generate discussion among the students?

Figure 3.4 provides a guide of the considerations for evaluating a text for instructional practices. This resource can also be found in Appendix E.

Figure 3.4 Evaluating Text for Instructional Practices Guide

Instructional Practice	Ask Yourself...
Read Aloud	- Is there a flow to the language that makes it enjoyable to read aloud? - Will the content engage the interest of the whole class? - Is there potential for the text to generate discussion? - Does it contain information that is critical for your unit of study? - Does the book inspire inquiry by prompting students to ask questions?
Literature Circles	- Will the text generate student discussion? - Will students benefit from the opportunity to discuss/extend their understanding of the content with peers? - Does the text provide a review of important content information or does the text provide an expansion of information that is well matched to the readers in the group?
Guided Reading	- Is the text at a level that students can read and comprehend with some support? - Does the text offer an opportunity for strategy instruction to help students grow as readers? - Does the text provide a review of content study information previously discussed in a whole-group setting, or does it provide an opportunity to expand on content information that is well matched to the readers in the group?
Independent Reading	- Is the text neither too hard nor too easy, offering the reader a chance to develop his or her reading abilities? - Does the text provide either a review of information previously learned or an expansion of content study information that is well matched to the reader's particular interests?
Whole-Class Reading	- Is the text a good match for your instructional purpose and content learning goals? - Can enough of the students in the class read and interpret the content independently? - Will the text generate discussion among the students?

Considering Utility: Instructional Purpose and Practice—An Example

In the previous sections, we have discussed the kinds of considerations we make related to our instructional purposes and practices. In Chapter Two, we considered the quality of a text and whether it was "good." In this chapter, we have been considering the different processes for determining "What is it good for?"

Let's go back to our initial consideration of Barbara Kerley's picture book biography *Those Rebels, John and Tom* (2012). At the end of Chapter Two, we shared our initial response to the book with you in narrative format, and then began to complete the Quality, Utility, and Complexity Chart as an example of our "shorthand thinking."

One of the many things that struck us about this book was the potential it had to play different roles within the social studies curriculum. Many fourth and fifth graders around the country study the American Revolution as part of their curriculum. As such, this book provides a snapshot of the complexity of that time, and an opportunity to teach both content standards and disciplinary literacy. It is a window into the lives of Jefferson and Adams, but also into our emerging national identity and regional differences that existed then as they do now. We can see that the book could be used to deliver content about the American Revolution and the Declaration of Independence while also exploring the multiple perspectives of people from different regions of the 13 colonies. In addition to the content about the specific time period of the American Revolution, the book is a lens through which we can explore political friendships and relationships in any time period, a jumping off point from which students can explore other relationships between allies and enemies.

The book has another role to play within both social studies and language arts—as a mentor text for writing biography. Furthermore, there are key aspects of the writing that could be highlighted in a lesson on transitional phrases and compare and contrast text structure.

We are not saying that we would do *all* of these instructional activities with *Those Rebels, John and Tom* with the fifth graders studying the American Revolution. These are options, a wide-open brainstorm of the possibilities for instruction. We think it's best to cast a wide net, consider many possibilities, and then narrow down our instructional purposes and refine our goals, a process that we address at an in-depth level in our previous book *Teaching with Text Sets* (Cappiello and Dawes 2012).

Now that you have learned more about how to consider a text for instructional purpose and practice, Figure 3.5 shows more of the *Quality, Utility, and Complexity Chart* completed for *Those Rebels, John and Tom*.

Figure 3.5 Sample Partially Completed *Quality, Utility, and Complexity Chart* for *Those Rebels, John and Tom*

Utility as a Teaching Tool: Instructional Possibilities (Purpose/Practice)
Instructional Purposes
Understanding Content
In social studies, the book could be used to explore political relationships in general, and as a lens for looking at how Congress functions today.
This book would also be useful as part of a text set of biographies of historical figures from the American Revolution, to better understand the time period.
Developing Disciplinary Literacies
This book could be read in the context of exploring the Declaration of Independence as a document, helping to scaffold student understanding of how the document was written. The document was created as a result of a process that involved more than one person. Who were those people? How did they work together? How is the Declaration of Independence an end product of their collaboration, not simply something set in stone from the very beginning?
Using as Mentor Text for Student Writing
As a "double portrait" mentor text in social studies, students can learn about how to write about two figures from any time period, for students to see figures as interconnected. Students could also read *George vs. George: The American Revolution as Seen by Both Sides* by Rosalyn Schanzer, about George Washington and King George of England, as another mentor text; as part of a composition study of parallel structure in writing comparisons and contrasts in language arts.
Teaching Literary Analysis and Genre Study
As part of a biography genre study in language arts, students can examine author's craft while reading this and *Worst of Friends*, another narrative book about the friendship between Thomas Jefferson and John Adams.
Developing Reading Skills
Reading this book allows students to hear some of the transitional phrases used to compare and contrast the two men, showing students how identifying the text structure supports their understanding of a nonfiction text.
Instructional Practices
This book works well as a read aloud for reading for understanding content, developing disciplinary literacy, analyzing mentor texts, and developing reading skills.
As a literature circle book, it could be used as one group's exploration of "founding fathers," while other groups read other perspectives.
For a biography genre study, it would be ideal for a whole-class read as a mentor text.

Conclusion

As this chapter shows, there are many different lenses that we can use to make decisions about which texts are used in our classrooms and why. The evaluation of a text for quality and utility encompasses that careful balance between "is it good?" and "what is it good for?" When considering what a text is "good for," we need to reflect on our instructional purposes. These instructional purposes can be separate and highly focused, or combined with one another. What purpose you adopt as the primary lens for selection will differ depending upon your role, and the grade level at which you teach. As you consider how the text will fit into the curriculum you are building or revising, you will also consider the classroom practice that best showcases the strengths of the text and its potential for teaching. In Chapter Four, we discuss the next step in the process of text selection: the deeper consideration of the range of readers in your classroom, and how to analyze the reader, text, and activity to determine the complexity of a text.

Questions for Reflection

1. How do the instructional purposes that we have discussed in this chapter mirror the lenses that you typically use when selecting texts?

2. How do the instructional practices that we have discussed in this chapter match your own classroom practices? Did your thinking about the way you use those practices shift?

3. In what ways does this process feel new to you?

Chapter 4
Considering Complexity

Now we are ready to dive into a conversation about text complexity. We have guided your thinking about the complexity of the reading process, the literary and artistic value of the book as an art form, and the utility of a book as a teaching tool. Chapter One detailed the different purposes, contexts, and lenses for reading that contribute to the complexity of the process. Chapter Two asked you to consider the quality of a book and whether or not you want to use it in your classroom. Chapter Three gave you the tools to consider the range of instructional goals that a text could help you meet. Within our three-part evaluation process, we are now ready to focus on our third step: the consideration of the complexity of the text as shown in Figure 4.1, and how the complexity of that text is interdependent on how you will use the text in your classroom and the specific reader(s) you have in mind.

Figure 4.1 Considerations for Text Selection

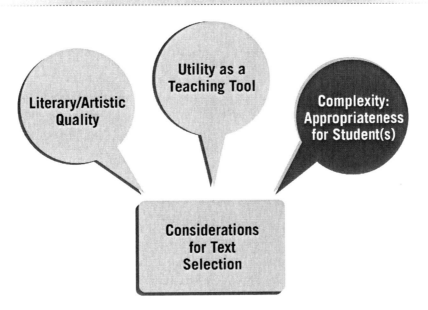

Multiple factors influence the complexity of a text for a particular reader at a particular time. The premise of our process for selecting texts for classroom use is our understanding that texts are complex based on how they are written, the content and the information they contain, who the reader is, and what the reader will be doing with the text and for what purpose. Essentially, we believe that the same text can be complex in different ways and in different contexts. And of course, with different readers.

There is no one number or measure that can determine how difficult a text is. There is no single label to measure any book. However, Common Core Reading Anchor Standard 10 for text complexity outlines specific goals for where students should be as readers by the end of certain grade levels or grade spans. Common Core Reading Anchor Standard 10 states "Read and comprehend complex literary and informational text independently and proficiently" (CCSSO 2010, 35). This is not something we can ignore, but it is something we can take ownership of and pull into the decisions that we make about developmental-appropriateness for our students, or what they read and when they read it.

We consider a conversation about text complexity as a natural part of our process of evaluating and selecting texts for classroom practice. To do this, we harness the evaluation criteria that we discussed in Chapter Two, which helps us to understand how a text operates; and the instructional purposes we discussed in Chapter Three, which helps us to see the range of roles any one text can have in the classroom, and use them concurrently as a foundation for determining the *complexity* of a text. In reality, a text is complex only in context. The fact that text complexity can be measured for a text in isolation is a myth.

In this chapter, we will first dissect some common misconceptions and concerns regarding the Common Core State Standards that impact discussions of Standard 10; detail the expectations of the standard as it is explicated in Appendix A; discuss how we harness those expectations as a part of our text selection process; and finally, discuss the implications of Standard 10 for school and district curriculum planning.

Common Misconceptions and Concerns

Many schools in America have spent the past decade "teaching to the test." Because of the punitive measures put in place by No Child Left Behind in 2001, schools have viewed the annual testing in grades 3 through 8 as the focal point for much of instruction. Curriculum has become synonymous in many schools with test preparation. Now, new assessments accompany the Common Core State Standards, and states are planning their roll out in different ways.

Because no changes have been made to the NCLB legislation, formerly known as the Elementary and Secondary Schools Act, schools are still fearful of the implications of test results. In states and districts that won Race to the Top grant funding from the federal government, new teacher assessment systems are being put into place, and a component in those evaluation systems includes the standardized test scores of students. Now, more than ever, particularly in Race to the Top states and districts, standardized tests are critical components of how teachers are viewed and evaluated by internal constituencies, such as principals and superintendents, and external constituencies, such as parents, community members, and the news media. This new use for standardized tests, regardless of whether one thinks of it as appropriate or inappropriate, puts new pressures on teachers, but it also puts a great deal of pressure and responsibility on the children and adolescents taking those tests.

Our concern with this continued emphasis on standardized tests and one that we know is shared by many teachers and colleagues, is that the most important instrument to measure reading growth is one that feels *authentic* to students and their families. Authentic measurements can only be established when teachers within a school and district have time to talk about common reading goals; they happen when teachers have time to talk with students and their parents about common reading goals on a personal level. This is not the same thing as providing students and families with numbers and test scores and reading levels.

The practice of reporting student progress in guided reading levels is common in the schools in which we work; however this practice, too, stems from a misconception. The innovators of these practices themselves say: "Educators have sometimes made the mistake of thinking that guided reading is the reading program or that all of the books students read should be leveled. We have argued against the overuse of levels. We have never recommended that the school library or classroom libraries be leveled or that levels be reported to parents" (Fountas and Pinnell 2013, 281). Like Fountas and Pinnell, we believe that the best measures of a student's growth in reading are what that student has to say about what he or she reads, how that develops from September to June, and the wide array of individual, small-group, and whole-class reading experiences he or she has. At the middle and high school level, these individual conversations are as important as at the elementary level. Student understanding of what they are reading, and why, in science and social studies, is as important as in language arts. These are the conversations that we must foster as individuals, teaching teams, and school-wide communities.

Schools and teachers are under a lot of pressure transitioning to the standards and anticipating the new assessments. Because of this pressure, Standard 10 has often been reduced to a focus on a number—a readability level for texts that students need to achieve. In many cases, this number is the Lexile number associated with a book, because it is something concrete and specific.

We also hear of schools creating curriculum around the books that are listed in Appendix B, because they have already been deemed appropriate for certain grade levels and make the selection process easier. In some cases, this list of *exemplar* texts is now being interpreted as a list of *required* texts. These books are merely examples, not a representative list of the kinds of books available to readers at different grade spans. In fact, the informational texts listed for middle school and high school almost completely sidestep the field of middle grade and young adult nonfiction, and the opportunities for student reading in a range of content areas these nonfiction texts provide. Because teachers and administrators are feeling overwhelmed, curriculum materials are being selected based on what other people have said about them, without a specific purpose or context in mind, and without teacher or student ownership.

These misconceptions influence, and make unclear, the important conversations that could be happening around text selection and complexity in schools. Genuine concern has been expressed specifically about the appropriateness of Standard 10 when it comes to the reality of student readers, particularly students who are struggling readers. We know that we can't wave a magic wand and ensure that students are reading, comprehending, and analyzing appropriately complex texts for their age. We also can't effectively meet Standard 10 if all we do is have students read texts that meet the quantitative measurements for text complexity for their grade level or band. We can't effectively meet Standard 10 if we ignore the very real strengths and weaknesses of students as readers and writers. We have trouble even articulating what an appropriately complex text as a Platonic ideal is because we can't separate the text from the context and the range of readers involved; "the complexity of a text is not static at all" (Nesi 2012, 20).

Ultimately, we believe that we can harness the elements of text complexity that are detailed in Standard 10 and appropriate them into the process that we have always used to determine whether a text was suitable for our classroom. We think other teachers can, too. This is not to say that we are always perfect in our choices. Each of us can think about times when we made missteps, when we thought students could read something that proved to be too challenging, or too dull to motivate them to get through it. This is all part of the messy process that is teaching. We and our students learn as much about the reading process from these experiences as we do when the selections we make are a good fit. It allows us all to understand the recalibration that has to happen when we are not reading well and it emphasizes the fundamental importance of self-monitoring. This way of thinking necessitates a degree of ownership over who in the school is making the choices about what students are reading and why. That ownership is at the core of this book. We don't think such ownership is an "add on" or a "luxury." We think a sense of agency, on the part of teachers and students, is at the core of student learning.

So, to be clear, we are going to walk a careful line in this chapter. We want to explain Standard 10 and equip you with an understanding of it. But we also want to demonstrate that, from our perspective, it is not the only, or even the most important piece of the puzzle, to pay attention to when it comes to choosing and using books in school. It is one piece of this process. To us, Standard 10 is the finish line, not the starting point. All of us want to make sure that our students are successful as readers, writers, and thinkers. All of us want to foster a love of reading. All of us need to have the highest of expectations for our students, combined with a realistic understanding of what they can and can't do in September, February, and May. As teachers, we understand that each year, students arrive in our classes with a range of reading capacities, experiences, and interests. We have many things to teach them. Our job is to move them forward. Having common goals is helpful. We are not teaching to the test, but to something far more complex—the real world. We are teaching to *complexity*.

Expectations of Range, Quality, and Complexity

So what does Standard 10 actually say? How is text complexity defined in the Common Core Standards? Technically, Standard 10 is called "Range, Quality, and Complexity." But the standard does not reveal a lot of detail about the range of texts or the quality of texts selected.

For the K–5 standards, they suggest that "[t]hrough extensive reading of stories, dramas, poems, and myths from diverse cultures and different time periods, students gain literary and cultural knowledge as well as familiarity with various text structures and elements. By reading texts in history/social studies, science, and other disciplines, students build a foundation of knowledge in these fields that will also give them the background to be better readers in all content areas. Students can only gain this foundation when the curriculum is intentionally and coherently structured to develop rich content knowledge within and across grades" (2010c, 10).

For the 6–12 standards, they suggest that "[t]hrough wide and deep reading of literature and literary nonfiction of steadily increasing sophistication, students gain a reservoir of literary and cultural knowledge, references, and images; the ability to evaluate intricate arguments; and the capacity to surmount the challenges posed by complex texts" (2010c, 35).

Within Standard 10 descriptors, there are a range of text types articulated by genre for grades K–5, and another for grades 6–12. The 2012 "Supplemental Information for Appendix A of the Common Core State Standards for English Language Arts and Literacy: New Research on Text Complexity" also clarifies that "[s]electing texts for student readings should not only depend on text complexity but also on considerations of quality and coherence" (2012d, 7). In essence, the standards demand that students read widely, and that the selections are well-written texts of all genres and modalities. Nothing to argue with, right? It all makes sense.

But what of the third component of Standard 10: complexity?

Figure 4.2 Common Core Standards Model of Text Complexity

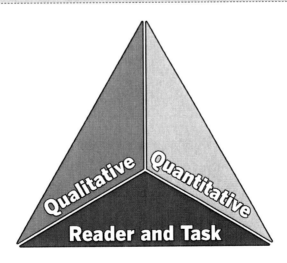

This triangle appears within Standard 10 and it details the balancing act that takes place when a teacher is determining if a text is an appropriate selection for the classroom. On the left side, is the Qualitative Analysis of the text's complexity; on the right side, is the Quantitative Analysis of the text's complexity. Serving as a foundation on the bottom is the consideration of the reader as well as the task, the purpose for reading. No one part of this triangle is any bigger than the other. In fact, Appendix A specifically affirms that the triangle "consists of three equally important parts" (2010a, 4). The three elements work together to inform one another and help a teacher determine whether or not a text is an appropriate fit for the reader(s) and the instructional purpose.

However, within the Qualitative Analysis of Appendix A, this method is described as "a necessary complement and sometimes as a corrective to quantitative measures" (5). This language seems to privilege the Quantitative Analysis, which makes us uncomfortable. Furthermore, Appendix A states that the description of each "should be considered only provisional; more precise, more accurate, and easier-to-use tools are urgently needed to help make text complexity a vital, everyday part of classroom instruction and curriculum planning" (5). All of these tools are a work in progress. We view this book as one set of tools to use toward making appropriate text selections. But professional development and teacher education may be the most powerful tool that is needed, not more computer programs or one-size-fits-all models. Empowering teachers and building their capacity to make decisions about texts and creating school-based processes for fostering these conversations is, from our standpoint, much more urgent.

In the sections that follow, we'll unpack each of the three elements of the text complexity triangle (see Figure 4.2), incorporating in our discussion a consideration of the quality of the text (using the evaluation criteria we described in Chapter Two) and the potential instructional uses for the text (using the criteria for consideration we described in Chapter Three).

Considering the Text

The standards suggest two methods to use as lenses for the complexity of any particular text: quantitative and qualitative. The quantitative methods are completed according to numeric computations, and they focus on certain measurable and quantifiable elements of the text. The qualitative method focuses more on how the text operates and the nuances of text, and is closely aligned with the analysis of text quality that we focused on in Chapter Two. We will discuss this more specifically later in the chapter.

Quantitative Analysis

Quantitative analysis is defined as the portion of the text complexity triangle as "those aspects of text complexity, such as word length or frequency, sentence length, and text cohesion, that are difficult if not impossible for a human reader to evaluate efficiently, especially in long texts, and are thus today typically measured by computer software" (2010).

Quantitative analysis of text complexity relies on computer-based computations based on scanned text excerpts.

The "Supplemental Information for Appendix A of the Common Core State Standards for English Language Arts and Literacy: New Research on Text Complexity" (2010d) details more specifically than the original standards the range of quantitative tools that currently exist. They consist of the following:

Figure 4.3 Quantitative Tools for Measuring Text Complexity

ATOS by Renaissance Learning
   http://www.renlearn.com/atos/

Degrees of Reading Power (DRP) by Questar Assessment, Inc.
   http://drp.questarai.com/home/

Flesch-Kincaid

The Lexile Framework for Reading by MetaMetrics
   http://www.lexile.com/

Reading Maturity Metric by Pearson Education
   http://www.readingmaturity.com/rmm-web/#/

TextEvaluator by Educational Testing Service
   https://texteval-pilot.ets.org/TextEvaluator/

Easability Indicator by Coh-Metrix
   http://141.225.42.101/cohmetrixgates/Home.aspx?Login=1

Some of these quantitative measurement systems require a subscription; others require that you sign up with an email account or username and password. Still others, like the Lexile Framework and ATOS, allow you to search their databases without subscribing or registering.

Since the publication of the Common Core State Standards, additional information has been provided to educators on the quantitative elements of text complexity in the "Supplemental Information for Appendix A of the Common Core State Standards for English Language Arts and Literacy: New Research on Text Complexity" (2012). The results of one research project determined that "all of the quantitative metrics were reliably and often highly correlated with grade level and student performance based measures of text difficulty across a variety of text sets and reference measures" (Supplemental to Appendix A 2010d, 3). Essentially, each system was evaluating texts with primarily consistent outcomes. A new "common scale for cross comparisons of the quantitative tools" was created, allowing teachers to work across the different measurement tools to select texts in the agreed-upon context of the scale's measurement of text complexity.

To create the scale, the researchers started with the reading material common in a first-year of college course or a vocational training program. Thus, the scale privileges the reading done by adults and then "recalibrates" in descending order the reduction of complexity in reading from the 11th to the 2nd grade levels. An example of the scale is shown as follows:

Figure 4.4 Updated Text Complexity Grade Bands and Associated Ranges from Multiple Measures

Common Core Band	ATOS	Degrees of Reading Power®	Flesch-Kinkaid	The Lexile Framework®	Reading Maturity	SourceRater
2nd–3rd	2.75–5.14	42–54	1.98–5.34	420–820	3.53–6.13	0.05–2.48
4th–5th	4.97–7.03	52–60	4.51–7.73	740–1010	5.42–7.92	0.84–5.75
6th–8th	7.00–9.98	57–67	6.51–10.34	925–1185	7.04–9.57	4.11–10.66
9th–10th	9.67–12.01	62–72	8.32–12.12	1050–1335	8.41–10.81	9.02–13.93
11th–CCR	11.20–14.10	67–74	10.34–14.2	1185–1385	9.57–12.00	12.30–14.50

(CCSSO 2010, Appendix A)

But what do these numbers reveal? What do they tell us? As "The Supplemental to Appendix A" suggests, "[t]he tools for measuring text complexity are at once useful and imperfect" (7).

We consider quantitative measurements with caution. As Olga Nesi (2012) reminds us, these measures "while profoundly comforting and easiest to determine, can be largely misleading… Quantitative measurements encourage us to slap a number, letter, or grade level on a text and be done with it. Librarians and classroom teachers know intuitively that these labels do not work" (20). They do not work precisely because they do not take into consideration variables related to readers and tasks.

There are additional concerns, particularly among elementary educators and researchers, regarding the ways in which this quantitative "staircase of complexity" has been constructed. Specifically, the Lexile® Framework, which was the primary quantitative method initially identified by the Common Core State Standards, recalibrated its grade band and Lexile matches to accommodate the new focus on college and career readiness. But, as Elfrieda Hiebert has asked, "what is the evidence that raising levels of text complexity, especially for primary-level texts, fosters the goal of college and career readiness?" (2011 and 2012, 26). Are we setting students up for failure in the primary and intermediate grades by pushing texts that are too complex too soon? For example, is there enough research to demonstrate that successful third grade readers in the past did not continue to be successful readers because the texts they read in third grade were not challenging enough (Hiebert 2011, 2012)? Hiebert encourages the education community to reconsider this new scale of complexity, arguing that "it is not at all clear that college and career readiness at high school graduation will be supported by raising the height of the staircase step at third grade and asking young students to jump higher and faster" (27).

Our greatest concern regarding an over-reliance on the quantitative measurement of a book is that these computer and mathematical computations focus exclusively on concrete elements like word length and frequency, sentence length, and structure. They can't read for content, nuance, or theme. Therefore, they have the potential to be highly inaccurate for determining text appropriateness. This is particularly true when attempting to calculate the complexity of narrative text. As the Supplemental to Appendix A cautions, "[r]esearch showed more disagreement among the quantitative measures when applied to narrative fiction in high complexity bands than with informational texts or texts in lower grade bands" (2012, 8). The informal language and dialogue of narrative fiction belies the complexity of its themes and content. There is no widely accepted system of quantitative measurement for poetry and drama, or beginner reader texts, because they are too difficult to quantify.

To illustrate the concerns about quantitative measurement, we consider Jacqueline Woodson's young adult novel *Behind You* (2004). *Behind You* receives a score of 720 on the Lexile Framework, and a 4.1 on the ATOS, placing it solidly in the middle of second grade to the end of 5th grade complexity bands. But this eloquently written novel is quite complex. Not only do the chapters alternate with different first person narrations, but the book focuses on sensitive issues of race, class, gender, and sexuality. The starting point of the book is the aftermath of a death; Jeremiah, an African-American teenager has been mistakenly shot and killed by police. It is not a book for elementary readers, despite the numerical score it receives. On the other hand, Woodson's fictional picture book, *Each Kindness* (2012), receives a Lexile score of 640, and an ATOS score of 3.4, putting it solidly in the 2nd to 3rd grade complexity band. We believe this makes sense for this book. Numerically, the books are not that far away from one another in their quantitative labels. But we know and understand because of our knowledge of the books that each would be read with very different groups of students.

The Common Core State Standards demand that we take the quantitative evaluation of a book into consideration. And so, we do. Oftentimes, we have little disagreement with the numbers the databases generate. We simply believe that our qualitative analysis of the text is more important. We also disagree with the process outlined in the Supplemental to Appendix A, which recommends (but does not require!) that a teacher first determine the grade band via a quantitative measurement and then use qualitative measures to "locate a text in a specific grade" (2012, 7). This would suggest that if we were 6th grade teachers, we would first determine the quantitative level of complexity, to ensure the book falls within the grades 6–8 band before qualitatively analyzing the book.

We believe it is more important to start with the qualitative assessment, and then we use the quantitative to shed a new perspective on our analysis. Furthermore, we take with caution the recommendation that "the overwhelming majority of texts that students read in a given year should fall within the quantitative range for that band" (8). If the texts were also appropriate for our readers and our content focus, this would be ideal. But the reality of the range of readers in our classroom may dictate a different calibration and range, and our understanding of the potential for books outside of that range to engage our students also suggests otherwise. Moving students through the year and through the grade bands over the years, we strive to transition to such a number. But we believe *we* are the most important arbitrators of text selection, not mathematical formulas.

Qualitative Analysis

The "Supplemental Information for Appendix A" document states that "considerations of quality and coherence should always be at play when selecting text," (7) and we couldn't agree more. That is why we want to parallel the criteria articulated by the Common Core State Standards for a *qualitative* determination of text complexity with our evaluation criteria for *quality*. It's all about qualifying. As we have said earlier in this book, we believe it is essential that you feel confident evaluating books in a number of ways—for their quality, their complexity, and the various roles they can play in the classroom. But first, we want to be clear about what the standards state about qualitative analysis of text complexity.

Appendix A of the Common Core State Standards states that "in the Standards, *qualitative dimensions* and *qualitative factors* refer to those aspects of text complexity best measured or only measurable by an attentive human reader, such as levels of meaning or purpose; structure; language conventionality and clarity; and knowledge demands" (2010, 4). These four categories outlined in Appendix A have become the foundation for conversations in and out of schools and in the education community about the qualitative aspects of text complexity.

Levels of Meaning/Purpose

Appendix A of the Common Core State Standards states that the *level of meaning* refers to a literary text, while the *purpose* refers to an informational text. Appendix A states that "[l]iterary texts with a single level of meaning tend to be easier to read than literary texts with multiple levels of meaning (such as satires, in which the author's literal message is intentionally at odds with his or her underlying message). Similarly, informational texts with an explicitly stated purpose are generally easier to comprehend than informational texts with an implicit, hidden, or obscure purpose" (2010, 5).

Structure

The second element of the qualitative analysis addresses text structure. Appendix A tells us that "[s]imple literary texts tend to relate events in chronological order, while complex literary texts make more frequent use of flashbacks, flash-forwards, and other manipulations of time and sequence. Simple informational texts are likely not to deviate from the conventions of common genres and subgenres, while complex informational texts are more likely to conform to the norms and conventions of a specific discipline" (2010, 5). While the focus is on structure; illustrations, format, and graphics are included in the discussion. "Graphics tend to be simple and either unnecessary or merely supplementary to the meaning of texts of low complexity, whereas texts of high complexity tend to have similarly complex graphics, graphics whose interpretation is essential to understanding the text, and graphics that provide an independent source of information within a text" (5). The document goes on to clarify that picture books for young readers "rely heavily on graphics to convey meaning" and are therefore "an exception to the above generalization" (5).

Language

Appendix A of the Common Core State Standards has very little to say about the language of a text and how it impacts complexity. The whole of the description consists of the following: "Texts that rely on literal, clear, contemporary, and conversational language tend to be easier to read than texts that rely on figurative, ironic, ambiguous, purposefully misleading, archaic or otherwise unfamiliar language or on general academic and domain-specific vocabulary" (2010, 5).

Knowledge Demands

Appendix A of the Common Core State Standards is equally brief about knowledge demands, stating: "Texts that make few assumptions about the extent of readers' life experiences and the depth of their cultural/literary and content/discipline knowledge are generally less complex than are texts that make many assumptions in one or more of those areas" (2010, 5).

Sharpening the Focus of the Qualitative Elements

To support teachers in their efforts to determine the qualitative complexity of a text, a bulleted diagram has been created on page six of Appendix A of the Common Core State Standards. Since the publication of that document, more detailed and specific rubrics for determining qualitative complexity have been created by the State Collaboratives on Assessment and Student Standards (SCASS). This collaborative is affiliated with the Council of Chief State School Officers, one of the driving forces behind the Common Core State Standards. The two rubrics—one for informational text and one for literary text—are available for teachers to use. They can be found at http://www.achievethecore.org/dashboard/300/search/1/1/0/1/2/3/4/5/6/7/8/9/10/11/12/page/656/finding-ccss-grade-levels-for-texts-scass-rubrics.

The four gradients created within these rubrics are designed to help teachers determine appropriate grade-band level of complexity of a text. As a companion to this rubric, yet another tool was created by Student Achievement Partners, the non-profit organization formed by the original authors of the Common Core State Standards, called the "Qualitative Scales." The purpose of these scales is to locate the grade level qualitative complexity of a text within a grade band, drawing upon an in-depth exploration of the qualitative elements described in the graphic on page six of Appendix A of the Common Core State Standards. These scales can be found at http://www.achievethecore.org/page/657/finding-ccss-grade-levels-for-texts-qualitative-scales.

Envisioning a New Focus for Qualitative Assessment

We believe that the foundation to making an informed qualitative assessment of the complexity of a text is far more important than the quantitative measurement of the text. We also believe that knowing and understanding how texts operate will allow teachers to make an informed qualitative assessment of the complexity of a text, and to determine what is a quality text worth spending time on in the classroom. We also recognize that one can't separate a text from its context in the classroom.

But before we move to the third part of the text complexity triangle, the consideration of the reader and the task, we want to pause and pivot our thinking. We believe there is a clear connection between the qualitative dimensions of text complexity and the reader and task considerations outlined in the Common Core State Standards and the evaluation criteria for text quality that we outlined in Chapter Two.

Here is how we believe they match up:

Figure 4.5 Aligning the Language of the Common Core with our Evaluation Categories

Common Core State Standards	Our Evaluation Categories
Level of Meaning and Purpose	Genre Characteristics
Structure	Text Structure Visuals: Illustrations and Book Design
Language	Language
Knowledge Demands	Content
Reader	Readers
Task	Utility: Considerations of Instructional Purposes and Practices

We think that it is actually more useful to consider the evaluation categories and their associated criteria as your primary focal point for determining complexity. By first determining the quality of a text and why you think it is good, you can then more carefully determine the level of complexity of the text and make the match between the readers and the specific instructional purposes you have in mind.

Figure 4.5 shows the relationship between the evaluation categories and the qualitative elements of text complexity as articulated by the Common Core State Standards. Figure 4.6 demonstrates how we appropriate those elements into our natural and authentic discussion of how texts operate. For the moment, we will consider just the elements of the text itself, and the following questions:

- How is it good?
- How is it complex?

Figure 4.6 Guide to Aligning an Evaluation of Quality with an Evaluation of Complexity

How Is It Good?	How Is It Complex?
Genre Characteristics - How does it meet established criteria?	**Genre Characteristics/Levels of Meaning** - How does the book meet and/or differ from genre characteristics? How does this impact accessibility?
Content - What is the book about?	**Content/Knowledge Demands** - How complex is the content for the intended audience? How does this impact accessibility?
Text Structure - How is the book organized? - What is the overall text structure?	**Text Structure** - Is the text structure simple or more complex? How does this impact accessibility?
Language - How is the language rich and interesting? What kind of sentence variation occurs?	**Language** - How challenging is the language? How does this impact accessibility?
Visuals: Illustrations and Design/Structure - How do the visuals engage the reader? How do they enhance the content? - How does the book design reinforce the content?	**Visuals: Illustrations and Design/Structure** - How do the visuals and design impact accessibility?

There is even yet another layer of specificity that we can achieve here, if we consider the genre-specific questions that we posed in Chapter Two. Over time, with use, you will incorporate those genre considerations into your thinking automatically. But as you begin to use the *Quality, Utility, and Complexity Chart* as a tool, you may want to look at the genre-specific sections of Chapter Two for assistance. (Also see Appendix E.)

Sociocultural Context

In the triangle representing the evaluation of text complexity found in Appendix A, the authors of the Common Core give equal weight across the consideration of qualitative factors, quantitative measures, and reader and task, noting that "[w]hile the prior two elements of the model focus on the inherent complexity of text, variables specific to particular readers (such as motivation, knowledge, and experiences) and to particular tasks (such as purpose and the complexity of the task assigned and the questions posed) must also be considered when determining whether a text is appropriate for a given student. Such assessments are best made by teachers employing their professional judgment, experience, and knowledge of their students and the subject" (2010, 4). We couldn't agree more. You know your readers best, understanding their abilities and interests. You also know your classroom, school, and community best, understanding your grade level goals and expectations in the context of your local setting. All of these factors play into a consideration of how complex a text is for a particular reader and for a particular purpose.

Think back to Chapter One and our discussion of theories on the process of reading. In the model of reading presented by the RAND Reading Study Group (2002) the act of comprehension involves the interaction between the reader, the text, and the activity embedded in a sociocultural context. We think about sociocultural context and its relationship to text complexity as a macro view of readers, texts, tasks and activities, and their influence on text complexity for a reader. Let's spend a moment doing this big picture thinking.

Sociocultural context has an overarching influence on readers, texts, activities, and tasks in the classroom. Considering the sociocultural context for reading means considering values around literacy that are both implicitly and explicitly expressed in particular settings. And, really, it is even more complex than we might think because sociocultural contexts are nested. The readers in your classroom are influenced by several sociocultural contexts—those of their homes, their classroom, their school, and their community. Through interactions in these various contexts, the readers in your classroom form their understandings about the purposes of the literacy practices of reading, writing, and thinking. Their ideas about why we read, why we write, and how we think about and go about *doing* reading and writing are influenced by the literacy practices they encounter at home, school, and in their community. Additionally, what they observe and what they participate in helps to construct a reading identity (Gee 1990; Heath 1982). To illustrate this point, let's consider the impact of assessment and instructional practices that heavily emphasize reading levels. A student in a classroom where reading instruction centers on progression through a system of leveled texts, might view learning to read as a process of reading 'harder' texts over time through practice. Alternatively, a student in a classroom where reading instruction is linked to or integrated with content-area study might view learning to read as a tool for learning about our world and how it works. These very different orientations to reading have a strong influence on interest and motivation.

So what does this have to do with text complexity? Students' conceptions of these purposes and processes influence how they approach any particular text. Let's oversimplify for a moment in order to provide an example: a student who has had a lot of coaching to sound out words that he or she does not recognize will likely have more difficulty with a text that includes less commonly used words (such as content-area specific vocabulary) than will a student who has received coaching on how to use context clues to support their understanding of unknown words in text. The first student has a conception of reading as a correct pronunciation of words, while the second student conceives of reading as a process of meaning-making (for a more complete discussion of this example, see Dawes 2007).

The big ideas that students have about reading purposes and processes influence their interaction with any particular text.

When considering sociocultural context and how it influences student reading experiences, ask yourself:

- Who are we as a classroom, as a school, as a community?
- What do we value?

- What are our literacy practices?
- How do our values influence our approach to reading instruction?
- How do our values influence the texts that we select?
- How do our values/perspectives influence the meaning that we construct from texts and what we do with texts?

Doing this big picture thinking about the sociocultural contexts that influence the readers in your classrooms can help to ground your global thinking about your readers and the reading experiences that you would like to create with them. This kind of thinking can shape your practice, but when you pick up a particular text to consider its use in your classroom, you will likely be thinking more immediately about how, and with whom, you will use the text.

Considering Readers

When considering a book for use in your classroom, of course, one of your primary considerations is how well you think the book will work for your particular readers. Lexile® levels and Guided Reading levels matched with student reading levels are a commonly used means for thinking about whether your students might be able to read and understand a particular book, but there are so many other factors at play. We think that, at best, quantitative evaluations can only serve as a very rough guide for book selection. They cannot predict with certainty whether a text will be a good match for a particular reader. To make a more informed selection of text for a particular student, we think about who that student is and what we know about his or her characteristics as a reader and learner.

Think for a moment of the readers in your classroom. Regardless of where you teach and at what grade level, we are confident that you have a very diverse group! The students with whom we work vary enormously in their home and language experiences, in what they know about the world and how they work, in their literacy knowledge and abilities, and in their interests and motivations. When considering a text for use in the classroom, we think about who our readers are and how they might possibly be using the book.

When we consider who the readers in our classroom are and how they might read, comprehend, and respond to a particular text, we think about the reader's abilities, content knowledge, language knowledge, motivation, and interest.

Reading Abilities

The concept of a student's reading ability is tricky to define. Students' reading abilities are highly connected to their knowledge about how the world works and their knowledge of how language works. Because of this interdependency, it is difficult to tease out what we might identify as a student's reading ability. In many classrooms that we have encountered, students self-identify as being at a certain reading level. We find this problematic for the same reasons that we find quantitative measurements of text levels problematic. Student reading levels are typically assessed by having students read and answer comprehension questions related to a series of benchmark texts, which progress in difficulty and are associated with different grade levels (either by standardized measures, or by locally agreed upon criteria). A student's success with the benchmark text can be influenced by his or her background knowledge; his or her desire to please the assessor; what might be going on in the student's personal life; and whether or not he or she is hungry, tired, or ill. If the reading level obtained is then used as a determinate for the texts that the student will be given to read in the classroom, we are especially unsettled. But we are not saying that a student's reading abilities are unmeasurable or unimportant. We think of reading ability as the student's body of sight word knowledge, the student's working vocabulary, and the student's critical-thinking and comprehension skills, all of which play into a student's ability to read, comprehend, and respond to a particular text at a particular time.

Content Knowledge

Consider how what one already knows before reading influences one's ability to connect with, understand, and process new information that one encounters in a text. What students know undoubtedly influences the level of complexity of text that they are able to access. This sounds obvious and on some level, yes, it is, but it can play out subtly in classrooms. Let's say for example that a text in a benchmark system used to assess student's reading levels (ability) is about a trip to a circus. Imagine the advantage that students who have actually been to a circus have over students who have not. Students who have attended the circus have been immersed in sensory and language experiences related to the who, what, where, when, and why of this particular event. Those who haven't need to work harder to make sense of the benchmark book that describes a circus. Students with less background knowledge related to particular assessment texts may test at a lower level of text complexity than if the text had been about something else. When we consider the work that students will need to do to make sense of a particular text, we take into account whether students will be able to make connections between what they already know and new content and concepts in the text. The more connections students can make, the easier it is to access the text. This becomes even more important as students progress through the grade levels and the content becomes even more sophisticated in discipline-specific texts.

Language Knowledge

In Chapter One, we highlighted the social and contextual nature of literacy practices. Linguist James Paul Gee (2001) calls our attention to how we vary our ways of speaking, reading, writing, and thinking depending on the context. This idea is at the heart of the notion of disciplinary literacies, developing students' abilities to identify and use the particular ways of speaking, reading, and writing associated with disciplines of study (supporting students as they learn to speak, read, write and think like scientists, historians, mathematicians, and artists). What does this have to do with text complexity? When we consider how easy or difficult it will be for a reader to comprehend a particular text, we need to think about the students' level of familiarity with how language is used in the text. This includes, and goes beyond, thinking about the readers' knowledge of the discipline-specific vocabulary the text contains. In addition to using specialized vocabulary terms, experts in their fields are members of a community who often share patterns in inquiry processes, strategies for thinking critically about the content, and accepted ways for theorizing and presenting their evolving understandings of the content. The degree to which students are familiar with these patterns of language use impacts how complex they will find a particular text to be.

It is very important to consider the language challenges that a text poses to English language learners. As Hadaway and Young (2010) remind us, "[u]nfortunately, teachers worry that English learners will not be able to handle authentic materials such as trade books given that they are often encountering the reading/writing process for the first time alongside learning English" (36). As a result, teachers have purchased materials comprised of artificial and inauthentic text, burdened by readability formulas and controlled vocabulary, which "rob English learners of an authentic language opportunity and may contribute to boredom, frustration, and the feeling that they are being labeled 'remedial'" (2010, 36). A more in-depth discussion of matching texts of appropriate complexity with English language learners is beyond the scope of this book. However, when you can unpack a text and understand how it operates, considering the cognitive load the content demands, text structure, and language demands, you will be better able to make matches between books and readers for all of the students in your room, including English language learners. For more on this subject, we recommend *Matching Books & Readers: Helping English Learners in Grades K–6* (Hadaway and Young 2010).

Interest and Motivation

Students' desire to read a text has a strong impact on their willingness to work at reading the text. When students really want to read a text, either because they are very interested in the content, because that particular book is all the rage with their peers at the moment, or because reading the book will allow them to do something they are interested in doing, we have seen them stretch beyond what we might have predicted their reading ability to be. They are able to read a more complex text than expected simply because they are highly motivated to do so (Guthrie and Wigfield 2000). We think it is very important for students to have lots of opportunities to self-select books across the course of their days at school, both in the classroom, and ideally from a well-stocked school library. Of course, self-selection is not always possible in the context of a unit of study, but we always try to shape our curriculum to leave room for students to personally connect with the content in some way.

Motivation and interest are also closely tied to a student's self-perception as a reader (Guthrie and Wigfield 2000). Our students arrive in our classrooms with a social history as readers. Some students have had lots of experiences reading and talking about texts in their homes. Some come from families and homes where discussion and oral storytelling has been more common than book reading experiences (Heath 1982). Some have encountered reading success as it has been defined in your school setting and some have been identified as struggling readers. Their level of confidence in their own reading abilities as well as their perception of whether a particular text looks challenging for them will influence how they will approach any particular text. We recognize that it is particularly challenging for secondary teachers to know their students' identities and beliefs as readers because they may see upwards of 100–200 students daily. It is very difficult to give this many students the individualized attention they need to grow as readers.

Considering students' reading abilities, content and language knowledge, and interest and motivation in relation to characteristics of the text, allows us to make an informed prediction of how well a particular reader may be able to read, comprehend, and respond to a particular text.

When considering how your readers may approach a particular text, ask yourself:

- What are their abilities to access (decode and interpret) the text?
- What are their abilities to analyze and critique text?
- What background knowledge do they have (content area knowledge, knowledge about the world and how it works)?
- What do they know about language and how it is used in different contexts (vocabulary and disciplinary literacies)?
- What are their interests and motivations?

Considering Activity/Task

As Figure 4.1 depicts, consideration of how well a book will work for the readers in one's classroom goes hand in hand with a consideration of the potential uses for the book in the context of one's curriculum. Like the consideration of readers, the consideration of activity or task has multiple facets to it. In Chapter Three we reviewed a range of instructional purposes for literacy and content-area learning; we also reviewed classroom practices that are used in service of these goals. These purposes and practices shape both how students will read a text and what they will do in response to the text. When we consider whether a text is useful for a particular instructional purpose or within a particular instructional practice—in other words, when we consider what a text is *"good for"*—we take into account the complexity of the text.

Considering Instructional Purposes and Complexity

When considering the relationship between our instructional purpose and the complexity of text, the guiding question that we ask ourselves is: To what degree will students need to interpret, analyze, and critique the information in the text in order to accomplish our instructional purpose? Implicit in this question are considerations of how thoroughly students will need to read and understand the text, and what they will do with the information that they gain from the text.

Each of the instructional purposes outlined in Chapter Three (Figures 3.1–3.5) suggests a specific consideration of text complexity.

Understanding Content: When evaluating the complexity of a text that we intend to use in a unit of study in the content areas, we ask ourselves how well students need to understand the content of the text. Within a unit of study, some of the texts that we use are a close match to the content outlined in our curriculum guidelines. These texts we want our students to be able to read and interpret deeply. Other texts may contain interesting information related to the topic that might inspire some students to further inquiry, but go beyond the content required in the standards. For texts with crucial information, text complexity matters more—we want students to be able to access and interpret that information. We carefully consider how well the text is written and the match between readers' content and language knowledge, and the content, language, and structure of the text. If students already know a lot about the topic, the text can be more complex. If students are less familiar with the content and vocabulary, we would seek a less complex text.

Developing Disciplinary Literacies: If our instructional goal is to support students as they experience and apprentice in different disciplinary literacies, our consideration of text complexity should focus on how text expresses language/vocabulary, processes of thought, and inquiry of the discipline. In other words, how much insider language is used and how is it contextualized for the reader. We seek to align the complexity of the text with readers' experience level of the language and content of the discipline. More experience means that the text can be more complex.

Developing Reading Skills: As we teach with well-written engaging texts across the content areas, we are continually working to develop students' reading skills and strategies. But sometimes we are selecting texts with this particular instructional purpose in mind. When we focus on developing students reading skills, we offer support in accessing and interpreting the text. If we are building students' abilities to access text independently we look for text that is matched to students' sight word knowledge and repertoire of decoding strategies. We seek a text at a level of complexity such that students can decode the text with little support, but with enough challenge to provide practice solving unknown words and vocabulary—we seek an appropriate level of challenge. We also focus on students' abilities to interpret the text, recognizing that reading involves both decoding and comprehending. We consider whether the text is at a level of complexity such that the reader can work to interpret the content of the text by drawing on content knowledge and background knowledge with the support of peers or a teacher.

Teaching Literary Analysis/Genre Study: When we select texts for the instructional purpose of helping students learn about a genre, and the characteristics of well-written examples of that genre, we are asking students to engage in analysis of the qualities of writing and to make inferences about the writing process. This deeper level of analysis is possible when students are able to access and interpret the text with relative ease. With this in mind, we match the complexity of the text to readers' abilities to decode and comprehend. Additionally, we consider that if students have more experience with reading and analyzing a genre, the text can be more complex.

Analyzing Mentor Text for Writing: When we consider the appropriate level of complexity of a mentor text for student writing, we carefully consider the reader's level of content and language knowledge. Sometimes students are using a text as a model for their own writing in a content area. In this case, the text may or may not be in the same genre as the writing that students will ultimately produce. Students may review texts about the content they will focus on across a range of genres in order to decide which genre format appeals to them for their own writing. In this case, when offering students a mentor text, we would evaluate the complexity of the text in relation to the reader's level of experience with the content and language. Ideally, students' knowledge of the content would allow them to easily access and interpret the information in the texts, so that they can focus on the writing and presentation choices of the author, considering these choices as possibilities for their own writing. Alternatively, we may require students to write in a particular genre and provide them with a text as an exemplar of that genre. In this case, we would also want the reader to be able to access and interpret the text with relative ease, freeing up his or her attention to focus on the characteristics and features of the genre and infer the writing process used by the author. Again, if the reader has greater familiarity with the genre, it is possible to use a more complex text.

Developing Critical Thinking: Critical thinking happens across content areas and across reading, writing, speaking and listening practices in the classroom. In some sense, we are always selecting texts to develop critical-thinking skills, but sometimes this focus is explicitly at the forefront of our text selection. The Common Core State Standards ask us to push our students' abilities to compare and contrast, and analyze and critique, information across related texts. They also ask us to develop students' abilities to respond to information and to express their learning in various forms of writing, including persuasive pieces. When students are analyzing and critiquing a text with the goal of creating an oral or written response to the perspectives on content expressed in the text, they need to engage in close reading of the text. Our considerations for text complexity when fostering critical thinking focus on providing readers with texts that are appropriately matched to their abilities, and content and language knowledge, while giving special consideration to the levels of meaning and perspectives expressed in the text. The complexity should allow students to be able to dig in to the content and consider a range of perspectives, and not get bogged down in a reading struggle to access the content.

Engaging in Inquiry and Research: When we select texts that students will use for research or inquiry, we can draw from a wide range of complexity. These are texts that students may not need to read in their entirety. Sometimes they will skim the text or read particular sections as opposed to reading the entire text. When choosing texts for this instructional purpose, we consider in particular how the text is organized and the text features it includes. A more complex text can be used if it's a highly-organized nonfiction text with many text features and an index because readers can more easily locate the information they need.

Fostering Reading Habits and Love of Reading: When considering texts to foster a love of reading, our primary lens for considering the complexity of the text is a full consideration of the characteristics of the reader. We want to offer a text that he or she can access and interpret independently (considering the reader's abilities, content, and language knowledge) and that is well matched to his or her interests and motivations as a reader. Figure 4.7 summarizes the considerations for instructional purpose and text complexity. This resource can also be found in Appendix E.

Figure 4.7 Considerations for Instructional Purposes and Text Complexity Guide

Instructional Purpose: Understanding Content	
When considering the text for this instructional purpose, ask yourself:	**The implications for text complexity are:**
What is the match between my content standards and the text?	It depends on the reader's content and language knowledge. The more knowledge they have, the more complex the text may be.
What is the match between my content standards and this text in relation to other texts on the topic?	If the content information and vocabulary is essential to the unit of study, the text may need to be less complex so that students access what they need to learn.
Is information presented in a way that will hook my students and get them even more interested in the unit topic?	
Does the information in this text go beyond the standards? How will that impact how my students read it?	

Instructional Purpose: Developing Disciplinary Literacies	
When considering the text for this instructional purpose, ask yourself:	**The implications for text complexity are:**
Is the vocabulary used in the text authentic to the discipline, but contextually defined in a manner that makes it accessible to my students?	A wide range of complexity is possible, depending on instructional practice considerations below.
Does the text model the inquiry and/or critical thinking processes of the discipline either implicitly (for example in an author's note) or explicitly (through direct description in the text)?	

Instructional Purpose: Developing Reading Skills	
When considering the text for this instructional purpose, ask yourself:	**The implications for text complexity are:**
Does this book appeal to students? Will it be worth working at?	The text should be at a level of complexity such that readers can decode it with little support; unknown words and vocabulary should provide an appropriate level of challenge.
How much background knowledge does the book require? Will students be able to comprehend as they decode?	The text is at a level of complexity such that the reader can "work" to interpret the content of the text, drawing on content knowledge and background knowledge with the support of peers or a teacher.
What kinds of words does it contain? What is the balance of sight words, monosyllabic and polysyllabic words?	
How long are the sentences? Too long? Too short? Just right?	

Instructional Purpose: Teaching Literary Analysis/Genre Study	
When considering the text for this instructional purpose, ask yourself: How does this book represent the genre we are studying? How does it accomplish this on its own and how does it accomplish this understanding in the context of other books of the same genre or of different genres that focus on the same topic? What literary elements are at work in the book? Does the author do anything unique with one or two in particular that stand out as very effective examples to use in instruction? What is the match between the literary elements that are required to teach according to your school's scope and sequence or state and district standards?	**The implications for text complexity are:** Generally, in order to analyze genre characteristics, students should be able to access the text with ease in order to focus on critically examining the text. Your selection is also dependent on the readers' prior knowledge of the genre. If they have more experience with the genre, the text can be more complex.

Instructional Purpose: Analyzing Mentor Texts	
When considering the text for this instructional purpose, ask yourself: If students are reading "like a writer," what do they learn about genre through this text? How does this particular text model a particular quality of good writing, for example, varied sentence length, for targeted writing practicing that skill? How does this particular text model the ways in which writing can be used to communicate knowledge to the world, by simply informing readers or informing and persuading readers simultaneously?	**The implications for text complexity are:** The complexity of the text is dependent on whether it is being used as a model for a demonstration of content learning or as a model of genre in genre study. In each case, you have to consider your readers' level of content, genre, and language knowledge). To use as a mentor text, students should be able to access and interpret the text to a degree that allows them to understand the writing process of the author.

Instructional Purpose: Developing Critical Thinking	
When considering the text for this instructional purpose, ask yourself: What are the key ideas and details in this text? What perspectives and points of view are offered within this text? Which are left out? What can a student learn by reading just this text? What does the student learn by reading this text in the context of other texts within a text set?	**The implications for text complexity are:** A wide range of complexity is possible, depending on the content and language knowledge of the reader. Special consideration should be given to the 'levels of meaning' and the perspectives expressed in the text. The complexity should allow students to be able to "dig in" to the content and consider a range of perspectives, and not get bogged down in a reading struggle to access the content.

Instructional Purpose: Engaging in Inquiry and Research	
When considering the text for this instructional purpose, ask yourself:	**The implications for text complexity are:**
What is the match between the text and the content we are learning about, either individually, in pairs, small groups, or as a class? Is this text well-researched? Does the back matter and bibliography demonstrate to my students how someone does thorough research using quality sources? Does this text represent "the literature of inquiry"? Does it model the inquiry process, the having of questions, and the ways around stumbling blocks and dead ends? Will it help my students persevere through their own research? Is this text going to help me model how I do research? Or is this text one that I will have my students explore? Or both? How does this text compare to other texts on the topic in terms of all of the above questions?	A wide range of complexity is possible as readers may skim or read sections as opposed to reading the whole text. Consider in particular how the text is organized and the access features it includes. A well-organized text can be more complex because readers can more easily locate the information they need.

Instructional Purpose: Building Reading Habits and a Love of Reading	
When considering the text for this instructional purpose, ask yourself:	**The implications for text complexity are:**
Who is the audience for this text? What about this book reflects my students' interests, passions, worries, or senses of humor? Who in my class this year, last year, or maybe in future years, might find this of interest? If the book is going to be a challenge read, is there enough of interest to hear to make it worth it for students to stick with it?	Text is at a level of complexity that the reader can access and interpret independently. Text content matches interests and motivations of the reader.

Considering Instructional Practices and Complexity

Figure 4.7 is a helpful thinking tool for considering the relationship between instructional purpose, evaluation of text utility, and text complexity; but we need to add another layer of consideration to an already complex picture. That layer is a consideration of the instructional practices that we will use to help achieve the instructional purposes described above. The main question that guides our consideration of the relationship between instructional practice and text complexity is: What supports will readers receive to interpret, analyze, and critique the information in the text in order to accomplish the instructional purposes? As a general rule of thumb, the more support (or scaffolding) that students receive to access and interpret the text, the more complex the text can be.

In this layer of consideration, we first consider how the students will access the text. We decide whether the student will read the text independently or if they will have support from a teacher, a parent, a peer, or technology. Technology provides us with more options to support student access of a text than we previously had available. Lively audio versions of novels, picture books, and nonfiction texts are often available. These options allow us to offer students more complex text to interpret and discuss with their teachers and peers.

Next, we consider how students will interpret the content of the text. If students have support in thinking through and responding to text ideas, they are able to work with more complex text than they might be able to understand independently. When considering student comprehension of text in the context of different instructional practices, and in relation to the complexity of the text, we ask ourselves: How will the students interpret the text—will they read and interpret the text independently or will they have the support of teachers or peers? Do they have the content and language knowledge to interpret, analyze, and critique the text independently? Or can the text be harder/more complex because they will have the opportunity to talk it over with others who will help them interpret and to consider multiple perspectives?

Beyond these general considerations, each of the instructional practices outlined in Chapter Three suggest a specific consideration of text complexity:

Reading Aloud: When we read aloud to our students we have the option of offering them more complex texts than they would be able to access independently. When selecting a text, we consider the content and language of the text in relation to students' background knowledge and experiences. We try to be sure that the ideas and concepts discussed in the text are accessible to most students with teacher and/or peer support.

Literature Circles: Students participating in literature circles generally read a text independently and then gather to discuss the content of the text. This does not preclude offering students assistance to access the text. Typically the level of text complexity should be well matched to readers' abilities, content and language knowledge, and interests and motivations; however text can be more complex if students have help accessing the text. Since students will have the opportunity to discuss, analyze, and critique the text with a peer group, the text can be more complex conceptually than if students did not have the benefit of peer support.

Guided Reading: In the guided reading structure, we are providing focused support to students as they access and interpret a text with the goal of providing specific coaching to help students develop as readers. When selecting a text for guided reading we choose an aspect of the text's complexity as a focus for instruction that will support the reader's ability to read increasingly complex texts. We try to make sure the text is at a level of complexity that the reader can access and interpret with some support from a teacher.

Independent Reading: When we guide students to select texts for independent reading, we are focused on the reader. Above all, we want to motivate students to read independently by choice in, and especially, out of, school settings. We want the students to have a successful reading experience with a text closely matched to their interests and motivations. Ideally this is a text that is at a level of complexity well suited to their abilities, content knowledge, and language knowledge.

Whole-Class Read: When we ask all students in a class to read the same text independently and then come together to discuss and analyze the text in small and large groups, we are focused on collective meaning-making. We want students to be successful in reading the text, and we recognize that some students will read the text more easily than others. Ideally, the text is at a level for most students to read independently without frustration. Whole-class and small-group instruction will shape students' interactions with the text and responses to the text. Some students will need more scaffolding than others.

Figure 4.8 provides an overview of the implications for text complexity of each instructional practice, as well as questions related to the appropriateness of the text for each instructional practice (drawn from Chapter 3). This figure can also be found in Appendix E.

Figure 4.8 Instructional Practices and Text Complexity Considerations Guide

Instructional Practice	Literacy and Content-Area Learning Considerations	Implications for Text Complexity
Read Aloud	Is there a flow to the language that makes it enjoyable to read aloud? Will the content engage the interest of the whole class? Is there potential for the text to generate discussion? Does it contain information that is critical for your unit of study? Does the book inspire inquiry by prompting students to ask questions?	Since the teacher reads the text aloud, the text can be more complex, but the ideas and concepts discussed in the text should be accessible to students with teacher and/or peer support.
Literature Circles	Will the text generate student discussion? Will students benefit from the opportunity to discuss/extend their understanding of the content with peers? Does the text provide a review of important content information or does the text provide an expansion of information that is well matched to the readers in the group?	Consider how students will access the text when determining the appropriate level of complexity. If students will read the text independently, it needs to be well matched to their abilities to decode and interpret. If students will access the text with audio or teacher/parent support, the text can be more complex. Since students will have the opportunity to discuss, analyze, and critique the text with a peer group, the text can be more complex conceptually than if students did not have the benefit of peer support.

Instructional Practice	Literacy and Content-Area Learning Considerations	Implications for Text Complexity
Guided Reading	Is the text at a reading level that students can read and comprehend with some support? Does the text offer an opportunity for strategy instruction to help students grow as readers? Does the text provide a review of content study information previously discussed in a whole group setting or does it provide an opportunity to expand on content information that is well matched to the readers in the group?	The text is at a level of complexity that the reader can access and interpret with *some* support from a teacher. You can identify an aspect of the text's complexity as a focus for instruction that will support the reader's ability to read increasingly complex texts.
Independent Reading	Is the text neither too hard nor too easy, offering the reader a chance to develop his or her reading abilities? Does the text provide either a review of information previously learned or an expansion of content study information that is well matched to the reader's particular interests?	The text is at a level of complexity matched to the reader's abilities, content and language knowledge and interest and motivation. The students should be able to confidently access and interpret the text independently.
Whole-Class Read	Is the text a good match for your instructional purpose and content learning goals? Can enough of the students in the class read and interpret the content independently? Will the text generate discussion among the students?	The text is at a level of complexity that allows for the majority of the students to read independently without frustration and interpret the text on different levels. Classroom instruction in small-group and whole-class settings will provide the scaffolding necessary to allow a range of readers to access the text with success. Like selection considerations for literature circles, the text of a whole-class read can be more complex conceptually than if students did not have the benefit of peer support.

Considering Complexity in Context—An Example

Considering text quality, your reader, and task are all important aspects of your instructional planning and determination of text complexity. We are simultaneously thinking about:

- What is the instructional purpose for using the text?
- What attributes make this text challenging? What attributes make it more accessible?
- How will students read or access the text in order to accomplish the task you intend?
- What will students do after reading the text and what is the complexity of the task?
- What kinds of critical thinking will students be doing to carry out the task?

All of these factors influence one another and represent the synergy of complexity that is represented in Standard 10's triangle.

When we try to capture a qualitative analysis of text complexity we have to take the reader, the text, the task, and the context into consideration. This is not simple! The good news is that teachers are probably already considering lots of these factors subconsciously or as an implicit aspect of their curriculum development. The current focus on text complexity can challenge us in a positive way to be even more deliberate about selecting the texts that will be the most effective learning tools for our students.

Considering quality, utility, and complexity is truly a recursive process. Each informs the other. The quality of the text matters because it tells us whether the text is worth spending time on in the classroom; but the categories that we use to articulate the quality of the text are the very same categories that we use to determine what makes the text more or less accessible. The utility of the text matters because it has to meet our instructional purposes. What we do with a text matters, and it impacts our consideration of the complexity of the text in the context of our instructional purpose. The more complex the task, the easier the text should be, and vice-

---

Resources and Perspectives on Text Complexity

If you are looking for additional resources and perspectives on text complexity, the following might be useful:

Council of Chief State School Officers: "Navigating Text Complexity" http://www.ccsso.org/Navigating_Text_Complexity.html

Teaching Channel: "Simplifying Text Complexity" https://www.teachingchannel.org/videos/simplifying-text-complexity

The Text Project: The Text Complexity Multi-Index http://www.textproject.org/professional-development/text-matters/the-text-complexity-multi-index/

Common Core State Standards Initiative: Other Resources http://www.corestandards.org/resources

Student Achievement Partners: Text Complexity Collection http://www.achievethecore.org/dashboard/300/search/1/1/0/1/2/3/4/5/6/7/8/9/10/11/12/page/642/text-complexity-collection

Terrell Young and Nancy Hadaway. *Matching Books and Readers: Helping English Learners in Grades K–6*. In the Solving Problems in the Teaching of Literacy Series, edited by Cathy Collins Block. Guilford Press, 2010.

versa. An understanding of our students as readers influences how we go about determining the tasks that we will have students do, and the instructional practices we follow to meet our instructional purposes. For example, depending on our instructional purpose, a more complex book may use the instructional practice of a read aloud rather than a whole-class read. It is really impossible to separate any one of these considerations, as much as we have tried to in the preceding chapters.

You will see all of these elements working together when you see the completed chart in Chapter Five. But in Figure 4.9 you will see how an example of our evaluation of the quality of the text informs our consideration of the qualitative complexity of the text. This "close reading" of the text demonstrates the nuanced examination of the book's strengths and suggests how it will be more or less accessible to students.

Figure 4.9 Sample Partially Completed *Quality, Utility, and Complexity Chart* for *Those Rebels, John and Tom*

Genre Characteristics: Literary and Artistic Value	Genre Characteristics: Complexity and Accessibility
How does it meet established criteria? As a "double portrait" it is a biography of two people, but a partial biography of each. As a double biography it shows parallel events in each of their lives chronologically, as one would expect. There is no invented dialogue (which would be problematic), but Kerley does use direct quotes from each man's writings to create a sense of immediacy with the reader. We get to "hear" each of them through her selective quotes. Research is well documented in the back matter, with citations for different source material and an author's note that explains the origins of the book and the relationship between the two after the Declaration of Independence was written.	*How does the book meet and/or differ from genre characteristics? How does this impact accessibility?* Most students are used to reading a single biography or a collected biography of a lot of people. As a "double portrait" of two historical figures this might be a new concept for most readers. But the comparison and contrast supports the reader in understanding the two men simultaneously and their common goal. If it were not as well-written, it would become a challenge. But the format makes this "deviation" from a typical single biography easier to access. The information provided in the author's note helps to put the narrative text in context for the reader. For some readers, it might be too much information, but reading the author's note is not central to understanding the narrative; it simply enhances the narrative.
Content: Literary and Artistic Value	**Content: Complexity and Accessibility**
What is the book about? It is a partial picture book biography about Thomas Jefferson and John Adams. It covers their childhood and early years, leading up to the writing and signing of the Declaration of Independence. The book focuses on how different they were and how they worked together as a team to get the Declaration both written and then approved by the Continental Congress.	*How complex is the content for the intended audience? How does this impact accessibility?* For much of the book, contrasts are drawn between John Adams and Thomas Jefferson. In this case, what makes the book complex is also what makes it accessible and therefore less complex. The comparison and contrast between the two allows the reader to understand how important it was that they shared so many of the same values despite their differences in upbringing, life experiences, and interests.

Text Structure: Literary and Artistic Value	Text Structure: Complexity and Accessibility
How is the book organized? What is the overall text structure? It is a chronological narrative. At the start, there is a page about John, then a page about Tom, and then a page about the two together. Sometimes the book talks about each separately on different sides of the two-page spread; when talking about events they were both involved in, it talks about them together.	*Is the text structure simple or more complex? How does this impact accessibility?* The text structure is what makes this book accessible to readers. Comparison and contrast is used within the paragraphs about each man. Each is written about in contrast to the other or an event that is unfolding. The narrative itself is straightforward because it follows chronological order moving from childhood to adulthood. However, it goes through their childhood fairly quickly and spends most of the narrative on the writing of the Declaration of Independence, which takes place over a short period of time. But this is clear, and should not confuse students, particularly if they are studying this for the purpose of understanding content about the American Revolution.

Language: Literary and Artistic Value	Language: Complexity and Accessibility
How is the language rich and interesting? What kind of sentence variation occurs? It starts off with a great hook that frames the whole narrative ("formed a surprising alliance, committed treason, and helped launch a new nation".) The book is filled with rich adjectives and parallel structure within paragraphs and pages. Direct quotes from each, taken from primary source materials, are included in quotation marks throughout. There is a jovial mood to the text in general.	*How challenging is the language? How does this impact accessibility?* The direct quotes are not difficult to read and understand because they are written into sentences as phrases, so the context supports the reader in understanding the point of view in the direct quote. It creates a sense of immediacy with Jefferson & Adams without slowing anything down or making the book more difficult. Adjectives and overall mood of the language make it more fun to read and slightly silly, which builds motivation in student readers.

Visuals: Literary and Artistic Value	Visuals: Complexity and Accessibility
How do the visuals engage the reader? How do they enhance the content? *How does the book design reinforce the content?* The book is illustrated with a palette of red, white, and blue, which reinforces the identity of the United States of America. The cover illustration and the final illustration are both allusions to famous images associated with the American Revolution. The cartoon drawings of Adams and Jefferson reinforce the comparisons and contrasts within the text. Background colors of white and navy also set up contrasts just as the book contrasts the two men. John and Tom are always mentioned in capital letters. Some sentences are in a larger bold font to emphasize their importance.	*How do the visuals and design impact accessibility?* The visuals make the book more accessible by illustrating with concrete images the differences between the two men. These illustrations can move readers from the concrete to the abstract in their thinking about the two men. The visuals also extend historical information to support students who might not have prior knowledge, making the book more accessible. For example, when discussing the occupation of Boston and the British navy patrol of the Atlantic seaboard, the book's illustrations bring to life the author's reference to "racket" in Boston (loud, occupied city controlled by the British army) and the "racket" in Virginia (the British navy's occupation of the Atlantic coast so that no ships could purchase colonial goods). By using a homonym (racket) the author compares and contrasts a very specific topic. But it is the illustrations that make the different meanings of that homonym clear to the reader who does not know the word, and demonstrates very clearly some of the activities of the British navy of which most students probably do not have prior knowledge.

Readers

Overall, in what ways does this book feel appropriate for some or all of the readers in your class?

Fifth graders will find the personal approach to history interesting. The use of humor in the text and the illustrations, and the humorous subtext and mood despite the serious topic, will engage students and make them want to keep reading. The more students view the illustrations, the more connections they will find between text and illustration, again, making the facts and concepts in the book more accessible and meaningful. The tightly written structure and book format will also help students navigate the text successfully. The personalities of Adams and Jefferson also make the book engaging to students, and therefore, more invested in reading for meaning and understanding.

Quantitative Evaluation of Text Complexity

Include one or two quantitative measurements of complexity to compare and contrast with your evaluation of the text.

Lexile® Range = 960 (upper parts of the 4–5 grade band)

ATOS/Accelerated Reader Bookfinder = 6.3 (middle of the 4th–5th band)

Our example in Figure 4.9 continues our examination of the picture book biography *Those Rebels, John and Tom* (Kerley 2012). One of the ways this book is unique is that it is a picture book biography of two people, not one. It is a focused look at the two men as separate individuals as well as an examination of their political friendship. From a quality standpoint, as we mentioned in Chapter Two, this makes the book relatively unique and quite interesting. It could make the book more difficult to read, because it deviates from the typical expectation of a picture book biography. However, because of the tightly written structure and the strength of the illustrations to convey conceptual understanding, we think that the book remains relatively accessible to fifth graders. Of course, this is a *generalization*. The calibration will be different teacher by teacher, class by class. Another category of evaluation is the content of the book: political friendship. Again, we think that the contrast allows for students to better access the individual attributes of each man, making the book sophisticated, but less complex because of the tight language.

There is also a sophisticated use of language play which could make the book more complex. For example, when discussing the British government's unfair policies, Kerley uses the homonym *racket*. When King George's troops occupied Boston, they created a racket. When the law required that colonists sell their goods only to England, it was considered a racket. However, the visuals support the language play. On one side of the page gutter, there is a picture of John Adams, kept awake by the loud noises made by the troops. On the opposing page, there is a picture of a British ship, loaded with bulging bags of goods, gold coins spilling off the top. Complex language is rendered less complex through artfully designed page composition and illustration.

Through these examples, you can see that the quality of the book makes it sophisticated, but less complex to read and understand. You also see that the categories overlap one another. Each informs the other in terms of both quality and complexity, even as we tease them out separately. The consideration of language complexity can't be done in isolation, since the illustrations render the text less complex. Similarly, the tightly woven compare and contrast text structure allows the content to be more accessible.

Conclusion

This chapter gave you a great deal to keep in mind when selecting texts for classroom use with a consideration of text quality and complexity. Your approach to text complexity may differ if you are a language arts teacher versus a content-area teacher or an elementary teacher fusing the two together. Depending on your role, you may have different responsibilities for moving students up the ladder of complexity. While evaluating texts for their quality and complexity, you have to take into consideration the vast array of readers you may have in your class, as well as the varying educational goals of language arts and content-area instruction.

In the next chapter, we will add yet another layer to this conversation, considering more fully how text complexity needs vary according to instructional purposes and practices and how teaching with multiple texts affects considerations of text complexity.

Questions for Reflection

1. How do you currently make decisions about the readability/reading level/complexity of the texts that you select for your students?

2. What are the challenges and possibilities embedded in the need to develop students' abilities to read more complex texts? How is this idea being interpreted in your school setting?

3. How can you develop a deeper understanding of who your students are as readers—their abilities, content knowledge, language knowledge, and interests and motivations?

4. How can the *Quality, Utility, and Complexity Chart* help you to evaluate text complexity in the context of your instructional purposes, practices, and the readers you teach?

Chapter 5

Complexity in Context

Remember the metaphor of the teacher as a juggler introduced in Chapter One? Teachers are, all at once, juggling the expectations and understandings of the various communities at work in their school, their instructional purposes, the students in their classroom, and the necessary decisions about text quality and complexity. How do we hold all of this thinking in our head at once? How do we use this information to inform curriculum design, lesson planning, and a range of assessments?

When examining a new work of fiction, nonfiction, or poetry, we look at each text with one or more lenses. There are many different reasons why we select texts to use in the classroom. We select books based on their quality; how they capture or defy genre expectations in new and engaging ways; for their utility as a teaching tool and the role the book can play in language arts and content area curriculum; and whether the book works best as a read aloud, small-group, or independent read. Sometimes we select a book for our classroom library, knowing that there will be an individual student for whom this book is the perfect intersection of interests and abilities. Sometimes, we are making decisions about a single text that the whole class will read.

We do not select a book exclusively for its complexity. Yet, we do not ignore complexity. Rather, as Chapter Four discusses, we consider the complexity in the context of the book's quality and utility—the particular role the book is going to play in the classroom. We first decide whether or not we think the book is worth spending time on in the classroom. Next, we decide whether the book is a good fit for our specific instructional purposes. Finally, we consider whether or not the book is an appropriate fit for our readers, given the instructional purpose it serves. The skillful incorporation of this consideration of quality, utility, and complexity into decision making does not happen automatically. It takes practice. The more books you read, the more skilled you become at making these judgments. The more you embrace this process with your colleagues, the easier it will be to have these conversations with one another. Remember what Deborah Stevenson (2006) asks us to consider: "Is it good? What is it good for?" Each new text we read gets incorporated into the map of literature in our head, and we consider each text on its own and in the context of our prior reading and teaching experiences.

From our point of view, meeting the expectations of today's standards requires a renewed focus on student-centered teaching and learning that embraces all modalities of literacy. In order for students to read ever-increasingly more complex texts, they need to have a great deal of practice with literacy—with speaking, listening, and writing around these texts—harnessing the different dimensions of literacy as a tool for meaning-making and understanding. We do not think the most important conversation is about setting up false dichotomies such as instructional levels versus complex texts, or fiction versus nonfiction. Different students need different calibrations; different instructional purposes demand different ways of viewing what happens in the classroom. Sometimes students are learning with texts that meet the grade-level or grade-span expectation of complexity. Sometimes they are working with texts that fall below or above those expectations. Students need robust experience with a range of texts—easy, difficult, and somewhere in between—in order to have their own personal toolkit for the decoding, comprehension, critical thinking, and synthesis that real-world reading at each grade level requires.

In our roles as teacher educators, we, like many literacy coaches and reading specialists, consider the K–12 possibilities of each and every book we read. Our approach to each text is to consider the range of possibilities that exist for classroom explorations. These possibilities include how the book could be used at different grade levels, contexts, and subject areas. From this perspective, text complexity is never static; it is a changing dynamic depending on the role the book plays in the curriculum and the identity and age of the readers.

If you are a classroom teacher working at a particular grade level, you most likely take a different approach to considering texts, the approaches we discussed in Chapter Three. You have specific gaps that you need to fill, new state or local standards to build curriculum around, or changes you want to make to further engage, support, or challenge your students. While our approaches may be different, we think that our broader context for thinking about texts may illuminate how you can sharpen your focus and fuse the consideration of quality, utility, and complexity.

We are now going to zoom in even further on our decision-making process. Our decision-making process involves activating our map of literature on many levels, for we rarely make decisions about texts in isolation. We consider one book in the context of other books we are considering, books we are familiar with, and the dynamic relationships between them. In this context as well, texts often become more or less complex depending on the other texts within the unit of study. This is at the heart of our work with text sets.

In this chapter, we want you to peek over our shoulders, and listen to what we have to say as we make these decisions. We will discuss how we:

- explore a single text for teaching possibilities at a range of grade levels and subject areas and consider the implications for text complexity;
- identify the different roles texts can play within a unit of study, and how that impacts our consideration of text complexity; and
- consider how other texts that the students are reading influence the complexity of each text and task.

Exploring the Possibilities: One Text, Many Contexts

The examples in Figures 5.1 and 5.2 illustrate how the same book can be used at different grade levels with readers of varying abilities, when used for different instructional purposes and with different instructional practices. We'll share with you our completed *Quality, Utility, and Complexity Chart* for each featured book and then outline several possible teaching ideas, highlighting the instructional purposes of each teaching idea and considerations for text complexity dependent on the intended grade level.

Those Rebels, John and Tom

We'll begin with the book that we have used across Chapters One through Four to illustrate the thinking process of evaluating for quality, utility, and complexity. By now, you probably feel quite familiar with Barbara Kerley's *Those Rebels, John and Tom,* illustrated by Edwin Fotheringham. We want to ground you with this familiarity so that you can see the ways in which we pivot from thinking about the book one way to thinking about the book in multiple contexts.

Throughout this resource, we have been considering the book for instruction in fifth grade social studies and language arts. In Figure 5.1, you will see an example of our considerations for the complexity of *Those Rebels, John and Tom* (Kerley 2012). This chart outlines the consideration of this book for fifth graders. But even when considering using the book with fifth graders, the complexity of a text is not static (Nesi 2012). The instructional purposes still vary.

If we are using this book in the context of an exploration of the American Revolution, students are going to be gaining background knowledge on that time period and on the specifics of the development of the Declaration of Independence. They will be able to use that information to access this text or this text will serve as a scaffold or introduction to the other texts and conversations that might follow on the contents of the Declaration of Independence. Later in this chapter, we will address more specifically the ways in which other texts work to shape and inform the complexity of any single text in a text set approach. But for now, it is important to consider that other texts on this topic in social studies can and will support students' historical analysis of this particular text, and that will impact how difficult this text is for them.

Instructional practice decisions will also impact the consideration of complexity. Sometimes the complexity suggests a certain practice, as we discussed in Chapter Four. But it is the instructional purpose combined with the complexity that truly suggests a particular instructional practice; complexity is considered in the context of both at once. For example, if a fifth grade teacher decides that everyone in the class should experience this book to frontload knowledge or multiple perspectives about the American Revolution, then the book would either be read aloud or treated as a whole-class read. Either way, there will be much more support for meaning-making than if the instructional purpose is to consider multiple perspectives on these two men and half of the class reads this book and one half reads *Worst of Friends: Thomas Jefferson, John Adams and the True Story of An American Feud* (Jurmain 2011). Having different groups read one or the other is a really interesting and engaging instructional possibility. But you have to decide whether or not your students can do that, and if they can do that with the particular texts under consideration. Instructional decisions for this kind of classroom planning will also take into consideration how students make sense of the book they read and consider the content of the *other* book read by their classmates. Yet another consideration of complexity takes place if the instructional purpose is to have students learn about different men and women who played pivotal roles during this period of American history. If each literature circle in class reads one of several picture book biographies, you have to consider how the students take notes and evaluate the information in the book they read, and how the books their classmates read shed light on their own. The texts selected for these literature circles have to meet that format.

Of course, it could be that you're considering using this book in a fifth grade biography genre study, and it is one example among many picture book biographies. The change in instructional purpose will have you looking at the complexity of the text and the other books being read alongside this particular book with a different lens. You will consider the elements of the text that make it complex and the elements of biography you want to showcase through this particular book. Whether or not the biography genre study takes place before, during, or after the study of the American Revolution will continue to influence your consideration of its complexity. If you have already completed the unit, or are conducting both concurrently, the book may be less complex than if students read it before the unit takes place in social studies.

Figure 5.1 Completed Sample *Quality, Utility, and Complexity Chart* for *Those Rebels, John and Tom*

Title: *Those Rebels, John and Tom*

Author: Barbara Kerley

Year of Publication: 2012

Notes from the Book Reviews
Booklist calls it a "double portrait," (2011) which is a good name to use in teaching with the book. Booklist also gave it a starred review and said, "[it]… is a terrific book to lead the charge in learning about the Revolution, as well as a lesson in how dedicated cooperation can achieve great ends. An obvious choice to pair with *Worst of Friends*." (*Booklist* 2011).
All reviews focus on how the book addresses the issue of class differences between them and the issue of slavery, since Jefferson was a slave owner.
All reviews address the focus on the two men and the story of the writing of the Declaration of Independence.
The *School Library Journal* review talks about the content of the author's note and their presidential years and changing relationship and an "authoritative" but "child-friendly" approach to history (Whitehurst 2012).

Genre Characteristics: Literary and Artistic Value	Genre Characteristics: Complexity and Accessibility
How does it meet established criteria? As a "double portrait" it is a biography of two people, but a partial biography of each. As a double biography it shows parallel events in each of their lives chronologically, as one would expect. There is no invented dialogue (which would be problematic), but Kerley does use direct quotes from each man's writings to create a sense of immediacy with the reader. We get to hear each of them through her selective quotes. Research is well documented in the back matter, with citations for different source material and an author's note that explains the origins of the book and the relationship between the two after the Declaration of Independence was written.	*How does the book meet and/or differ from genre characteristics? How does this impact accessibility?* Most students are used to reading a single biography or a collected biography of a lot of people. As a "double portrait" of two historical figures this might be a new concept for most readers. But the comparison and contrast supports the reader in understanding the two men simultaneously and their common goal. If it were not as well written, it would become a challenge. But the format makes this deviation from a typical single biography easier to access. The information provided in the author's note helps to put the narrative text in context for the reader. For some readers, it might be too much information, but reading the author's note is not central to understanding the narrative; it simply enhances the narrative.

Content: Literary and Artistic Value	Content: Complexity and Accessibility
What is the book about? It is a partial picture book biography about Thomas Jefferson and John Adams. It covers their childhood and early years, leading up to the writing and signing of the Declaration of Independence. The book focuses on how different they were and how they worked together as a team to get the Declaration both written and then approved by the Continental Congress.	*How complex is the content for the intended audience? How does this impact accessibility?* For much of the book, contrasts are drawn between John Adams and Thomas Jefferson. In this case, what makes the book complex is also what makes it accessible and therefore less complex. The comparison and contrast between the two allows the reader to understand how important it was that they shared so many of the same values despite their differences in upbringing, life experiences, and interests.

Text Structure: Literary and Artistic Value	Text Structure: Complexity and Accessibility
How is the book organized? What is the overall text structure? It is a chronological narrative. At the start, there is a page about John, then a page about Tom, and then a page about the two together. Sometimes the book talks about each separately on different sides of the two-page spread; when talking about events they were both involved in, it talks about them together.	*Is the text structure simple or more complex? How does this impact accessibility?* The text structure is what makes this book accessible to readers. Comparison and contrast is used within the paragraphs about each man. Each is written about in contrast to the other or an event that is unfolding. The narrative itself is straightforward because it follows chronological order moving from childhood to adulthood. However, it goes through their childhood fairly quickly and spends most of the narrative on the writing of the Declaration of Independence, which takes place over a short period of time. But this is clear, and should not confuse students, particularly if they are studying this for the purpose of understanding content about the American Revolution.

Language: Literary and Artistic Value	Language: Complexity and Accessibility
How is the language rich and interesting? What kind of sentence variation occurs? It starts off with a great hook that frames the whole narrative ("formed a surprising alliance, committed treason, and helped launch a new nation"). The book is filled with rich adjectives and parallel structure within paragraphs and pages. Direct quotes from each, taken from primary source materials, are included in quotation marks throughout. There is a jovial mood to the text in general.	*How challenging is the language? How does this impact accessibility?* The direct quotes are not difficult to read and understand because they are written into sentences as phrases, so the context supports the reader in understanding the point of view in the direct quote. It creates a sense of immediacy with Jefferson and Adams without slowing anything down or making the book more difficult. Adjectives and overall mood of the language make it more fun to read and slightly silly, which builds motivation in student readers.

Visuals: Literary and Artistic Value	Visuals: Complexity and Accessibility
How do the visuals engage the reader? How do they enhance the content? *How does the book design reinforce the content?* The book is illustrated with a palette of red, white, and blue, which reinforces the identity of the United States of America. The cover illustration and the final illustration are both allusions to famous images associated with the American Revolution. The cartoon drawings of Adams and Jefferson reinforce the comparisons and contrasts within the text. Background colors of white and navy also set up contrasts just as the book contrasts the two men. John and Tom are always mentioned in capital letters. Some sentences are in a larger bold font to emphasize their importance.	*How do the visuals and design impact accessibility?* The visuals make the book more accessible by illustrating with concrete images the differences between the two men. These illustrations can move readers from the concrete to the abstract in their thinking about the two men. The visuals also extend historical information to support students who might not have prior knowledge, making the book more accessible. For example, when discussing the occupation of Boston and the British navy patrol of the Atlantic seaboard, the book's illustrations bring to life the author's reference to "racket" in Boston (loud, occupied city controlled by the British army) and the "racket" in Virginia (the British navy's occupation of the Atlantic coast so that no ships could purchase colonial goods). By using a homonym (racket) the author compares and contrasts a very specific topic. But it is the illustrations that make the different meanings of that homonym clear to the reader who does not know the word, and demonstrates very clearly some of the activities of the British navy of which most students probably do not have prior knowledge.

Readers

Overall, in what ways does this book feel appropriate for some or all of the readers in your class?

Fifth graders will find the personal approach to history interesting. The use of humor in the text and the illustrations, and the humorous subtext and mood despite the serious topic, will engage students and make them want to keep reading. The more students view the illustrations, the more connections they will find between text and illustration, again, making the facts and concepts in the book more accessible and meaningful. The tightly written structure and book format will also help students navigate the text successfully. The personalities of Adams and Jefferson also make the book engaging to students, and therefore, more invested in reading for meaning and understanding.

Utility as a Teaching Tool: Instructional Possibilities (Purpose/Practice)

Instructional Purposes

Understanding Content

The book could be used to explore political relationships in general, and as a lens for looking at how Congress functions today in social studies.

This book would also be useful as part of a text set of biographies of historical figures from the American Revolution, to better understand the time period.

Developing Disciplinary Literacies

This book could be read in the context of exploring the Declaration of Independence as a document, helping to scaffold student understanding of how the document was written. The document was created as a result of a process that involved more than one person. Who were those people? How did they work together? How is the Declaration of Independence an end product of their collaboration, not simply something set in stone from the very beginning?

Using Mentor Text for Student Writing

As a "double portrait" mentor text in social studies, students can learn about how to write about two figures from any time period, for students to see figures as interconnected. Students could also read *George vs. George* by Rosalyn Schanzer, about George Washington and King George of England, as another mentor text. As part of a composition study of parallel structure in writing comparisons and contrasts in English Language Arts.

Teaching Literary Analysis and Genre Study

As part of a biography genre study in English Language Arts, students can examine the author's craft while reading this and *Worst of Friends,* another narrative book about the friendship between Thomas Jefferson and John Adams.

Developing Reading Skills

Reading this book allows students to hear some of the transitional phrases used to compare and contrast the two men, showing students how identifying the text structure supports their understanding of a nonfiction text.

Instructional Practices

It works well as a read aloud for reading for understanding content, developing disciplinary literacy, analyzing mentor texts, and developing reading skills.

As a literature circle book, it could be used as one group's exploration of founding fathers, while other groups read other perspectives.

For a biography genre study, it would be ideal for a whole class read as a mentor text.

Quantitative Evaluation of Text Complexity

Include one or two quantitative measurements of complexity to compare and contrast with your evaluation of the text.

Lexile® Range = 960L (upper parts of the 4–5 grade band)

ATOS/Accelerated Reader Bookfinder = 6.3 (middle of the 4th–5th band)

But what would it be like to teach this book with students who are not in fifth grade? Let's explore.

Political Friendships

Instructional Purposes: Understanding Content—Social Studies: Political Friendships

Grade Level: 7

In many states, 7th grade social studies classes explore early United States history, from pre-colonial times through the Civil War. The Civil War is typically studied toward the end of the year. Have students read *Those Rebels, John and Tom* paired with Russell Freedman's chapter-length nonfiction book *Abraham Lincoln and Frederick Douglas: The Story Behind an American Friendship* (2012). Read the picture book aloud or have multiple copies for students to explore in small groups. Ask students to document how the friendship between the two men helped them to craft the Declaration of Independence. Then, have students use 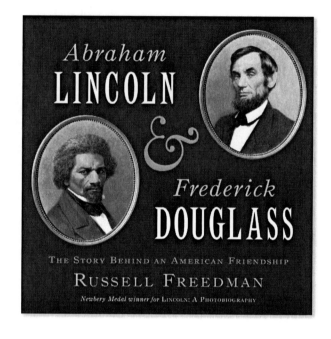 the theme of this book, the potential of friendship, as a lens for reading Freedman's book on Abraham Lincoln and Frederick Douglas. Have students explore what the relationships between Lincoln and Douglas did toward ending the Civil War and slavery in the United States. You may also want to extend this conversation to an exploration of friendships "across the aisle" in Congress today. What members of Congress are friends with one another despite being in different political parties? How have those friendships impacted legislation and policy today? How have they failed to make an impact?

Considerations for Text Complexity: This picture book would not be a challenging read for most 7th graders who have studied the American Revolution earlier in the school year. The book is fairly simple in its comparison and contrast, which provides a stepping stone for the reading of *Abraham Lincoln and Frederick Douglas: The Story Behind an American Friendship*, a longer and more complex book. By introducing students to the concept of political friendships, and what the two accomplished despite their differences, students can use that theme as a strategy for reading the longer nonfiction work that focuses on a different period of time. Reading the nonfiction book in social studies while studying the Civil War allows students to reinforce the other content they are learning about the time period, generally, and the question of slavery as a moral and political matter, specifically.

Russell Freedman has also written *Give Me Liberty! The Story of the Declaration of Independence* (2000). This nonfiction chapter book would work equally well paired with *Those Rebels, John and Tom* (2012) in a focused exploration on the ideas and history behind the Declaration of Independence in seventh grade social studies.

Biography Genre Study

Instructional Purposes: Teaching Literary Analysis/Genre Study—English: Biography

Grade Level: 10

Biography styles have changed a great deal over the past 30 years. Writers of popular literary nonfiction often use the literary device of theme as a way to hook their writers and focus their cradle-to-grave biographies more precisely on a range of themes that can be identified within a subject's life. As an introduction to a student research project that involves researching and writing their own biographies, have students conduct a combined picture book biography and author study of Barbara Kerley's picture book biographies: *Those Rebels, John and Tom* (2012), *The Dinosaurs of Waterhouse Hawkins* (2001), *What to Do About Alice?* (2008), and *A Home for Mr. Emerson* (2014). High school teachers might be surprised to think about using picture book biographies for a lesson in author's craft. But picture books provide a quick pathway to important writing lessons that can be learned in context and carried into longer student works. Have students respond to questions such as what themes are at work in each individual picture book biography? How does the author connect those themes to the time and place in which the subject lived? Use these biographies as mentor texts for students' first approach to writing biographies on subjects of interest to them. You might also want to have students read excerpts from well-written biographies of adults, such as David McCullough's *John Adams* (2001). As they conduct their research, what themes do they see emerging in the figure's life? What themes do they decide to concentrate on in their own writing? Why?

Considerations for Text Complexity: These picture book biographies will be simple reads for most 10th grade students, with the exception of English language learners who may be new to the United States and not have the same grasp of American history that other students might have. Regardless, these picture book biographies will still be able to ground readers in a manageable dose of biographical writing that can inform their own decision-making as they research and write. Picture book biographies will help to make the biographies written for adults more accessible as mentor texts, and less complex. If students can understand how theme works in a picture book, it can then be used as a reading strategy as students read full-length books, articles, and book chapter written for adults.

The teaching ideas for 5th grade included in the *Quality, Utility, and Complexity Chart* and these for 7th grade and 10th grade illustrate the different ways that this picture book biography can be used at different grade levels for different instructional purposes.

Now let's consider a second example.

It's Our Garden

It's Our Garden: From Seeds to Harvest in a School Garden by George Ancona (2013) is a book that invites exploration at first glance. The attractive cover includes the title in varying hues of green, student artwork depicting the flora and fauna of a garden and five photographs depicting multicultural students at work caretaking and harvesting. Photo-essayist George Ancona offers readers the opportunity to experience a year alongside these children, their teachers, parents, and community members as they work, learn, and play together in a vibrant courtyard garden. Ancona's insightful photographs depict the 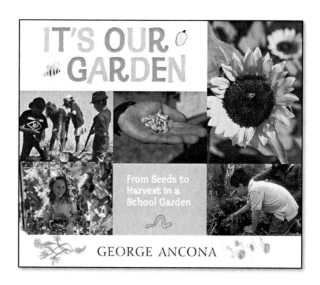 carefully designed space, illustrate the processes of gardening, and capture the intensity and joy of the gardeners. As an added bonus, student artwork provides a wonderful complement to carefully placed photos and generous white space. Clear and engaging text elaborates the images, and readers will gain a sense of the cyclical nature of gardening, the hard work involved, and the many rewards reaped by the gardeners. Throughout the book, Ancona highlights the integration of school curriculum with gardening activities; a teacher seeking a compelling argument for the establishment of a school garden need look no further than this book.

But a discussion of school gardens is only the most obvious possible curriculum focus for this title. Let's take a closer look to examine the versatility of this particular title.

Figure 5.2 Completed Sample *Quality, Utility, and Complexity Chart* for *It's Our Garden*

Title: *It's Our Garden: From Seeds to Harvest in a School Garden*

Author: George Ancona

Year of Publication: 2013

Notes from the Book Reviews
"clearly written text works seamlessly with the two kinds of color illustrations" (Booklist 2013)
"Ancona's no nonsense style is perfectly suited for newly independent readers" (Horn Book 2013)
School Library Journal (2012) review emphasizes the sensory experiences highlighted by the author.
Several reviewers note that teachers and students will be inspired to create their own school gardens after reading the book.

Genre Characteristics: Literary and Artistic Quality	Genre Characteristics: Literary and Artistic Quality
How does it meet established criteria? Book is a photo essay (documentary style): Photos play a strong role in conveying the content. Specialized Nonfiction: specifically tracks a year in this particular elementary school garden. As a documentary, the accuracy of the content is based on firsthand experience, documentation through photographs, observation, and interview. Includes recommended books and websites.	*How does the book meet and/or differ from genre characteristics? How does this impact accessibility?* Text and photos play an equal role in conveying the activities in this garden over the course of a year. The inclusion of the photos makes the text more accessible by providing visual supports.

Content: Literary and Artistic Quality	Content: Complexity and Accessibility
What is the book about? The book introduces the school garden at Acequia Madre elementary school—first by describing the planning and construction of the garden. The author spent a year documenting the activities in the school garden and a sequential recounting of the activities is the main focus of the text. Additionally, gardening concepts and scientific processes such as pollination, composting, plant life cycles, and animals and insect garden creatures are described. Different kinds of plants are named and illustrated with photographs. The author also makes note of the curriculum connections that teachers make with the garden—students read, write, paint, calculate and document their observations.	*How complex is the content for the intended audience? How does this impact accessibility?* Students' levels of experiences with gardening will vary. The author provides concise explanations of gardening processes. For example, the description of pollination reads: Flowers produce a sweet liquid called nectar. *"When a bird, a bee, or a butterfly goes into a flower to drink the nectar, a powder called pollen sticks to them..."* These processes are also depicted with photographs. There is a clear match between the text and photo illustrations so that less familiar content is well supported visually.

Text Structure: Literary and Artistic Quality	Text Structure: Complexity and Accessibility
How is the book organized? What is the overall text structure? Following a brief introduction that describes the beginnings of the garden and people who played key roles in its design, the text chronologically tracks the activities in the gardening, progressing from spring through the following winter, describing the necessary tasks associated with each season.	*Is the text structure simple or more complex? How does this impact accessibility?* The narrative chronological structure is a familiar structure for students. This makes the text easier to follow.
Language: Literary and Artistic Quality	**Language: Complexity and Accessibility**
How is the language rich and interesting? What kind of sentence variation occurs? The language used evokes sensory experiences. For example, the opening sentence: "The school bell sounds… and the classrooms explode with the noise of books closing, chairs sliding on the floor, and kids chattering."	*How challenging is the language? How does this impact accessibility?* Language is straightforward. When garden-specific vocabulary is introduced, words are defined/contextualized within the text. Sensory descriptions are reinforced by the photographs—when the text describes the process of using adobe to make a bread oven, a young girl is depicted with mud-coated hands outstretched.
Visuals: Literary and Artistic Quality	**Visuals: Complexity and Accessibility**
How do the visuals engage the reader? How do they enhance the content? *How does the book design reinforce the content?* Visuals play a strong role in conveying and reinforcing the content. Children's art is included—this increases child appeal, and demonstrates children's involvement in and learning from the gardening processes. Layout is exceptional—careful placement of the images enhance the pacing of the content while working to reinforce the information conveyed in the text. Variation in placements provides visual interest—holds the attention of the young reader. Close-ups, cameos, and panorama views are included. Vivid green endpapers feature children's art. The photo collage on the cover balances close-up and portrait images.	*How do the visuals and design impact accessibility?* Throughout the book the close alignment between the text content and the photos chosen by the author support comprehension. Sequences of photos are used to depict processes, such as pizza making, that occur in the garden.

Utility as a Teaching Tool: Instructional Possibilities (Purpose/Practice)

Instructional Purposes

<u>Understanding Content</u>

Appropriate in the context of these areas of study:

- community
- gardening
- life cycles
- animal/plant relationships
- seasonal changes

<u>Analyzing Writing as a Mentor Text</u>

Mentor text for the genre of a photo essay. Students will be inspired to document and write about an aspect of their school or community life.

Instructional Practices

Appropriate across a range of grade levels. Engaging *read aloud* for the primary and intermediate grades. It is a longer text, but could be read across multiple sittings.

Excellent potential as a *guided reading* text in the intermediate grades and for more capable readers in first and second grade.

Readers

Overall, in what ways does this book feel appropriate for some or all of the readers in your class?

Due to its engaging visuals, this text has broad appeal. The clear concise text, with embedded definitions and explanations, combined with the close alignment between the text and photos on each page make the book highly accessible.

The focus on the students as gardeners portrays children as active, capable persons—students will identify with these children.

Multicultural families are depicted and there is an emphasis on the garden as a gathering place for community members.

Quantitative Evaluation of Text Complexity

Include one or two quantitative measurements of complexity to compare and contrast with your evaluation of the text.

Lexile® : AD910L

ATOS (Accelerated Reader website) 5.1

Grade Level Band 4–5

Figure 5.2 represents our evaluation of the quality, utility, and complexity of *It's Our Garden* and includes a brainstorm of some possible curriculum connections and classroom uses. We can explore some of these possibilities in greater depth, selecting examples from three different grade levels, while considering the implications for text complexity.

Comparing Garden Stories

Instructional Purposes: Developing Reading Skills—Compare and Contrast; Understanding Content—Life Science (Gardening), Social Studies (Community)

Grade Level: 1

Pair a reading of *It's Our Garden* with a reading of Robbin Gourley's *First Garden: The White House Garden and How it Grew* (2011). Compare the origins, goals, and outcomes of the creation of each garden, constructing a comparison chart to document student thinking. Be sure to compare the photographs on the back of each dust jacket! As an extension, select a local garden, either at your school, in your community, or at a local historical site or museum. Have students interview the garden's caretakers to learn the story of how and why this garden was established and how it is cared for. If time allows, work with your students to co-author a story about the local garden you have come to know.

Considerations for Text Complexity: In this activity, you are integrating language arts, science, and social studies instruction, developing reading comprehension skills while simultaneously building science and social studies content knowledge. Since the texts are at a level of complexity beyond the reading abilities of most 1st graders, you would most likely read aloud *It's Our Garden* to your students; the books would be a stretch for small-group or independent reading. However, the embedded explanations and definitions for garden vocabulary terms provide strong support for student comprehension of both *It's Our Garden* and a subsequent reading aloud of *First Garden: The White House Garden and How it Grew*. Since students can easily be supported to access and interpret the texts, they can engage in the more complex task of comparing and contrasting the garden creation and processes described in two texts. In this example, the text is of appropriate complexity in order to facilitate the critical-thinking skills of comparison.

Garden Helpers

Instructional Purposes: Understanding Content—Life Science; Engaging in Inquiry and Research

Grade Level: 3

Child-drawn images of bees, butterflies, and ladybugs adorn the end papers of *It's Our Garden*. The text describes the roles that insects and worms play in supporting plant growth in the garden. Allow students to learn more about creatures beneficial to the garden by reading books such as *Bug Shots: The Good, The Bad, and the Bugly* (Siy 2011), *The Beetle Book* (Jenkins 2012), *The Honeybee Man* (Nargi 2011), *Ladybugs* (Gibbons 1991), *Insect Detectives* (Voake 2010), and *Yucky Worms* (French 2009). Have students work in small groups to become experts on an assigned type of creature by reading these texts. Then have them make notes on their findings and prepare a presentation for their classmates.

Considerations for Text Complexity: In this example, *It's Our Garden* is one title in a text set that explores the roles of insects, arachnids, and arthropods in the ecosystem of a garden. Your purpose in using this text set is to support student learning about the characteristics and behaviors of these animals. Although a quantitative analysis of the complexity of *It's Our Garden* places it slightly above the reading level of some third grade students, our qualitative analysis of the text helps us to be confident that by working in pairs or groups, students will be able to access and interpret the content of the text; due to the clear explanatory language used in the text and the strong support provided by a close match between the visuals and the text.

Genre Study of The Photo Essay

Instructional Purposes: Teaching Literary Analysis and Genre Study; Analyzing a Mentor Text for Writing

Grade Level: 5

It's Our Garden is a striking example of creative formatting in a photo essay. The integration of children's art makes the book unusual and the placement and shape of the images makes it a standout. Pair this book with another gardening photo essay, *Watch Me Grow: A Down-to-Earth Look at Growing Food in the City* (Hodge 2011) and have students discuss the choices authors and photographers make when crafting a photo essay. Then have students look at other photo essays written by George Ancona, for example, *Come and Eat* (2011). How do the visual images work to enhance the messages of the text? Use *It's Our Garden* as a mentor text for student-created texts about an aspect of your school. The school garden is a unique feature of the Acequia Madre School—what is unique about your school?

Considerations for Text Complexity: In this example, *It's Our Garden* is employed as a mentor text for student writing in the study of a nonfiction subgenre: the photo essay. To maximize the benefit of a mentor text, students must engage in close reading of the texts, going beyond the processes of accessing and interpreting the content to deconstructing, understanding, and articulating the author's writing processes. Since a qualitative review of *It's Our Garden* assures us that the text and visuals are highly supportive of readers' comprehension, and a quantitative analysis placed the book in a grade 4–5 range, we can be fairly confident that students will be able to engage in the kind of close reading that the task requires, recognizing that some teacher support will be needed.

What we learn from this exploration of *It's Our Garden* at three different grade levels is that it is ripe for teaching possibilities with a range of instructional purposes. The evaluation of the quality of the book remains a constant. However, the variety of teaching possibilities, the audience, and the consideration of text complexity are an ever-changing dynamic rooted in the instructional purposes.

We walked through this brainstorm of teaching possibilities at different grade levels and in different subject areas to showcase more precisely the ways in which text complexity is never fixed when we consider the interactions between the reader, text, and task. When we change who the reader is and what the tasks are, the complexity of the text itself shifts.

A Book's Role in a Unit of Study: Considerations for Complexity

We rarely use a book in isolation. Typically, we use texts in combination with other texts. When we set up texts strategically, we often say that the texts are "talking" to one another. This conversation *between* the texts affects the complexity of each text, because the dialogue that takes place *across* the texts informs the students, sharpens classroom focus, and supports students' comprehension. The reading of one text informs the reading of the other and renders each more accessible than they would be if read on their own. The use of text sets allows you to focus on content and differentiate reading instruction simultaneously (Cappiello and Dawes 2013). Within a text set you can offer a range of texts at the appropriate level of complexity for different groups of students or even individuals, while also fostering their critical thinking as they share what they are learning across the different texts and perspectives.

In our previous book, *Teaching with Text Sets,* we shared our strategies for developing text sets along with a set of instructional models for teaching with multimodal, multigenre text sets. Here, we would like to focus on the different roles a text can play within a text set and the implications that the role has for considerations of text complexity. A text can play the following roles:

- scaffold
- immersion
- extension

Within the context of a unit of study, texts can serve different roles. We refer to some texts in a text set as **scaffolds**. These scaffolds are usually selected because they frontload important content and introduce a theme or genre. Scaffold texts inspire interest and curiosity and can generate important student questions. Scaffold texts are often shorter than other texts within the text set, so that students can get through them quickly and move into a deeper exploration within the unit. When using text sets, we often rely on multimodal texts as scaffolds, because they provide important access to the focal point of a unit without a lot of heavy reading.

Some texts in a text set are **immersion** texts. These immersion texts are longer texts that go into greater depth. Students will spend more time with these texts and perhaps receive more support to access and interpret the content. Or, conversely, perhaps these are the texts you expect students to work at to access and interpret independently, depending upon your instructional purposes. The use of multiple texts in a text set allows you to differentiate instruction based on the needs of the readers in your classroom. When students read multiple texts, you support them to layer content and vocabulary understanding. There is a logical progression of reading and an intentional positioning of texts to maximize student understanding and inquiry.

Finally, some texts in a text set are considered **extension** texts. They extend student understanding of whatever it is they are studying. The readers need the information in the previous texts to fully understand these texts. They would not be ready to access them fully at the beginning of a unit, because of their level of complexity and the students' lack of prior knowledge. Often, these texts can prompt action—they can serve as a jumping-off point for critical literacy or for doing something out in the real world with their newfound knowledge and experiences. Some extension texts can be used with a portion of the class, or arranged individually or by small groups, so that students are appropriately challenged by their areas of interest, reading abilities, and/or preferred literacy practices.

In Figure 5.3, we highlight the three different roles texts can play in a text set, and the implications of each role when considering text complexity.

Figure 5.3 Text Roles and Considerations for Complexity

Text Role	Implications for Complexity
Scaffold	Scaffolds serve as an introduction to the unit of study so the text should not be overwhelmingly complex.
	If multiple texts are used to present a diversity of perspectives, the texts can be more complex than when used singly.
	Consideration of complexity is superseded by the consideration of how well the text inspires interest and inquiry in the unit.
Immersion	Texts are selected as immersion texts because they are well-matched to the focus of the unit of study (important content). Students should be able to thoroughly access and interpret the text.
	If multiple texts are used to present a diversity of perspectives, the texts can be more complex than when used singly.
	The complexity of the text is appropriately matched with instructional practice. Consider the level of support students will receive to access and interpret the text. The more teacher-provided support throughout means a text can be more complex.
Extension	Extension texts may go beyond essential content and as such be more appropriate to be used with a subsection of the class as an extension.
	Perhaps not all students in the class will be reading the text. The complexity of the text can be matched with the abilities and interests of the readers reading it.
	Extension texts are a great way to support all of the readers in your room from the most experienced and skillful to those needing a lot of teacher-directed support.

In the teaching examples for using *Those Rebels, John and Tom* (Kerley 2012) in 7th grade social studies and 10th grade English, the picture book biography served as a scaffold. In 7th grade, the book served to introduce the concept of political friendships. The immersion text was Russell Freedman's *Abraham Lincoln and Frederick Douglas: The Story Behind an American Friendship* (2012). Contemporary articles and digital texts on the friendships between current members of Congress would form the extension texts. In the 10th grade biography genre study, Barbara Kerley's picture book biographies are used to scaffold the concept of theme within biography. Students can apply what they learn about theme in Kerley's work not just to the books and articles they read as part of their research, but to their process of composing biographies as well.

For yet another specific example of how texts can serve as scaffold, immersion, and extension, we want to share with you a unit on monarch butterflies that two teachers and a literacy coach in Maine developed for third graders. In this context, the text set is comprised of three parts, and each part is closely aligned with a different guiding question.

This unit was prompted by the sudden disappearance of monarch butterflies in North America during the summer of 2013. In this district, teachers who normally gather chrysalises from the school garden in September were unable to find any. This prompted an exploration of the reason why no monarchs could be found. We supported the teachers in helping to find and locate a range of digital and print texts that could ground the students in an immediate exploration of where the monarchs were (and were not), but also to extend it as a critical literacy exercise that explores why animals are in crisis and what kids can do to try and help.

Figure 5.4 lists the different texts that were used in this unit of study, describing the guiding questions that structure the unit and the roles played by the texts, with notes on our considerations of text complexity.

Figure 5.4 Text Roles and Complexity Considerations for the Monarch Text Set

Guiding Question	Scaffold
Where are the monarchs?	These digital texts frontload content by revealing that all across New England, monarchs were not to be found during the summer of 2013.
	The multimodal texts provide access without heavy reading.
Texts	
American University Radio http://thedianerehmshow.org/shows/2013-10-01/environmental-outlook-shrinking-monarch-butterfly-population Vermont Public Radio http://digital.vpr.net/post/vt-monarch-butterfly-population-dwindles New Hampshire Public Radio http://nhpr.org/post/natures-obligate-relationships Maine Public radio http://www.mpbn.net/	

Guiding Question	Immersion
Why are the monarchs disappearing? What is happening to other animals? Are they connected?	Texts are longer and go into greater depth. Most are appropriate for third grade readers, but we have included some challenge immersion texts for experienced advanced readers. Some students can be reading about climate change, habitat loss, and clean water as problems, while other students can be studying butterflies specifically, and still others can explore other animals who have been put in jeopardy and what some of the common causes have been. Connections can be made between the sudden loss of monarchs, the sudden loss of bees, and the sudden loss of golden frogs.

Texts

Why are the Monarchs Disappearing?

<u>Articles from Children's Magazines:</u>

Costello, Emily. (2008). Safe Haven. (cover story). *Science World*, 64 (11), 8.

McCormack, Fiona. (2005). Bye, Bye, Butterfly? *Scholastic News* 67 (19), 6.

<u>Children's Literature:</u>

Bang, Molly. (1997). *Common Ground: The Water, Earth, and Air We Share.* New York: Blue Sky Press.

Frost, Helen. (2008). *Monarch and Milkweed.* Ill. by Leonid. Gore. New York: Atheneum.

Royston, Angela. (2008). *Global Warming.* [Protect our planet series.] Chicago, IL: Heinemann Library.

Simon, Seymour. (2011). *Global Warming.* [Smithsonian series.] New York: Collins.

Stewart, Melissa. (2006). *A Place for Butterflies.* Atlanta, GA: Peachtree.

Challenge Text Read Aloud: Chapter "Butterflies Change Their Range"

Cherry, Lynn, Braasch, Gary. (2008). *How We Know What We Know About Our Changing Climate: Scientists and Kids Explore Global Warming.* Nevada City, CA: Dawn Publications.

What is Happening to Other Animals? What are the Connections?

<u>Digital Texts:</u>

"Back Home on the Range: Biologists Help Black-Footed Ferrets Come Back From the Brink of Extinction"
http://www.scholastic.com/browse/article.jsp?id=3757471

National Geographic Kids: Honey Bee Mystery
http://kids.nationalgeographic.com/kids/stories/animalsnature/honey-bee-mystery/

<u>Articles from Children's Magazines:</u>

Howling Success. (2008). *Scholastic News—Edition* 76 (14): 3.

Goodstein, Carol. (1997). Where Have All the Pollinators Gone? Science World, 53 (12): 12.

Anonymous. Out of the Woods. 2006. *Scholastic News* 63 (3): 2.

Graber, C. (2008). The Case of the Disappearing Bees. *Ask*, 7 (7), 14.

Smith, N. (2010). Bees Feel the Sting. (cover story). *Scholastic News—Edition 4*, 72 (22), 4.

Golden Opportunity. (2012). *Scholastic News—Edition 4*, 75 (1), 3.

Texts
Children's Literature:
George, J.C. (2013). *The Eagles Are Back*. Ill. by W. Minor. New York: Dutton.
George, J.C. (2008). *The Wolves Are Back*. Ill. by W. Minor. New York: Dutton.
Rotner, S., Woodhull, A. (2010). *The Buzz On Bees: Why Are They Disappearing?* New York: Holiday House. Challenge Texts:
Challenge Texts:
Burns, Loree G. (2010). *The Hive Detectives: Chronicle of a Honey Bee Catastrophe*. [Scientists in the field series.] Ill. by E. Harasimowicz. Boston: Houghton Mifflin.
Markle, Sandra. (2013). *The Case of the Vanishing Honeybee: A Scientific Mystery*. Minneapolis, MN: Millbrook Press.
Markle, Sandra. (2011). *The Case of the Vanishing Golden Frogs: A Scientific Mystery*. Minneapolis, MN: Millbrook Press.

Guiding Question(s)	Extension
What can I do to save the monarchs?	The complexity of these extension texts varied. Teachers considered both students' reading abilities and interests when selecting texts during this section of the unit of study.
	These books require a level of abstraction for students to use them. They provide role models of other people, in several cases children, taking action to improve Earth.
	Students read these books not for the content connected to the disappearing monarchs, but as models of ways that they can organize and take action in their community.
	These books also offer hope, so that students can see how humans can reverse their impact and help bring back polluted environments and endangered species.

Texts
Bouler, Olivia. (2011). *Olivia's Birds: Saving the Gulf*. New York: Sterling.
Burns, Loree G. (2012). *Citizen Scientists: Be a Part of Scientific Discovery From Your Own Backyard*. Ill. by E. Harasimowicz. New York: Macmillan.
Drummond, Allan. (2011). *Energy Island: How One Community Harnessed the Wind and Changed their World*. New York: Farrar, Straus, Giroux.
Kamkwamba, William, Mealer, B. (2012). *The Boy Who Harnessed the Wind*. Ill. by E. Zunon. New York: Dial Books.
Lawler, L. (2012). *Rachel Carson and Her Book That Changed the World*. Ill. by L. Beingessner. New York: Holiday House.
Yezerski, Thomas. (2011). *Meadowlands: A Wetlands Survival Story*. New York: Farrar, Straus, Giroux.

In this particular example, each grouping of texts within the text set serves either as a scaffold, immersion, or extension. Sometimes just a single text serves in each role. It all depends on the length of the texts, the instructional purpose, and the particular text set model that is used.

We highlight the roles books can play when used as scaffolds, immersion, and extension texts in a text set to emphasize the point that when texts sets are used the issue of text complexity becomes less critical. We focus not on finding the precise level of complexity for each particular reader and instead focus on the content of the books and our students' abilities to access and interpret that content over the course of a unit of study, not necessarily in any one book.

As we said at the beginning of this chapter, we do not choose a book based on its level of complexity. But this does not mean we ignore text complexity. We want our students, regardless of their age, to continue to grow as readers and to stretch their reading and comprehension abilities. If we want them to be able to read increasingly more sophisticated texts over time, we are confident that keeping our focus on selecting engaging, high-quality books that present related content and concepts from multiple perspectives, with a consideration of our readers' abilities to access and interpret that content with and without support, will result in that growth.

Conclusion

Ultimately, this book is about a range of processes. It is about the process of selecting texts for curriculum planning. It is about the process of grounding your text choices in specific goals and instructional purposes.

But this also a book about how you can feel empowered to make choices about the kinds of texts in your language arts, social studies, mathematics, science, and arts curriculum. It is about reading closely for authentic purposes in order to select texts that serve your curricular needs and your students' needs and interests.

Finally, it is a book about possibilities—about choosing books that will make school interesting and engaging, about asking students to think deeply and critically about these texts, and about ideas and issues, themes and concepts that matter to all of us.

Questions for Reflection

1. How does considering a text's complexity differ when considering a text on its own versus considering a text as part of a text set?

2. How has reading this book affected your view of the concept and importance of text complexity?

3. What questions about text complexity do you have after reading this book?

References Cited

Adams, Caralee J., Erik W. Robelen, and Nirvi Shah. 2012. "Civil Rights Data Show Retention Disparities." *Education Week* 31 (23). http://www.edweek.org/ew/articles/2012/03/07/23data_ep.h31.html?qs=civil+righ

Allington, Richard L. 2009. "If They Don't Read Much . . . 30 Years Later." In *Reading More, Reading Better*, edited by Elfrieda H. Hiebert, 30–54. New York, NY: Guilford.

Bamford, Rosemary, and Jan Kristo. 2002. *Making Facts Come Alive: Choosing and Using Nonfiction Literature K-8*, 2nd ed. Norwood, MA: Christopher Gordon Publishers.

Banks, James A., and Cherry A. McGee Banks, eds. 2007. *Multicultural Education: Issues and Perspectives*, 6th ed. San Francisco, CA: Wiley/Jossey-Bass Education.

Beers, Kylene. 2002. *When Kids Can't Read: What Teachers Can Do*. Portsmouth, NH: Heinemann.

———. 2003. *When Kids Can't Read, What Teachers Can Do: Guide for Teachers 6–12*. Portsmouth, NH: Heinemann.

Berenyi, Jessica R. 2008. "'Appropriate action,' Inappropriately Defined: Amending the Equal Educational Opportunities Act of 1974." *Washington and Lee Law Review* 65: 639–657.

Buehl, Doug. 2011. *Developing Readers in the Academic Disciplines*. International Reading Association.

Cappiello, Mary Ann, and Erika Thulin Dawes. 2012. *Teaching with Text Sets*. Huntington Beach, CA: Shell Education.

Cazden, Courtney, Bill Cope, Norman Fairclough, and Jim Gee et al. 1996. "A "Pedagogy of Multiliteracies: Designing Social Futures." *Harvard Educational Review* 66 (1): 60–92.

Chatton, Barbara. 2010. *Using Poetry across the Curriculum: Learning to Love Language*, 2nd ed. Santa Barbara, CA: Libraries Unlimited.

Crawford, Patricia A., and Vicky Zygouris-Coe. 2008. "Those Were the Days: Learning About History through Literature." *Childhood Education* 84 (4): 197–203.

Daniels, Harvey. 2002. *Literature Circles: Voice and Choice in Book Clubs and Reading Groups*. 2nd ed. Portland, ME: Stenhouse Publishers.

Dawes, Erika Thulin. 2007. "Constructing Reading: Building Conceptions of Literacy in a Volunteer Read-Aloud Program." *Language Arts* 85 (1): 10–19.

Faltis, Kelly. 2011. "Bilingual, ESL, and English Immersion: Educational Models for Limited English Proficient Students in Texas." *Pepperdine Policy Review* 4: 81–98.

Frey, Nancy, and Douglas Fisher. 2007. *Reading for Information in Elementary School: Content Literacy Strategies to Build Comprehension.* New York: Pearson/ Merrill Prentice Hall.

Fisher, Douglas, and Nancy Frey. 2011. *Improving Adolescent Literacy: Content Area Strategies at Work*, 3rd ed. New York: Pearson/ Merrill Prentice Hall.

Fountas, Irene C., and Gay Su Pinnell. 1996. *Guided Reading: Good First Teaching for All Children.* Portsmouth, NH: Heinemann.

———. 2001. *Guiding Readers and Writers, Grades 3–6: Teaching Comprehension, Genre, and Content Literacy.* Portsmouth, NH: Heinemann.

———. 2012. "Guided Reading: The Romance and the Reality." *The Reading Teacher* 66 (4): 268–284.

———. 2013. *The Critical Role of Text Complexity in Teaching Children to Read.* Portsmouth, NH: Heinemann.

Gee, James Paul. 1990. *Social Linguistics and Literacies: Ideology in Discourses.* New York, NY: Routledge.

———. 2001. "Reading as Situated Language: A Sociocognitive Perspective." *Journal of Adolescent & Adult Literacy* 44 (8): 714–725.

Guthrie, John T., and Wigfield, Allan. 2000. "Engagement and Motivation in Reading." In *Handbook of Reading Research*, vol. 3, ed. Michael L. Kamil, Peter B. Rosenthal, P. David Pearson, and Rebecca Barr. Mahwah, NJ: Lawrence Erlbaum Associates. 403–422.

Hadaway, Nancy L., and Terrell Young. 2010. *Matching Books and Readers: Helping English Learners in Grades K–6.* New York, NY: The Guilford Press.

Halliday, Michael A.K. 1975. *Learning How to Mean: Exploration in the Development of Language.* London: Edward Arnold.

Harvey, Stephanie. 1998. *Nonfiction Matters: Reading, Writing, and Researching in Grades 3–8.* Portland, ME: Stenhouse Publishing.

Harvey, Stephanie, and Anne Goudvis. 2007. *Strategies That Work: Teaching Comprehension for Understanding and Engagement*, 2nd ed. Portland, ME: Stenhouse Publishers.

Harvey, Stephanie, and Harvey Daniels. 2009. *Comprehension and Collaboration: Inquiry Circles in Action*. Portsmouth, NH: Heinemann.

Heard, Georgia. 1998. *Awakening the Heart: Exploring Poetry in Elementary and Middle School.* Portsmouth, NH: Heinemann.

Heath, Shirley Brice. 1982. "What No Bedtime Story Means: Narrative Skills at Home and School." *Language in Society* 11 (1): 49–76.

Hiebert, Elfrieda. December 2011, January 2012. "The Common Core's Staircase of Text Complexity: Getting the Size of the First Step Right." *Reading Today* 29 (3): 26–27.

Holbrook, Sara. 2005. *Practical Poetry: A Nonstandard Approach to Meeting Content-Area Standards.* Portsmouth, NH: Heinemann.

Horning, Kathleen T. 2010. *From Cover to Cover: Evaluating and Reviewing Children's Books.* New York, NY: HarperCollins.

Issacs, Kathleen T. 2013. *Picturing the World: Informational Picture Books for Children.* Chicago: American Library Association.

Janeczko, Paul B., ed., and Chris Raschka (illus.). 2005. *A Kick in the Head: An Everyday Guide to Poetic Forms.* Somerville, MA: Candlewick Press.

Kiefer, Barbara Z. 2010. *Charlotte Huck's Children's Literature.* 10th ed. Boston, MA: McGraw-Hill Higher Education.

Kihuen, Mariana. 2009. "Leaving No Child Behind: A Civil Right." *American University Journal of Gender Social Policy and Law* 17: 113–147.

Lee, Carol D., and Anika Spratley. 2010. "Reading in the Disciplines: The Challenges of Adolescent Literacy." New York, NY: Carnegie Corporation of New York.

Levstik, Linda, and David Barton. 2010. *Doing History: Investigating with Children in Elementary and Middle School.* New York, NY: Routledge.

Lindfors, Judith Wells. 2008. *Children's Language: Connecting Reading, Writing, and Talk.* New York, NY: Teachers College Press.

Lukens, Rebecca J., Jacquelin J. Smith, and Cynthia Miller Coffer. 2012. *A Critical Handbook of Children's Literature.* 9th ed. Boston, MA: Pearson.

Marcus, Leonard S. 2009. *The Wand and the Word: Conversations with Writers of Fantasy*. Somerville, MA: Candlewick Press.

Martin, Dave, and Beth Brooke. 2002. "Getting Personal: Making Effective Use of Historical Fiction in the History Classroom." *Teaching History* 108: 30.

Maxwell, Lesli. A. 2014. "U.S. School Enrollment Hits Majority-Minority Milestone." *Education Week* (August). http://www.edweek.org/ew/articles/2014/08/20/01demographics.h34.html?tkn=VYNFm4GWnl5JqsPp1DF7zfKLh1F%2BZ4qZck1T&print=1.

Mishra, Punya, and Matthew J. Koehler. 2006. "Technological Pedagogical Content Knowledge: A Framework for Teacher Knowledge." *Teachers College Record* 108 (6): 1017–1054.

Moje, Elizabeth Birr. 2008. "Foregrounding the Disciplines in Secondary Literacy Teaching and Learning: A Call for Change." *Journal of Adolescent & Adult Literacy* 5 (2): 96–107.

Moss, Barbara. 2002. *Exploring the Literature of Fact: Children's Nonfiction Trade Books in the Elementary Classroom*. New York: Guilford Press.

Moyers, Bill. 1995. *The Language of Life: A Festival of Poets*. New York, NY: Bantam Doubleday Dell.

National Council of Teachers of English. 2013. "NCTE Definition of 21st Century Literacies." http://www.ncte.org/positions/statements/21stcentdefinition.

National Governors Association (NGA) Center for Best Practices and Council of Chief State School Officers (CCSSO). 2010a. "Common Core States Standards: Appendix A." Washington, D.C.: National Governors Association Center for Best Practices, Council of Chief State School Officers. www.corestandards.org.

———. 2010b. "Common Core States Standards: Appendix B." Washington, D.C.: National Governors Association Center for Best Practices, Council of Chief State School Officers. www.corestandards.org.

———. 2010c. "Common Core States Standards: English Language Arts Standards." Washington, D.C.: National Governors Association Center for Best Practices, Council of Chief State School Officers. www.corestandards.org.

———. 2010d. "Common Core States Standards: Supplemental to Appendix A: New Research on Text Complexity." Washington, D.C.: National Governors Association Center for Best Practices, Council of Chief State School Officers. www.corestandards.org.

Nesi, Olga. 2012. "The Question of Text Complexity." *School Library Journal* 58 (10): 20.

Rainey, Emily, and Elizabeth Birr Moje. 2012. "Building Insider Knowledge: Teaching Students to Read, Write, and Think within ELA and across the Disciplines." *English Education* 45 (1): 71–90.

RAND Reading Study Group. 2002. *Reading for Understanding: Toward an R&D Program in Reading Comprehension*. RAND Corporation.

Rosenblatt, Louise M. 1978. *The Reader, the Text, the Poem: The Transactional Theory of the Literary Work*. Carbondale, IL: Southern Illinois University.

Shanahan, Timothy, and Cynthia Shanahan. 2008. "Teaching Disciplinary Literacy to Adolescents: Rethinking Content-Area Literacy." *Harvard Educational Review* 78 (1): 40–59.

Stevenson, Deborah. 2006. "Finding Literary Goodness in a Pluralistic World." *The Horn Book Magazine* 82 (5): 511–517.

Tomlinson, Carol A. 2012. "Teaching Today's Students: A Case for Differentiated Instruction" (presentation, Knox College, Galesburg, IL, February 9).

Tovani, Cris. 2000. *I Read It, but I Don't Get It: Comprehension Strategies for Adolescent Readers*. Portland, ME: Stenhouse Publishers.

Tunnell, Michael, and Richard Ammon, eds. 1992. *The Story of Ourselves: Teaching History through Children's Literature*. Portsmouth, NH: Heinemann.

Vygotsky, Lev. 1986. *Thought and Language*, ed. Alex Kozulin. Cambridge, MA: The MIT Press.

Wiley, Terrence G., and Wayne E. Wright. 2004. "Against the Undertow: Language-Minority Education Policy and Politics in the 'Age Of Accountability'." *Educational Policy* 18 (1): 142–168. doi:10.1177/0895904803260030.

Zarnowski, Myra. 2003. *History Makers: A Questioning Approach to Reading and Writing Biography*. Portsmouth, NH: Heinemann.

Zarnowski, Myra, and Susan Turkel. 2011. "Nonfiction Literature that Highlights Inquiry: How 'Real' People Solve 'Real' Problems." *Journal of Children's Literature* 37 (1): 30–37.

Book Reviews Cited

Betty Carter, review of *Penny and Her Marble*, by Kevin Henkes, The Horn Book, March/April 2013.

Booklist, review of *Interrupting Chickens*, by David Ezra Stein, September 15, 2010.

Booklist, review of *Those Rebels, John and Tom*, by Barbara Kerley, December 1, 2011.

Booklist, review of *Worst of Friends: Thomas Jefferson, John Adams, and the True Story of an American Feud*, by Suzanne Tripp Jurmain, December 1, 2011.

Carolyn Phelan, review of *It's Our Garden: From Seeds to Harvest in a School Garden*, by George Ancona, Booklist. February 15, 2013.

Carolyn Phelan, review of *Penny and Her Marble*, by Kevin Henkes, Booklist, December 15, 2012.

Danielle J. Ford, review of *Parrots Over Puerto Rico*, by Susan L. Roth and Cindy Trumbore, The Horn Book Magazine, January/February 2014.

Dean Schneider, review of *The Great Trouble: A Mystery of London, the Blue Death, and a Boy Called Eel*, The Horn Book Magazine, November/December 2013.

Donna Cardon, review of *Dreaming Up: A Celebration of Building*, by Christy Hale, School Library Journal, October 1, 2012.

Frances E. Millhouser, review of *It's Our Garden: From Seeds to Harvest in a School Garden*, by George Ancona, School Library Journal. December 1, 2012.

Gay Lynn Van Vleck, review of *Interrupting Chickens*, by David Ezra Stein. School Library Journal, July 1, 2010.

Harvey Daniels and Stephanie Harvey, *Comprehension and Collaboration: Inquiry Circles in Action*, Heinmann, 2009.

Horn Book, review of *Those Rebels, John and Tom*, by Barbara Kerley, Fall 2012.

Jody Kopple, review of *The Port Chicago 50: Disaster, Mutiny, and the Fight for Civil Rights*, by Steve Sheinkin, School Library Journal, February 1, 2014.

Kathy Piehl, review of *Parrots Over Puerto Rico*, by Susan L. Roth and Cindy Trumbore, School Library Journal, October 1, 2013.

Kirkus, review of *Dreaming Up: A Celebration of Building*, by Christy Hale, September 15, 2012.

Kirkus, review of *Interrupting Chickens*, by David Ezra Stein, July 1, 2010.

Kirkus, review of *Parrots Over Puerto Rico*, by Susan L. Roth and Cindy Trumbore, September 1, 2013.

Kirkus, review of *The Great Trouble: A Mystery of London, the Blue Death, and a Boy Called Eel*, by Deborah Hopkinson, August 15, 2013.

Kirkus, review of *The Port Chicago 50: Disaster, Mutiny, and the Fight for Civil Rights*, by Steve Sheinkin, December 15, 2013.

Kirkus, review of *Those Rebels, John and Tom*, by Barbara Kerley, November 15, 2011.

Linda Ludke, review of *Penny and Her Marble*, by Kevin Henkes. School Library Journal, February 1, 2013.

Lynne Christianson, review of *Those Rebels, John and Tom*, by Barbara Kerley, Library Media Connection, March/April 2012.

Publisher's Weekly, review of *The Great Trouble: A Mystery of London, the Blue Death, and a Boy Called Eel*, by Deborah Hopkinson, September 2, 2013.

Publisher's Weekly, review of *The Port Chicago 50: Disaster, Mutiny, and the Fight for Civil Rights*, by Steve Sheinkin, November 11, 2013.

Publisher's Weekly, review of *Those Rebels, John and Tom*, by Barbara Kerley, November 14, 2011.

Regan O'Malley, review of *The Great Trouble: A Mystery of London, the Blue Death, and a Boy Called Eel*, by Deborah Hopkinson, School Library Journal, October 1, 2013.

Roger Sutton, review of *The Port Chicago 50: Disaster, Mutiny, and the Fight for Civil Rights*, by Steve Sheinkin, The Horn Book Magazine, March/April 2014.

Sam Bloom, review of *It's Our Garden: From Seeds to Harvest in a School Garden*, by George Ancona, Horn Book, March/April, 2013.

Sarah Bean Thompson, review of *The Great Trouble: A Mystery of London, the Blue Death, and a Boy Called Eel*, by Deborah Hopkinson, Booklist, October 15, 2013.

Sarah Hunter, review of *The Port Chicago 50: Disaster, Mutiny, and the Fight for Civil Rights*, by Steve Sheinkin, Booklist, February 1, 2014.

Whitehurst, Lucinda Schneider, review of *Those Rebels, John and Tom*, by Barbara Kerley, School Library Journal, January 1, 2012.

Woodward, Linda, review of *Dreaming Up: A Celebration of Building*, by Christy Hale, Library Media Connection, May/June 2013.

Children's Literature Cited

Ancona, George. 2013. *It's Our Garden: From Seeds to Harvest in a School Garden.* Somerville, MA: Candlewick Press.

Ancona, George. 2011. *Come and Eat!* Watertown, MA: Charlesbridge Press.

Anonymous. 2006. "Out of the Woods." *Scholastic News* 63 (3): 2.

Anonymous. 2012. "Golden Opportunity." *Scholastic News* 75 (1): 3.

Bang, Molly. 1997. *Common Ground: The Water, Earth, and Air We Share.* New York, NY: Blue Sky Press.

Bouler, Olivia. 2011. *Olivia's Birds: Saving the Gulf.* New York, NY: Sterling.

Brownlee, Christine. 2012. "Back Home on the Range: Scientists Help Black-Footed Ferrets Come Back From the Brink of Extinction." *Science World.* http://www.scholastic.com/browse/article.jsp?id=3757471

Bryant, Jen. 2013. *A Splash of Red: The Life and Art of Horace Pippin.* New York, NY: Books for Young Readers.

Burns, Loree Griffin. 2009. *The Hive Detectives: Chronicle of a Honey Bee Catastrophe.* Boston, MA: Houghton Mifflin Books for Children.

———. 2012. *Citizen Scientists: Be a Part of Scientific Discovery from Your Own Backyard.* New York, NY: Henry Holt and Company.

———. 2014. *Handle with Care: An Unusual Butterfly Journey.* Minneapolis, MN: Millbrook Press.

Cherry, Lynne, and Gary Braasch. 2008. *How We Know What We Know About our Changing Climate: Scientists and Kids Explore Global Warming.* Nevada City, CA: Dawn Publications.

Collier, James Lincoln, and Christopher Collier. 1987. *War Comes to Willy Freeman.* New York, NY: Dell Yearling.

Appendix C • Children's Literature Cited

Collins, Suzanne. 2008. *The Hunger Games.* New York, NY: Scholastic.

Costello, E. 2008. "Safe Haven." *Science World* 64 (11): 8.

Creech, Sharon. 2001. *Love that Dog.* New York, NY: HarperCollins.

Curlee, Lynn. 2007. *Skyscraper.* New York: Atheneum Books for Young Readers.

Daerr, Elizabeth G. 2008. "A Howling Success." *Scholastic News* 70 (20): 2.

Davies, Nicola. 2012. *Outside Your Window: A First Book of Nature.* Somerville, MA: Candlewick Press.

Drummond, Allan. 2011. *Energy Island: How One Community Harnessed the Wind and Changed Their World.* New York, NY: Farrar, Straus, Giroux.

Elliot, David. 2010. *In the Wild.* Somerville, MA: Candlewick Press.

Farmer, Nancy. 2002. *The House of the Scorpion.* New York, NY: Simon & Shuster.

Florian, Douglas. 2010. *Poetrees.* New York, NY: Beach Lane Books.

Franco, Betsy. 2011. *A Dazzling Display of Dogs: Concrete Poems by Betsy Franco.* New York, NY: Tricycle Press.

Freedman, Russell. 2012. *Abraham Lincoln and Frederick Douglass: The Story Behind an American Friendship.* Boston, MA: Clarion Books.

Freedman, Russell. 2000. *Give Me Liberty! The Story of the Declaration of Independence.* New York, NY: Holiday House.

French, Vivian. 2009. *Yucky Worms.* Somerville, MA: Candlewick Press.

Frost, Helen. 2008. *Monarch and Milkweed.* New York, NY: Atheneum Books for Young Readers.

George, Jean Craighead. 2008. *The Wolves Are Back.* New York, NY: Dutton.

George, Jean Craighead. 2013. *The Eagles Are Back.* New York, NY: Dial.

Gibbons, Gail. 2012. *Ladybugs.* New York, NY: Holiday House.

Goodman, Joan Elizabeth. 1998. *Hope's Crossing.* Boston, MA: Houghton Mifflin.

Goodstein, Carol. 1997. "Where Have All the Pollinators Gone?" *Science World* 53 (12): 12.

Gourley, Robin. 2011. *First Garden: The White House Garden and How It Grew.* Boston, MA: Clarion Books.

Graber, C. 2008. "The Case of the Disappearing Bees." *Ask* 7 (7): 14.

Grimes, Nikki. 2013. *Words with Wings.* Honesdale, PA: Wordsong.

Harley, Avis. 2008. *The Monarch's Progress: Poems with Wings.* Honesdale, PA: Wordsong.

Hesse, Karen. 1997. *A Time of Angels.* New York, NY: Disney-Hyperion.

Hinds, Gareth. 2007. *Beowulf.* Cambridge, MA: Candlewick Press.

Hodge, Deborah. 2011. *Watch Me Grow! A Down-To-Earth Look at Growing Food in the City.* Toronto, CN: Kids Can Press.

Hopkins, Lee Bennett. 2012. *Nasty bugs.* New York, NY: Dial.

Hopkinson, Deborah. 2006. *Sky Boys: How They Built the Empire State Building.* New York, NY: Schwartz and Wade Books.

———. 2012. *A Boy Called Dickens.* New York, NY: Schwartz and Wade Books.

———. 2013. *The Great Trouble: A Mystery of London, the Blue Death, and a Boy Called Eel.* New York, NY: Schwartz and Wade Books.

Horvath, Polly. 2012. *Mr. and Mrs. Bunny—Detectives Extraordinaire.* New York, NY: Schwartz and Wade.

Janeczko, Paul. 2001. *A Poke in the I: A Collection of Concrete Poems.* Somerville, MA: Candlewick Press.

Jenkins, Steve. 2012. *The Beetle Book.* Boston, MA: Houghton Mifflin Books for Children.

Jurmain, Suzanne Trip. 2011. *The Worst of Friends: Thomas Jefferson, John Adams, and the True Story of an American Feud.* New York, NY: Dutton.

Kamkwamba, William, and Bryan Mealer. 2012. *The Boy Who Harnessed the Wind: Creating Currents of Electricity and Hope.* New York, NY: Dial Books for Young Readers.

Kerley, Barbara. 2001. *The Dinosaurs of Waterhouse Hawkins.* New York, NY: Scholastic.

———. 2008. *What To Do About Alice?* New York, NY: Scholastic.

———. 2012. *Those Rebels, John and Tom.* New York, NY: Scholastic.

———. 2014. *A Home for Mr. Emerson*. New York, NY: Scholastic.

Lawler, Laurie. 2013. *Rachel Carson and Her Book That Changed the World*. New York, NY: Holiday House.

Lowry, Lois. 1994. *The Giver*. New York: Houghton Mifflin.

———. 2011. *Like the Willow Tree*. New York, NY: Scholastic.

Markle, Sandra. 2011. *The Case of the Vanishing Golden Frogs: A Scientific Mystery*. Minneapolis, MN: Millbrook Press.

Markle, S. 2013. *The Case of the Vanishing Honeybee: A Scientific Mystery*. Minneapolis, MN: Millbrook Press.

McCormack, F. 2005. "Bye, Bye, Butterfly?" *Scholastic News* 67 (19): 6.

McCullough, David. 2001. *John Adams*. New York, NY: Simon and Schuster.

Milne, A.A. 1928. *The House at Pooh Corner*. New York, NY: Dutton Children's Books.

Murphy, Jim. 2003. *An American Plague: The True and Terrifying Story of the Yellow Fever Epidemic of 1793*. New York, NY: Clarion Books.

Nargi, Lela. 2011. *The Honeybee Man*. New York, NY: Schwartz and Wade.

Nelson, Marilyn. *Fortune's Bones: The Manumission Requiem*. Honesdale, PA: Front Street Press, 2004.

Newman, Leslea. 2012. *October Mourning: A Song for Matthew Shepard*. Somerville, MA: Candlewick Press.

Roth, Susan L., and Cindy Trumbore. 2013. *Parrots Over Puerto Rico*. New York, NY: Lee and Low Books.

Rotner, Shelley, and Anne Woodhull. 2010. *The Buzz on Bees: Why Are They Disappearing?* New York, NY: Holiday House.

Rowling, J.K. 1998. *Harry Potter and the Sorcerer's Stone*. New York, NY: Scholastic.

Royston, Angela. 2008. *Global Warming*. Chicago, IL: Heinemann.

Schanzer, Rosalyn. 2007. *George vs. George: The American Revolution as Seen from Both Sides*. Washington, DC: National Geographic Children's Books.

Sidman, Joyce. 2010. *Ubiquitous: Celebrating Nature's Survivors*. Boston, MA: Houghton Mifflin Books for Children.

Sidman, Joyce. 2006. *Meow Ruff, A Story in Concrete Poetry*. Boston, MA: Houghton Mifflin Books for Children.

Simon, Seymour. 2010. *Global Warming*. New York, NY: Harper Collins.

Siy, Alexandra. 2011. *Bug Shots: The Good, the Bad, and the Bugly*. New York, NY: Holiday House.

Smith, N. 2010. "Bees Feel the Sting." *Scholastic News* 72 (22): 4.

Stewart, Melissa. 2014. *A Place for Butterflies*. Atlanta, GA: Peachtree Publishers.

Stone, Tanya Lee. 2009. *Almost Astronauts: 13 Women Who Dared to Dream*. Somerville, MA: Candlewick Press.

Sweet, Melissa. 2011. *Balloons Over Broadway: The True Story of the Puppeteer of Macy's Parade*. Boston, MA: Houghton Mifflin Books for Children.

Turner, Pamela S. 2013. *The Dolphins of Shark Bay*. Boston, MA: Houghton Mifflin Books for Children.

Voake, Steve. 2010. *Insect Detective*. Somerville, MA: Candlewick Press.

Woodson, Jaqueline. 2004. *Behind You*. New York, NY: Puffin.

———. 2012. *Each Kindness*. New York, NY: Nancy Paulsen Books.

Yezierski, Thomas F. 2011. *Meadowlands: A Wetlands Survival Story*. New York, NY: Farrar, Straus Giroux.

Yolen, Jane, and Andrew Fusek Peters. 2007. *Here's a Little Poem: A Very First Book of Poetry*. Somerville, MA: Candlewick Press.

Resources for Locating Children's Literature

Online Book Reviews

The Horn Book Magazine
http://www.hbook.com/

School Library Journal
http://www.slj.com

Follett Titlewave
http://www.titlewave.com

Children's and Young Adult Book Awards

The Boston Globe-Horn Book Awards (picture book, fiction/poetry, nonfiction)
http://www.hbook.com/boston-globe-horn-book-awards/

Caldecott Medal (ALA)
http://www.ala.org/alsc/awardsgrants/bookmedia/caldecottmedal/caldecottmedal

Coretta Scott King Book Awards (ALA)
http://www.ala.org/emiert/cskbookawards

Newbery Medal (ALA)
http://www.ala.org/alsc/awardsgrants/bookmedia/newberymedal/newberymedal

Notable Books for a Global Society (IRA)
http://clrsig.org/nbgs.php

Notable Social Studies Trade Books for Young People (NCSS-CBC)
http://www.socialstudies.org/notable

Orbis Pictus Award for Outstanding Nonfiction for Children (NCTE)
http://www.ncte.org/awards/orbispictus

Outstanding Science Trade Books for Students K-12 (NCTE-CBC)
http://www.nsta.org/publications/ostb/

Michael L. Printz Award (ALA)
http://www.ala.org/yalsa/printz-award

Robert F. Sibert Informational Book Medal (ALA)
http://www.ala.org/alsc/awardsgrants/bookmedia/sibertmedal

YALSA Award for Excellence in Nonfiction for Young Adults (ALA)
http://www.ala.org/yalsa/nonfiction

Schneider Family Book Award (ALA)
http://www.ala.org/awardsgrants/schneider-family-book-award

NCTE Award for Excellence in Poetry for Children
http://www.ncte.org/awards/poetry

Theodore S. Geisel Award
http://www.ala.org/alsc/awardsgrants/bookmedia/geiselaward

Blogs and Websites

The Classroom Bookshelf
http://www.classroombookshelf.blogspot.com

Cooperative Children's Book Center (CCBC)
http://ccbc.education.wisc.edu/

Cooperative Children's Book Center (Bibliographies and Booklists)
http://ccbc.education.wisc.edu/books/bibBio.asp

I.N.K. Interesting Nonfiction for Kids Blog
http://inkrethink.blogspot.com/

I.N.K. Think Tank
http://www.inkthinktank.com

International Children's Digital Library
http://en.childrenslibrary.org/

School Library Journal Blogs
http://www.slj.com/slj-blog-network/

Genre-Specific Evaluation Resources

NCTE: Anti-Censorship Center
http://www.ncte.org/action/anti-censorship

Cooperative Children's Book Center: Multicultural Literature
http://ccbc.education.wisc.edu/books/multicultural.asp

Cynthia Leitich Smith: Children's and YA Fantasy Novels
http://www.cynthialeitichsmith.com/lit_resources/favorites/by_genre/fantasy.html

Mythopoeic Society
http://www.mythsoc.org

National Public Radio: Children's Fantasy Lit in the Modern World
http://www.npr.org/templates/story/story.php?storyId=5039319

The Poetry Foundation
http://www.poetryfoundation.org

Favorite Poem Project
http://www.favoritepoem.org

Library of Congress: Poetry 180: A Poem a Day for American High Schools
http://www.loc.gov/poetry/180/

"Purposeful Poetry" by Susan Dove Lemke
http://archive.hbook.com/magazine/articles/2005/may05_lempke.asp

The Uncommon Corps
http://www.nonfictionandthecommoncore.blogspot.com

ATOS by Renaissance Learning
http://www.renlearn.com/atos/

Degrees of Reading Power (DRP) by Questar Assessment, Inc.
http://drp.questarai.com/home/

The Lexile® Framework for Reading by MetaMetrics
http://www.Lexile.com/

Reading Maturity Metric by Pearson Education
http://www.readingmaturity.com/rmm-web/#/

TextEvaluator by Educational Testing Service
https://texteval-pilot.ets.org/TextEvaluator/

Appendix D ■ Resources for Locating Children's Literature

Easability Indicator by Coh-Metrix
http://141.225.42.101/cohmetrixgates/Home.aspx?Login=1

Council of Chief State School Officers: "Navigating Text Complexity"
http://www.ccsso.org/Navigating_Text_Complexity.html

Teaching Channel: "Simplifying Text Complexity"
https://www.teachingchannel.org/videos/simplifying-text-complexity

The Text Project: The Text Complexity Multi-Index
http://www.textproject.org/professional-development/text-matters/the-text-complexity-multi-index/

Common Core State Standards Initiative: Other Resources
http://www.corestandards.org/resources

Student Achievement Partners: Text Complexity Collection
http://www.achievethecore.org/dashboard/300/search/1/1/0/1/2/3/4/5/6/7/8/9/10/11/12/page/642/text-complexity-collection

Sample *Quality, Utility, and Complexity Charts*

Title: *Those Rebels, John and Tom*

Author: Barbara Kerley

Year of Publication: 2012

Notes from the Book Reviews
Booklist calls it a "double portrait," (2011) which is a good name to use in teaching with the book. Booklist also gave it a starred review and said, it "… is a terrific book to lead the charge in learning about the Revolution, as well as a lesson in how dedicated cooperation can achieve great ends. An obvious choice to pair with *Worst of Friends*." (*Booklist* 2011).
All reviews focus on how the book addresses the issue of class differences between them and the issue of slavery, since Jefferson was a slave owner.
All reviews address the focus on the two men and the story of the writing of the Declaration of Independence.
The *School Library Journal* review talks about the content of the author's note and their presidential years and changing relationship and an "authoritative" but "child-friendly" approach to history (Whitehurst 2012).

Appendix E ▪ Resources for Evaluating Texts

Genre Characteristics: Literary and Artistic Value	Genre Characteristics: Complexity and Accessibility
How does it meet established criteria? As a "double portrait" it is a biography of two people, but a partial biography of each. As a double biography it shows parallel events in each of their lives chronologically, as one would expect. There is no invented dialogue (which would be problematic), but Kerley does use direct quotes from each man's writings to create a sense of immediacy with the reader. We get to hear each of them through her selective quotes. Research is well documented in the back matter, with citations for different source material and an author's note that explains the origins of the book and the relationship between the two after the Declaration of Independence was written.	*How does the book meet and/or differ from genre characteristics? How does this impact accessibility?* Most students are used to reading a single biography or a collected biography of a lot of people. As a "double portrait" of two historical figures this might be a new concept for most readers. But the comparison and contrast supports the reader in understanding the two men simultaneously and their common goal. If it were not as well written, it would become a challenge. But the format makes this deviation from a typical single biography easier to access. The information provided in the author's note helps to put the narrative text in context for the reader. For some readers, it might be too much information, but reading the author's note is not central to understanding the narrative; it simply enhances the narrative.

Content: Literary and Artistic Value	Content: Complexity and Accessibility
What is the book about? It is a partial picture book biography about Thomas Jefferson and John Adams. It covers their childhood and early years, leading up to the writing and signing of the Declaration of Independence. The book focuses on how different they were and how they worked together as a team to get the Declaration both written and then approved by the Continental Congress.	*How complex is the content for the intended audience? How does this impact accessibility?* For much of the book, contrasts are drawn between John Adams and Thomas Jefferson. In this case, what makes the book complex is also what makes it accessible and therefore less complex. The comparison and contrast between the two allows the reader to understand how important it was that they shared so many of the same values despite their differences in upbringing, life experiences, and interests.

Text Structure: Literary and Artistic Value	Text Structure: Complexity and Accessibility
How is the book organized? What is the overall text structure? It is a chronological narrative. At the start, there is a page about John, then a page about Tom, and then a page about the two together. Sometimes the book talks about each separately on different sides of the two-page spread; when talking about events they were both involved in, it talks about them together.	*Is the text structure simple or more complex? How does this impact accessibility?* The text structure is what makes this book accessible to readers. Comparison and contrast is used within the paragraphs about each man. Each is written about in contrast to the other or an event that is unfolding. The narrative itself is straightforward because it follows chronological order moving from childhood to adulthood. However, it goes through their childhood fairly quickly and spends most of the narrative on the writing of the Declaration of Independence, which takes place over a short period of time. But this is clear, and should not confuse students, particularly if they are studying this for the purpose of understanding content about the American Revolution.

Language: Literary and Artistic Value	Language: Complexity and Accessibility
How is the language rich and interesting? What kind of sentence variation occurs? It starts off with a great hook that frames the whole narrative ("formed a surprising alliance, committed treason, and helped launch a new nation"). The book is filled with rich adjectives and parallel structure within paragraphs and pages. Direct quotes from each, taken from primary source materials, are included in quotation marks throughout. There is a jovial mood to the text in general.	*How challenging is the language? How does this impact accessibility?* The direct quotes are not difficult to read and understand because they are written into sentences as phrases, so the context supports the reader in understanding the point of view in the direct quote. It creates a sense of immediacy with Jefferson and Adams without slowing anything down or making the book more difficult. Adjectives and overall mood of the language make it more fun to read and slightly silly, which builds motivation in student readers.

Visuals: Literary and Artistic Value	Visuals: Complexity and Accessibility
How do the visuals engage the reader? How do they enhance the content? *How does the book design reinforce the content?* The book is illustrated with a palette of red, white, and blue, which reinforces the identity of the United States of America. The cover illustration and the final illustration are both allusions to famous images associated with the American Revolution. The cartoon drawings of Adams and Jefferson reinforce the comparisons and contrasts within the text. Background colors of white and navy also set up contrasts just as the book contrasts the two men. John and Tom are always mentioned in capital letters. Some sentences are in a larger bold font to emphasize their importance.	*How do the visuals and design impact accessibility?* The visuals make the book more accessible by illustrating with concrete images the differences between the two men. These illustrations can move readers from the concrete to the abstract in their thinking about the two men. The visuals also extend historical information to support students who might not have prior knowledge, making the book more accessible. For example, when discussing the occupation of Boston and the British navy patrol of the Atlantic seaboard, the book's illustrations bring to life the author's reference to "racket" in Boston (loud, occupied city controlled by the British army) and the "racket" in Virginia (the British navy's occupation of the Atlantic coast so that no ships could purchase colonial goods). By using a homonym (racket) the author compares and contrasts a very specific topic. But it is the illustrations that make the different meanings of that homonym clear to the reader who does not know the word, and demonstrates very clearly some of the activities of the British navy of which most students probably do not have prior knowledge.

Resources for Evaluating Texts • Appendix E

Readers
Overall, in what ways does this book feel appropriate for some or all of the readers in your class?
Fifth graders will find the personal approach to history interesting. The use of humor in the text and the illustrations, and the humorous subtext and mood despite the serious topic, will engage students and make them want to keep reading. The more students view the illustrations, the more connections they will find between text and illustration, again, making the facts and concepts in the book more accessible and meaningful. The tightly written structure and book format will also help students navigate the text successfully. The personalities of Adams and Jefferson also make the book engaging to students, and therefore, more invested in reading for meaning and understanding.

Utility as a Teaching Tool: Instructional Possibilities (Purpose/Practice)

Instructional Purposes

Understanding Content

The book could be used to explore political relationships in general, and as a lens for looking at how Congress functions today in social studies.

This book would also be useful as part of a text set of biographies of historical figures from the American Revolution, to better understand the time period.

Developing Disciplinary Literacies

This book could be read in the context of exploring the Declaration of Independence as a document, helping to scaffold student understanding of how the document was written. The document was created as a result of a process that involved more than one person. Who were those people? How did they work together? How is the Declaration of Independence an end product of their collaboration, not simply something set in stone from the very beginning?

Using Mentor Text for Student Writing

As a "double portrait" mentor text in social studies, students can learn about how to write about two figures from any time period, for students to see figures as interconnected. Students could also read *George vs. George* by Rosalyn Schanzer, about George Washington and King George of England, as another mentor text. As part of a composition study of parallel structure in writing comparisons and contrasts in English Language Arts.

Appendix E ▪ Resources for Evaluating Texts

Utility as a Teaching Tool: Instructional Possibilities (Purpose/Practice) *(cont.)*

Teaching Literary Analysis and Genre Study

As part of a biography genre study in English Language Arts, students can examine the author's craft while reading this and *Worst of Friends*, another narrative book about the friendship between Thomas Jefferson and John Adams.

Developing Reading Skills

Reading this book allows students to hear some of the transitional phrases used to compare and contrast the two men, showing students how identifying the text structure supports their understanding of a nonfiction text.

Instructional Practices

It works well as a read aloud for reading for understanding content, developing disciplinary literacy, analyzing mentor texts, and developing reading skills.

As a literature circle book, it could be used as one group's exploration of founding fathers, while other groups read other perspectives.

For a biography genre study, it would be ideal for a whole class read as a mentor text.

Quantitative Evaluation of Text Complexity

Include one or two quantitative measurements of complexity to compare and contrast with your evaluation of the text.

Lexile® Range = 960L (upper parts of the 4–5 grade band)

ATOS/Accelerated Reader Bookfinder = 6.3 (middle of the 4th–5th band)

Sample *Quality, Utility, and Complexity Charts* (cont.)

Title: *It's Our Garden: From Seeds to Harvest in a School Garden*

Author: George Ancona

Year of Publication: 2013

Notes from the Book Reviews
"clearly written text works seamlessly with the two kinds of color illustrations" (Booklist 2013)
"Ancona's no nonsense style is perfectly suited for newly independent readers" (Horn Book 2013)
School Library Journal (2012) review emphasizes the sensory experiences highlighted by the author.
Several reviewers note that teachers and students will be inspired to create their own school gardens after reading the book.

Genre Characteristics: Literary and Artistic Quality	Genre Characteristics: Complexity and Accessibility
How does it meet established criteria? Book is a photo essay (documentary style): Photos play a strong role in conveying the content. Specialized Nonfiction: specifically tracks a year in this particular elementary school garden. As a documentary, the accuracy of the content is based on firsthand experience, documentation through photographs, observation, and interview. Includes recommended books and websites.	*How does the book meet and/or differ from genre characteristics? How does this impact accessibility?* Text and photos play an equal role in conveying the activities in this garden over the course of a year. The inclusion of the photos makes the text more accessible by providing visual supports.

Appendix E ▪ Resources for Evaluating Texts

Content: Literary and Artistic Quality	Content: Complexity and Accessibility
What is the book about? The book introduces the school garden at Acequia Madre elementary school—first by describing the planning and construction of the garden. The author spent a year documenting the activities in the school garden and a sequential recounting of the activities is the main focus of the text. Additionally, gardening concepts and scientific processes such as pollination, composting, plant life cycles, and animals and insect garden creatures are described. Different kinds of plants are named and illustrated with photographs. The author also makes note of the curriculum connections that teachers make with the garden—students read, write, paint, calculate and document their observations.	*How complex is the content for the intended audience? How does this impact accessibility?* Students' levels of experiences with gardening will vary. The author provides concise explanations of gardening processes. For example, the description of pollination reads: Flowers produce a sweet liquid called nectar. *"When a bird, a bee, or a butterfly goes into a flower to drink the nectar, a powder called pollen sticks to them..."* These processes are also depicted with photographs. There is a clear match between the text and photo illustrations so that less familiar content is well supported visually.

Text Structure: Literary and Artistic Quality	Text Structure: Complexity and Accessibility
How is the book organized? What is the overall text structure? Following a brief introduction that describes the beginnings of the garden and people who played key roles in its design, the text chronologically tracks the activities in the gardening, progressing from spring through the following winter, describing the necessary tasks associated with each season.	*Is the text structure simple or more complex? How does this impact accessibility?* The narrative chronological structure is a familiar structure for students. This makes the text easier to follow.

Language: Literary and Artistic Quality	Language: Complexity and Accessibility
How is the language rich and interesting? What kind of sentence variation occurs? The language used evokes sensory experiences. For example, the opening sentence: "The school bell sounds… and the classrooms explode with the noise of books closing, chairs sliding on the floor, and kids chattering."	*How challenging is the language? How does this impact accessibility?* Language is straightforward. When garden-specific vocabulary is introduced, words are defined/contextualized within the text. Sensory descriptions are reinforced by the photographs—when the text describes the process of using adobe to make a bread oven, a young girl is depicted with mud-coated hands outstretched.

Visuals: Literary and Artistic Quality	Visuals: Complexity and Accessibility
How do the visuals engage the reader? How do they enhance the content? *How does the book design reinforce the content?* Visuals play a strong role in conveying and reinforcing the content. Children's art is included—this increases child appeal, and demonstrates children's involvement in and learning from the gardening processes. Layout is exceptional—careful placement of the images enhance the pacing of the content while working to reinforce the information conveyed in the text. Variation in placements provides visual interest—holds the attention of the young reader. Close-ups, cameos, and panorama views are included. Vivid green endpapers feature children's art. The photo collage on the cover balances close-up and portrait images.	*How do the visuals and design impact accessibility?* Throughout the book the close alignment between the text content and the photos chosen by the author support comprehension. Sequences of photos are used to depict processes, such as pizza making, that occur in the garden.

Appendix E ▪ Resources for Evaluating Texts

Utility as a Teaching Tool: Instructional Possibilities (Purpose/Practice)

Instructional Purposes

<u>Understanding Content</u>

Appropriate in the context of these areas of study:

- community
- gardening
- life cycles
- animal/plant relationships
- seasonal changes

<u>Analyzing Writing as a Mentor Text</u>

Mentor text for the genre of a photo essay. Students will be inspired to document and write about an aspect of their school or community life.

Instructional Practices

Appropriate across a range of grade levels. Engaging *read-aloud* for the primary and intermediate grades. It is a longer text, but could be read across multiple sittings.

Excellent potential as a *guided reading* text in the intermediate grades and for more capable readers in first and second grade.

Readers

Overall, in what ways does this book feel appropriate for some or all of the readers in your class?

Due to its engaging visuals, this text has broad appeal. The clear concise text, with embedded definitions and explanations, combined with the close alignment between the text and photos on each page make the book highly accessible.

The focus on the students as gardeners portrays children as active, capable persons—students will identify with these children.

Multicultural families are depicted and there is an emphasis on the garden as a gathering place for community members.

Quantitative Evaluation of Text Complexity
Include one or two quantitative measurements of complexity to compare and contrast with your evaluation of the text.   Lexile® Range = AD910L   ATOS (Accelerated Reader website) = 5.1   Grade Level Band 4–5

Appendix E ■ Resources for Evaluating Texts

Sample *Quality, Utility, and Complexity Charts* (cont.)

Title: *Dreaming Up: A Celebration of Building* (poetry)

Author: Christy Hale

Year of Publication: 2012

Notes from the Book Reviews

"Hale turns her educated eye to modern and contemporary architecture and produces a book that is at once groundbreaking, child-friendly and marvelously inclusive." Starred review (*Kirkus* 2012).

"Back matter includes brief paragraphs about each building and mini portraits and paragraphs about the architects, who come from a variety of countries; most are men." *School Library Journal* review (Cardon 2012).

"This is a unique picture book that will attract all ages on several different levels." Highly recommended in *Library Media Connection* (Woodward 2013).

Genre Characteristics: Literary and Artistic Quality	Genre Characteristics: Complexity and Accessibility
How does it meet established criteria? This is a collection of concrete poems in picture book format. The book is truly a picture book in that the illustrations (which include mixed media and photographs) play an equal part in conveying the meaning of the text. Back matter is included to expand upon the content.	*How does the book meet and/or differ from genre characteristics? How does this impact accessibility?* This collection of concrete poetry has a clear and consistent format. This format makes the text more accessible to readers as they know what to expect from each double page spread.

Content: Literary and Artistic Quality	Content: Complexity and Accessibility
What is the book about? The poems and illustrations in the book compare children's constructions from various materials to well known buildings around the globe. Short and highly visual concrete poems describe the children's constructions. Within the main body of the book, the featured "real" building is simply depicted by a photograph. More information about the buildings and the architects who designed the buildings is included in the back matter.	*How complex is the content for the intended audience? How does this impact accessibility?* It is likely that many children have experimented with building constructions of their own using the same materials that the children depicted in this book are using. This "hands-on" familiarity with the building process and materials makes the text of the concrete poems more accessible/less complex.

Text Structure: Literary and Artistic Quality	Text Structure: Complexity and Accessibility
How is the book organized? What is the overall text structure? The text is formatted in double page spreads that feature on one side: an illustration of children building a structure using varied materials and a concrete poem describing the structure. The other side of the spread is a full page photograph of a building that is similar in some way to the structure being constructed by the children in the illustration on the opposing page. Back matter is included, providing additional information about the buildings depicted in the photographs and the architects who designed them. A listing of the author's sources is also included.	*Is the text structure simple or more complex? How does this impact accessibility?* The structure of the book is consistent throughout. Once students understand the pattern / concept of comparison, they know what to expect on subsequent double page spreads. This makes the text more accessible. The back matter is more complex for preschool and primary grade readers. These students would need additional teacher support to access and understand this information.

Appendix E ▪ Resources for Evaluating Texts

Language: Literary and Artistic Quality	Language: Complexity and Accessibility
How is the language rich and interesting? What kind of sentence variation occurs? These concrete poems vary in length and shape. The shape (line breaks and placement) is conceptually related to the mixed media illustration on the page of a child engaged with building materials. The vocabulary used in the concrete poems is not complex. In some cases the poems rhyme, in other cases they do not. The lines of the poems are not complete sentences, nor do they match the grammatical patterns of "talking." The back matter includes expository text that describes the featured buildings and architects in short paragraphs.	*How challenging is the language? How does this impact accessibility?* The simple and familiar vocabulary of poems make them less complex for primary grade readers. The less familiar grammatical patterns of poetry makes the text more complex for young readers. The expository text of the back matter is more complex because it includes more sophisticated vocabulary. Primary grade students would need support to access this text.

Visuals: Literary and Artistic Quality	Visuals: Complexity and Accessibility
How do the visuals engage the reader? How do they enhance the content? *How does the book design reinforce the content?* Clear mixed media illustrations depict the children engaged in the activity described in each poem. A full-page photograph on the facing page depicts a 'real world' building that employs similar construction. The back matter repeats in small scale the photographic images of the "real world" building and adds a mixed media illustration of the building's architect. A composite image on the cover places a child builder in front of the multiple "real world" building images.	*How do the visuals and design impact accessibility?* The book design and illustrations enhance the accessibility of the text content by providing visual reinforcement of the described building process.

Readers

Overall, in what ways does this book feel appropriate for some or all of the readers in your class?

The book has strong child appeal because it recognizes their building interests and talents, comparing their work to those of the 'greats.' There is a diversity of ages and cultures included in the author/artist's depiction of children at work. Additionally, many children are intrigued by the visual interest of concrete poetry as a poetic form.

Utility as a Teaching Tool: Instructional Possibilities (Purposes/Practices)

Instructional Purposes

<u>Teaching Literary Analysis/Genre Study</u>

The book could be a mentor text for the form of concrete poetry. Included in a collection of texts that feature this poetic form, it can serve as a model for students' composition of concrete poetry. Other texts featuring concrete poems: *A Poke in the I* (Janeczko 2001), *Meow Ruff* (Sidman 2006) and *A Dazzling Display of Dogs* (Franco 2011).

<u>Understanding Content and Engaging in Inquiry and Research</u>

Architecture and Building: This book could serve as a launching point for student research either on the featured buildings or architects. Students could work individually or in small groups to conduct their research—they could share their findings with classmates through presentations or multigenre projects.

Instructional Practices

Reading Aloud—The book is an excellent choice for reading aloud. Large font size and clear visual images (illustrations and photographs) make it easy for a large group of students to follow along.

Guided Reading—Excerpts (double page spreads) could be used as guided reading material.

Independent Reading—The book could be offered as an independent reading choice for a child interested in concrete poetry and/or buildings and architects.

Appendix E ▪ Resources for Evaluating Texts

Quantitative Evaluation of Text Complexity

Include one or two quantitative measurements of complexity to compare and contrast with your evaluation of the text.

Titlewave Reading Level = 2.6

Guided Reading Level = 1

Sample *Quality, Utility, and Complexity Charts* (cont.)

Title: *The Great Trouble: A Mystery of London, the Blue Death, and a Boy Called Eel* (historical fiction)

Author: Deborah Hopkinson   **Year of Publication**: 2013

Notes from the Book Reviews
The book got two starred reviews, which speaks to its quality.
It's a blend of genres per Booklist "[e]qual parts medical mystery, historical novel, and survival story" (2013) and that the "book uses a fictional story to teach readers about science, medicine, and history." It also offers research opportunities, as the review states that it "offers readers a way to observe—and, hopefully, ask questions about—the scientific method" (2013).
Kirkus says that the book has a "convincingly childcentric focus" (2013).
All reviews emphasize the book as a medical mystery.
This book details the cholera outbreak of 1854 in London, which is when epidemiologist Dr. John Snow (the "father" of public health) determined that cholera was spread through water not air.
Several reviews make reference to Charles Dickens—that the book has the same kind of spirit to it that Dickens' writing (from that time) possesses.

Appendix E ▪ Resources for Evaluating Texts

Genre Characteristics: Literary and Artistic Value	Genre Characteristics: Complexity and Accessibility
How does it meet established criteria? As a historical novel, it blends fact and fiction. Eel, the main character, is invented, but Dr. John Snow, Reverend Whitehead, and other characters actually lived. A very thorough Author's Note details sources used and the research process and provides additional information about cholera.	*How does the book meet and/or differ from genre characteristics? How does this impact accessibility?* Because of the detailed Author's Note, by the end of the book it will be clear to students what was "real" and what was "invented." The descriptive writing and mystery plot help to make the story more accessible; the historical mystery dominates, and makes it easier to access perhaps than if it focused just on the cholera itself.

Content: Literary and Artistic Value	Content: Complexity and Accessibility
What is the book about? The book focuses on the cholera outbreak in London in 1854. The story starts in the neighborhood where the outbreak began; it isn't until the end of the story that the characters realize that the water pump supplying the neighborhood with water is what is spreading the disease. Much of the plot centers on how the disease is spreading; however, the other plotline is Eel's own life story, and why he is on the "run" from certain men in London. When the story begins, Eel, a self-sufficient orphan, is a "mudlark," who swims in the filthy Thames River to find things to sell in order to support his younger brother who secretly lives elsewhere.	*How complex is the content for the intended audience? How does this impact accessibility?* Because we are introduced to the characters who live in the neighborhood where the pump is before anyone gets sick, we get to know the neighborhood and care about it. Therefore, when cholera breaks out, the reader cares about finding out how the disease is spread, since the reader cares about the characters. The fact that Eel is a mudlark is also a hook that helps to bridge the historical differences between Eel's life and the lives of children in most parts of the US today. Children in the US may be surprised to learn after reading the book that access to clean water is still an ongoing issue for millions of people, and cholera remains a problem even though we know how it starts and gets spread.

Text Structure: Literary and Artistic Value	Text Structure: Complexity and Accessibility
How is the book organized? What is the overall text structure? The book follows the typical narrative arc. It is told in the first person from Eel's point of view, and while it is a straight chronological narrative, Eel writes about events that have taken place in the past which provide important clues to why he is living the life that he is living.	*Is the text structure simple or more complex? How does this impact accessibility?* Eel's voice is strong and engaging, and one that readers may identify with. His voice as narrator serves as almost "tour guide" through the past, but in an authentic way, he doesn't speak to the reader "in the future." Because he is telling the story, the flashbacks that occur are told as memories, and are therefore less confusing to the reader than if they appeared as separate chapters.

Language: Literary and Artistic Value	Language: Complexity and Accessibility
How is the language rich and interesting? What kind of sentence variation occurs? The language is made interesting because of Eel's personality; we hear about London of 1854 through his eyes. His voice is clearly that of a young adolescent.	*How challenging is the language? How does this impact accessibility?* Although there are a lot of words that are specific to the 19th century, the reader can figure them out in context. The important details, such as the historical figures like Dr. Snow, are clearly explained. The details about everyday life, class differences, etc. are "shown" rather than "told," which help the reader to absorb the details in the context of the narrative.

Visuals: Literary and Artistic Value	Visuals: Complexity and Accessibility
How do the visuals engage the reader? How do they enhance the content? *How does the book design reinforce the content?* The book does not have any illustrations, but for the cover, which evokes a collage. The cover is very blue, and cholera was referred to as "the blue death," (as the subtitle suggests), and so the cover image reinforces this connection. There is a skeleton sitting upright on the cover, clippings from a historical newspaper in the center top, and a picture of London along the Thames at the very bottom. In the middle is the silhouette of a young boy (presumably Eel). On the top right is a picture of the actual pump, which spread the disease.	*How do the visuals and design impact accessibility?* The cover image provides important clues to to the reader about the details of the story, specifically, it shows that the pump could be an important piece of the puzzle. But this requires the reader to infer such a detail at the very beginning, or to carry the question about what makes it important enough to be a cover image as he or she reads.

Readers

Overall, in what ways does this book feel appropriate for some or all of the readers in your class?

As a mystery, this book is a hook for any reader who enjoys suspense. As historical fiction, it's a hook for those who love the genre.

As a read aloud, the book is a great introduction to the genre of historical fiction for 3rd–5th graders, because of the personal and the historical mysteries that are intertwined. Eel is very likable and his independence at age 12 will be fascinating for those students.

For 5th–8th graders, the fact that Eel is approximately their age will be of interest. They will be able to identify with his friendships and aspire towards aspects of his self-sufficiency.

The quick pacing of the chapters cultivates a sense of anticipation and mystery that propels readers forward in the plot.

Utility as a Teaching Tool: Instructional Possibilities (Purposes/Practices)

Instructional Purposes

Understanding Content

This book could used in social studies class at the middle level to explore urbanization and industrialization in the 19th century, along with primary source information from the time available online.

Understanding Disciplinary Literacy

This book models the scientific process as Dr. Snow attempts to figure out the cause of cholera. In his work mapping the outbreak and centering on the Broad Street Pump demonstrate public health in action, the kinds of questions posed and methods used.

This book could be read in conjunction with other historical novels and nonfiction works about disease, in which students in literature circles could explore different diseases: *An American Plague* (Murphy 2003), *A Time of Angels* (Hesse 1997), and *Like the Willow* (Lowry 2011).

Teaching Genre and Literary Elements

This is a great book to unpack the elements of historical fiction as a genre. Using the generous Author's Note as a resource, students can explore the resources that Hopkinson used to research and write the book and examine more closely what was invented and what was factual within the book. This book is also great if you are studying the motifs of the 19th century novel. Students can read the book and compare and contrast it with excerpts from Dickens's novels from that era and other novels written for children during that time period. How does this book "sound" like one of the books from the actual time period? Students could compare and contrast the Victorian London of The Great Trouble with the picture book biography Hopkinson wrote, *A Boy Called Dickens*.

Developing Reading Skills

Layered with several ongoing mysteries, this book is great for focusing students on the ways in which they predict and infer while reading. The layers of historic and scientific content add a more sophisticated "heft" to the process of making those predictions and inferences.

(For more teaching ideas, see The Classroom Bookshelf entry for *The Great Trouble* at: http://classroombookshelf.blogspot.com)

Appendix E ▪ Resources for Evaluating Texts

Utility as a Teaching Tool: Instructional Possibilities (Purposes/Practices) *(cont.)*

Instructional Practices

Eel's first person narration is very engaging, so for 4th–5th graders (maybe 3rd) with little to no prior knowledge of 19th century Victorian England, this book is powerful as a read aloud. The intertwined personal and medical mysteries create a sense of suspense as part of the read aloud, which further prompts engagement.

For 5th–8th graders, this book would be ideal in literature circles or a whole class read. The first person narration is straightforward, and middle grade readers are then better able to access and focus on the more sophisticated historical and scientific content.

Quantitative Evaluation of Text Complexity

Include one or two quantitative measurements of complexity to compare and contrast with your evaluation of the text.

Lexile® Range = 660L (which puts it in the 2nd–3rd grade band)

ATOS/Accelerated Reader Bookfinder (Renaissance Learning) = 4.6 (middle of the 2nd–3rd grade band)

Despite the quantitative assessments placing this book in grades 2–3, this is not appropriate for guided reading groups, literature circles, or independent reading in these grades (but for exceptionally advanced readers and history buffs). Most 2nd and 3rd graders do not have the reading stamina to get through a book with this much depth and vocabulary. The historical and scientific content would be particularly challenging for these students.

Resources for Evaluating Texts ▪ Appendix E

Sample *Quality, Utility, and Complexity Charts* (cont.)

Title: *Interrupting Chicken* (picture book, fiction)

Author: David Ezra Stein

Year of Publication: 2010

Notes from the Book Reviews
Each of the reviews focuses on the ways in which the book contains elements from traditional stories (Hansel and Gretel, Chicken Little, and Little Red Riding Hood)
Each review focuses on the father-daughter relationship and the going-to-bed ritual of reading aloud.
The difference between the illustrations that tell the story versus the illustrations within the stories being read aloud within the story are noted as a strength of the book.

Genre Characteristics: Literary and Artistic Value	Genre Characteristics: Complexity and Accessibility
How does it meet established criteria? This book is a fictional picture book that is both animal fantasy (chickens as stand-ins for people) and yet it is also a retelling of traditional stories in that it has the content from fairy tales. The narrative follows a chronological narrative arc that most fictional stories follow. But there are four other narratives within the story.	*How does the book meet and/or differ from genre characteristics? How does this impact accessibility?* The narrative follows a chronological narrative arc that most fictional stories follow. The other narratives within the story make it more difficult for students to access.

Appendix E ▪ Resources for Evaluating Texts

Content: Literary and Artistic Value	Content: Complexity and Accessibility
What is the book about? In a nutshell, the story is about a tired dad trying to put his daughter to bed by reading a story. The daughter keeps interrupting the story before he can finish reading it, so he starts another. Finally, he asks his daughter to tell a story, but his snoring interrupts her story. But there is additional content, because the stories they are reading are traditional stories: "Little Red Riding Hood," "Hansel and Gretel," and "Chicken Little."	*How complex is the content for the intended audience? How does this impact accessibility?* If students are unfamiliar with the three traditional stories within this narrative, it may make it harder for them to read. Without that knowledge, they may not fully understand *why* Little Red Chicken is interrupting her father to warn the participants of those other stories.

Text Structure: Literary and Artistic Value	Text Structure: Complexity and Accessibility
How is the book organized? What is the overall text structure? Chronological narrative with conflict, rising action, and resolution but within that the beginnings of three traditional stories and one more invented story appear. Each of these four stories stopped midway through.	*Is the text structure simple or more complex? How does this impact accessibility?* Again, the disruption to the overarching narrative as well as the other narratives may be confusing for students.

Language: Literary & Artistic Value	Language: Complexity and Accessibility
How is the language rich and interesting? What kind of sentence variation occurs? The language itself is very simple. It consists almost entirely of dialogue between the father and daughter, or narrative of one of the stories being read aloud.	*How challenging is the language? How does this impact accessibility?* The language on its own would be difficult to follow but because this is a picture book the visual support of the illustrations that equally share the meaning-making support readers through the shifting speakers within the dialogue and the reading aloud of the stories within the story.

Visuals: Literary and Artistic Value	Visuals: Complexity and Accessibility
How do the visuals engage the reader? How do they enhance the content? *How does the book design reinforce the content?* The mixed media visuals are very strong. The home in which the story takes place is warm and cozy with soft lighting, establishing the context of bedtime. The illustration style changes drastically when showing the open book that the dad is reading to his daughter, to distinguish between the primary narrative and the narratives within that narrative. Little Red Chicken appears within the page of the open book her father is reading her, to show her interruption of the story he is reading aloud.	*How do the visuals and design impact accessibility?* If students were only hearing the story, it would be very difficult, if not impossible to follow the complex dialogue that takes place around the reading of stories. Stein's illustrations literally show readers that Little Red Chicken is jumping into the telling of the story to save the character from danger. Her interruptions not only interrupt her father—they interrupt the very illustrations on the page of the storybook. In this sense, there is a literal and concrete demonstration of what Little Red Chicken is trying to do, which makes it easier for students to access and understand.

Readers:

Overall, in what ways does this book feel appropriate for some or all of the readers in your class?

This book is very engaging for preschool and primary grade students who are most familiar with the bedtime routine of parent-child read aloud.

For students who can't help but verbally and even physically react to a book while it is being read, this book is a wonderful mirror!

For students in the primary and elementary grades, folktales and fairy tales are often stories they are most familiar with, and this iteration of the tales is a quick demonstration of all the ways in which these stories get told, retold, and reworked in different ways.

For students who struggle with temporal sequencing in a story, or students who do not have a foundation in the three traditional tales within this narrative, reading the book independently could be a challenge, even with the strong visual support of the illustrations.

Appendix E ▪ Resources for Evaluating Texts

Utility as a Teaching Tool: Instructional Possibilities (Purpose/Practice)

Instructional Purposes

<u>Teaching Genre and Literary Elements</u>

This book is ideal for showing students how traditional stories get changed and evolve over time. Within the context of a study of folktales and fairy tales, this book can be an example of how writers continue to draw on these stories and "use them" in different ways. It is also an opportunity to teach students the concept of "intertextuality," that stories often refer to other stories, and we miss the reference if we don't know those other stories.

<u>Developing Reading Skills</u>

This book is ideal for focusing on how we connect with our prior knowledge to understand a text while reading (prior knowledge of fairy tales and folktales). This book is also ideal for showing how we predict what will happen next (that Little Red Chicken will interrupt the reading *again*).

Instructional Practices

For kindergarten and 1st grade, this book works best as a read aloud, where students can collectively hear the story, predict when Little Red Chicken might interrupt next, and work together to understand the layers of narrative at work.

For 2nd grade and up, this book is ideal for literature circles within an exploration of folktales and fairy tales.

For the intermediate and middle grade students, reading this book aloud quickly is a way to introduce and frontload the concept of intertextuality in a way that all students should be able to access. Students could then consider intertextuality at work in other, more age-appropriate texts of longer length, where the intertextuality is more subtle. These other texts could be novelized versions of fairy tale variants or books that heavily reference other texts or text types.

Quantitative Evaluation of Text Complexity:

Include one or two quantitative measurements of complexity to compare and contrast with your evaluation of the text.

Lexile® Range = AD300L (Below 2nd grade)

ATOS/Accelerated Reader Bookfinder (Renaissance Learning) = 2.2 (Below 2nd grade)

Sample *Quality, Utility, and Complexity Charts* (cont.)

Title: *Penny and Her Marble* (beginning reader)

Author: Kevin Henkes

Year of Publication: 2013

Notes from the Book Reviews

"Told in short sentences and simple words with a natural cadence, the story lays out a moral dilemma, lets the heroine find her own solution, and concludes with a reassuringly good outcome." Starred review. (*Booklist* 2012)

"Thoughts, imaginings, and dreams appear in unboxed frames, while concrete action is shown within borders. That respect for the beginning reader's emerging skills beautifully matches Henkes's respect for Penny and this common crisis of childhood." Starred review in *The Horn Book*. (Carter 2013)

"The short sentences with plenty of repetition and superb pacing make this title perfect for beginning readers." *School Library Journal* review. (Ludke 2013)

2014 Theodor S. Geisel Award Honor Book

Genre Characteristics: Literary and Artistic Quality	Genre Characteristics: Complexity and Accessibility
How does it meet established criteria? A beginning reader book. Meets expected format. Four chapters each approximately ten pages long. This is a work of fiction. The characters are mice, but they are stand-ins for human characters; it is more like contemporary realistic fiction than it is like fantasy (despite talking mice).	*How does the book meet and/or differ from genre characteristics? How does this impact accessibility?* The book clearly meets the criteria for a beginning reader chapter book. This story of familiar childhood experiences and emotion is told in a traditional narrative format. It is likely that young children have been read (or have read themselves) similar stories. This makes the text more accessible.

Appendix E ▪ Resources for Evaluating Texts

Content: Literary and Artistic Quality	Content: Complexity and Accessibility
What is the book about? Penny finds a marble in her neighbor's yard, falls in love with it, and slips it in her pocket to bring home. She then worries overnight that she was wrong to take it. The next morning she returns it and talks with her neighbor who encourages her to keep it. This moral dilemma will likely be familiar to young readers who have 'wanted' items that do not belong to them. Penny has two parents who are attentive and concerned over her worried behavior. She also has a neighbor who understands that a child would find a bright blue marble very appealing. Penny enjoys the freedom to take a walk on her own—this appeals to the child's desire for independence. Penny also engages in imaginary play with her doll, an activity that will feel familiar to children.	*How complex is the content for the intended audience? How does this impact accessibility?* The authentic and familiar representation of child emotions and activity will make the text less complex for young readers.

Text Structure: Literary and Artistic Quality	Text Structure: Complexity and Accessibility
How is the book organized? What is the overall text structure? The book is organized by four short chapters that chronologically narrate the story of Penny finding, taking, returning, and finally, receiving the marble. The chapter breaks occur at changes in location or large jumps in time sequences.	*Is the text structure simple or more complex? How does this impact accessibility?* The narrative chronological structure is a familiar structure for students. This makes the text easier to follow. Chronological narrative is the simplest version of narrative.

Language: Literary and Artistic Quality	Language: Complexity and Accessibility
How is the language rich and interesting? What kind of sentence variation occurs? Compared to Henkes's other "mouse books" the language is considerably less varied, engaging, and interesting. However, considered within the genre of a beginning reading book, the language is more natural than other examples in the genre.	*How challenging is the language? How does this impact accessibility?* The book makes use of a controlled vocabulary—many high frequency words and sight words are used, making it simpler for students. Repetition of phrases and patterned language can be found throughout, allowing for students to make predictions as they read about what words come next. Short sentences allow for easier access to meaning-making.

Visuals: Literary and Artistic Quality	Visuals: Complexity and Accessibility
How do the visuals engage the reader? How do they enhance the content? *How does the book design reinforce the content?* Illustrations play a strong role in conveying and reinforcing the content, particularly in conveying characterization. The book is the standard trim size for a beginning chapter book.	*How do the visuals and design impact accessibility?* Throughout the book the alignment between the text content and the illustrations support comprehension. The illustrations offer further insight into the strength of Penny's emotional turmoil, giving beginner readers additional clues to the meaning of the story.

Readers:
Overall, in what ways does this book feel appropriate for some or all of the readers in your class?   The close match between text and illustration, controlled vocabulary, and universally relatable theme make the book appealing to a range of primary grade readers. With a girl protagonist and an abundance of flowers and pastel colors in the visuals, the book will have greater appeal to girls as an independent reading choice.

Appendix E ■ Resources for Evaluating Texts

Utility as a Teaching Tool: Instructional Possibilities
Instructional Purposes   Understanding Content and Developing Critical Thinking   Social Emotional Learning Ethics   The book provides wonderful material for an ethics focused discussion on whether or not Penny should have taken (and returned) the marble. The expression "finders keepers" could generalize the discussion beyond this particular book.   Developing Reading Skills and Strategies   With its controlled vocabulary, engaging plot, and images that support meaning-making, the book is an excellent site for newly independent readers to practice reading skills and strategies. Students could be "coached" to practice these skills in a guided reading session.   **Instructional Practices**   Offer as an independent reading text.   Excellent potential as a guided reading text in grades 1 and 2.   Could be used as a read aloud with the opportunity for students to reread independently after the group reading.

Quantitative Evaluation of Text Complexity:
Include one or two quantitative measurements of complexity to compare and contrast with your evaluation of the text.   Titlewave Reading Level = 1.5   Lexile® Range = 350L   Guided Reading Level = Kindergarten

Sample *Quality, Utility, and Complexity Charts* (cont.)

Title: *The Port Chicago Fifty: Disaster, Mutiny, and the Fight for Civil Rights* (nonfiction chapter book)

Author: Steve Sheinkin   **Year of Publication**: 2014

Notes from the Book Reviews
The book got several starred reviews, which speaks to its quality. All of the book reviews point to the significance of this unknown event and the Civil Rights Movement, that this event was a precursor to that movement and a catalyst for desegregating the military. "In this thoroughly researched and well-documented drama, Sheinkin lets the participants tell the story, masterfully lacing the narrative with extensive quotations drawn from oral histories, information from trial transcripts and archival photographs. The event, little known today, is brought to life and placed in historical context, with Eleanor Roosevelt, Thurgood Marshall and Jackie Robinson figuring in the story." (Kirkus 2013). This tells me that the author did a great job including quotes from the people involved throughout, and that he also wrote about this event in the context of more well-known historical figures about whom students (and myself) have more background knowledge.

Appendix E ▪ Resources for Evaluating Texts

Genre Characteristics: Literary and Artistic Value	Genre Characteristics: Complexity and Accessibility
How does it meet established criteria? As a specialized work of nonfiction book, the book focuses very specifically on one event that took place during World War II. The research is meticulously documented, and the sources used (from oral histories) are scaffolded into the text as direct quotes. The events within the book are contextualized with the larger history of World War II and the history of the Civil Rights Movement. A range of perspectives and points of view are represented throughout the book, so the reader is fully immersed in the event. The focus is on the experiences of the African-American sailors, but the context is more comprehensive.	*How does the book meet and/or differ from genre characteristics? How does this impact accessibility?* The well-documented contextualizing of this particular event with larger history (World War II, Civil Rights Movement) allows readers to draw on their prior knowledge of those events. If you don't have prior knowledge of those events, it will not impede your reading of this book, as the narrative is clearly outlined. Having that knowledge simply deepens your reading. The immediacy of the first person quotes also makes it more accessible and "immediate" to readers, as they hear the voices of the historical figures represented.

Content: Literary and Artistic Value	Content: Complexity and Accessibility
What is the book about? The book centers on the segregated military during World War II, and specifically events that unfolded at the Port Chicago naval station in California. The first group of African-Americans allowed to enlist in the U.S. Navy as something other than mess attendants (cooks/stewards) were sent to Port Chicago not to fight or sail on ships, but to load ships with dangerous explosive weapons. These men received virtually no training on how to handle explosives; an explosion took place that killed over 300 people. When a core group of fifty men refused to go back to work without receiving proper training, they were tried and convicted as mutineers. They are still considered mutineers today. Their refusal to go back to work led the way to the desegregation of the military after the conclusion of World War II.	*How complex is the content for the intended audience? How does this impact accessibility?* Few Americans know about what happened in Port Chicago during World War II or know of the "Port Chicago 50." Most middle school students have a developing understanding of the history of civil rights for African Americans in the United States; by high school, they should have a solid understanding. In either case, students can read and understand this book as a separate, and interconnected, piece of that history. You don't need the prior knowledge to understand this story, though it enriches. The conflict is clearly articulated. The complexity lies in trying to fathom the government's treatment of these men, which makes "unpacking" this book important and discussion an important component of reading it.

Resources for Evaluating Texts • Appendix E

Text Structure: Literary and Artistic Value	Text Structure: Complexity and Accessibility
How is the book organized? What is the overall text structure? The book is organized in chronological order with short chapters. As narrative nonfiction, it has a strong narrative arc that makes it read a lot like fiction.	*Is the text structure simple or more complex? How does this impact accessibility?* The short chapters and fast pacing of the book allow readers to move through the narrative with the cognitive breaks that come with chapter beginnings and endings. For students who prefer fiction to nonfiction, the fact that this reads as such as strong narrative will appeal to them.

Language: Literary and Artistic Value	Language: Complexity and Accessibility
How is the language rich and interesting? What kind of sentence variation occurs? The writing is filled with dramatic tension; Sheinkin writes his nonfiction books with a strong narrative voice. The book is filled with direct quotes from oral histories conducted with members of the Port Chicago fifty, and their voices bring the book to life as well.	*How challenging is the language? How does this impact accessibility?* Primary source quotes can sometimes be a challenge for students to read, particularly if they disrupt the narrative thread. The quotes in this case are so well blended into sentences or the narrative itself that the opposite occurs, and they make the book even more immediate and accessible.

Visuals: Literary and Artistic Value	Visuals: Complexity and Accessibility
How do the visuals engage the reader? How do they enhance the content? *How does the book design reinforce the content?* Unlike many chapter book works of nonfiction published today, this book is not highly visual. There are sporadic photographs of Port Chicago included throughout. The cover image has five African-American sailors from the chest up, portrayed with determined looks. Behind them, an explosion occurs.	*How do the visuals and design impact accessibility?* The cover provides a preview of the essential conflict of the story, but readers have to infer what that might mean before they start reading. The visual components of the book enhance the book's narrative, but they are not a narrative on their own. The pictures and visuals are not enough to create their own narrative arc from which students can make meaning. Those accustomed to such visual narratives, either in nonfiction picture books or highly illustrated photo essays like the Scientists in the Field series, may wish for more visuals. But the book is not densely-written, so they need not *rely* on visuals to understand what is happening, as other books might require.

Readers:

Overall, in what ways does this book feel appropriate for some or all of the readers in your class?

The short chapters, strong structure, and quick pacing will make this book an accessible read for those who are reluctant to tackle nonfiction or who can't sustain the reading of long chapters and chunks of information.

For most students in grades 7 and up, reading this book independently is not a problem from a content or a syntax standpoint. But how it is used in class will impact the degree to which students are invested in reading the book.

The injustices presented in this book (that continue to this day because the mutineer conviction has not been retracted by the U.S. Navy) will outrage many students and engage them in passionate debate about the government's decisions as well as the individual choices each man had to make. Young adolescents and teenagers are often interested in fairness and equity. Students will be interested in discussing the question of when it is "right" to do something that may be "wrong."

Students who are very interested in American history and/or the history of the Civil Rights Movement may find this book very engaging. Additionally, students with a strong interest in military history may be interested in this book.

For students who prefer informational text that presents facts in a highly structured exposition with short chunks of text, and/or with lots of visual supports (and color), this book may be less engaging (or at least at first).

Appendix E ■ Resources for Evaluating Texts

Utility as a Teaching Tool: Instructional Possibilities (Purpose/Practice)

Instructional Purposes

Understanding Content

This book can be an important part of an exploration of World War II on the homefront. Students can read other books that focus on the ways in which socially accepted prejudice limited roles for certain Americans during the war. The book could also be explored in the context of the African-American Civil Rights Movement of the twentieth century, as one of the catalysts for desegregation of the military and an example of non-violent protest in the face of prejudice and unsafe working conditions.

Understanding Disciplinary Literacies

Much of the first-person quotations within the book come from oral histories that a college professor conducted with surviving members of the Port Chicago fifty in the 1970s. After reading the book and seeing how oral histories shape the narrative, have students attempt to conduct their own. In a social studies class or an integrated ELA/social studies unit, you could explore the nature of oral histories and the protocols and processes involved. How are oral histories different from the traditional work of the historian? How are they "true"? How are they "not true"?

Analyzing Mentor Text

Students can analyze Sheinkin's book as they read it. How does he structure the narrative? Build suspense? Introduce and carry certain themes across the manuscript? Students can then research and write their own narratives modeled on his style. This could be combined with the oral history project listed above, as an outgrowth of it.

Engaging in Inquiry and Research

Growing out of the focus on content or disciplinary literacies, have students conduct research with primary and secondary sources to further extend their understanding of World War II, the Civil Rights Era and/or the time period or event upon which their oral histories center.

Utility as a Teaching Tool: Instructional Possibilities (Purpose/Practice) *(cont.)*

Critical Thinking

When is it right to do something wrong? Students can debate the moral questions that surface while reading this book, and after. Why wasn't there any training at Port Chicago for those handling munitions? Should the Port Chicago fifty now have their conviction overturned? What are some of the ways in which the U.S. military is still not always providing proper safety conditions to sailors?

(For more teaching ideas see The Classroom Bookshelf entry at http://classroombookshelf.blogspot.com)

Instructional Practices

For any students grades 5 and up, this book is ideal as a read aloud. The strong narrative writing, quick pacing, and the clear injustice of the situation will have students excited to share the experience of reading this book in a social context. For students in grades 5 and 6 for whom the narrative is too difficult, a read aloud will give them access to this interesting piece of history.

For students in grades 7 and up this book can work for independent reading, literature circles, or a whole class read. As a literature circle option, it is ideal for exploring the content discussed above (prejudice on the Homefront in World War II and the Civil Rights Movement). As a whole class read, it is a wonderful catalyst for exploring oral histories.

The first chapter or two could be used in a guided reading group at the middle level, as a self-contained reading packed with rich information to "unpack" and explore from a comprehension standpoint.

Quantitative Evaluation of Text Complexity:

Include one or two quantitative measurements of complexity to compare and contrast with your evaluation of the text.

Lexile Range = 950L (upper parts of the 6th–8th grade band)

ATOS/Accelerated Reader Bookfinder (Renaissance Learning) = 6.7 (middle of the 4th–5th grade band)

Appendix E ▪ Resources for Evaluating Texts

The Quality, Utility, and Complexity Chart

Title: _____

Author: _____ Year of Publication: _____

Notes from the Book Reviews

Genre Characteristics: Literary and Artistic Quality	**Genre Characteristics: Complexity and Accessibility**
How does it meet established criteria?	*How does the book meet and/or differ from genre characteristics? How does this impact accessibility?*

Resources for Evaluating Texts ▪ Appendix E

Content: Literary and Artistic Quality	Content: Complexity and Accessibility
What is the book about?	How complex is the content for the intended audience? How does this impact accessibility?

Text Structure: Literary and Artistic Quality	Text Structure: Complexity and Accessibility
How is the book organized? What is the overall text structure?	Is the text structure simple or more complex? How does this impact accessibility?

Language: Literary and Artistic Quality	Language: Complexity and Accessibility
How is the language rich and interesting? What kind of sentence variation occurs?	How challenging is the language? How does this impact accessibility?

© Shell Education   #51460—Teaching to Complexity: A Framework to Evaluate Literary and Content-Area Texts

Appendix E ▪ Resources for Evaluating Texts

Visuals: Literary and Artistic Quality

How do the visuals engage the reader? How do they enhance the content?

How does the book design reinforce the content?

Visuals: Complexity and Accessibility

How do the visuals and design impact accessibility?

Readers

Overall, in what way does this book feel appropriate for some or all of the readers in your class?

Resources for Evaluating Texts • Appendix E

Utility as a Teaching Tool: Instructional Possibilities (Purpose/Practice)

Quantitative Evaluation of Text Complexity

Include one or two quantitative measurements of complexity to compare and contrast with your evaluation of the text.

Appendix E ▪ Resources for Evaluating Texts

General Text Evaluation Considerations for Quality Guide

General Text Evaluation Considerations for Quality	Ask yourself:
Genre Characteristics	▪ How does it meet established criteria?
Content	▪ What is it about?
Text Structure	▪ How is the text organized? ▪ What is the overall text structure?
Language	▪ How is the language rich and interesting? ▪ What kind of sentence variation occurs?
Visuals: Illustration and Book Design	▪ How do the visuals engage the reader? ▪ How do they enhance the content? ▪ How does the book design reinforce the content?
Appeal	▪ How will it appeal to the particularities and preferences of the readers in one's class?

Contemporary Realistic Fiction Text Evaluation Considerations for Quality Guide

Text Evaluation Considerations for Quality	Ask Yourself...
Genre Characteristics	■ Are the events, conflict, and resolution of the book plausible, engaging and meaningful? ■ Will young readers relate to the characters of the book? Do the characters develop over the course of the story? ■ Is the setting of the story fully imagined and does it serve to enhance the characters and events? ■ Who narrates the story? Whose story is being told and how?
Content	■ Does the theme of the story prompt critical thinking/reflection on the realities of life in our world? ■ Is the content developmentally appropriate for the age of the students with whom we work? ■ Does the theme/content expand students' worldviews by offering them new perspectives on daily life? ■ Does the book include an authentic and multifaceted representation of diversity in our society?
Text Structure	■ Does the story follow a sequential narrative arc, or are shifts in time incorporated into the narrative arc? ■ Are there changes in point of view or narration that are linked with shifts in time sequence?

Appendix E ▪ Resources for Evaluating Texts

Text Evaluation Considerations for Quality	Ask Yourself…
Language	▪ Does the 'feel' of the writing, or the writing style, help to convey a sense of the plot, characters, setting, and themes of the book? ▪ Will the readers in my classroom (or a particular reader) find this writing style engaging?
Visuals: Illustration and Design	▪ How do the illustrations enhance the reader's understanding of the story that is being told?

Traditional Literature Text Evaluation Considerations for Quality Guide

Text Evaluation Considerations for Quality	Ask Yourself...
Genre Characteristics	▪ What type of traditional literature is this? Is it a myth, legend, history, folktale, fairy tale, tall tale, or fable?
Content	▪ How does this story explain a natural phenomenon, human behavior, or imagined history? ▪ How does this book fuse a particular traditional story within the context of our modern world? ▪ Does the book say when the story originated orally and/or when it was first written down?
Text Structure	▪ Does this story follow the same narrative arc as other forms of the story? If not, how does it differ? ▪ Are there other structures at work that help frame the narrative structure of the story, such as the length of a day, season, month, or year?
Language	▪ What vocabulary words represent the culture from which this story originates? ▪ How does the dialogue represent the culture from which the story originates or is set?
Visuals: Illustration and Design	▪ What media is used to illustrate this story? Is there any connection between it and the time or culture in which the story is set? ▪ How does the illustration convey the magical elements, if any, of the story?

Fantasy/Science Fiction Text Evaluation Considerations Quality Guide

Text Evaluation Considerations for Quality	Ask Yourself...
Genre Characteristics	■ What subgenre of fantasy is this? ■ Are the events, conflict, and resolution of the book plausible, engaging, and meaningful? ■ Will young readers relate to the characters of the book? Do the characters develop over the course of the story? ■ Is the setting of the story fully imagined and does it serve to enhance the characters and events? ■ Who narrates the story? Whose story is being told and how? ■ Is there consistency in the imaginary world(s) that the author has created for the reader?
Content	■ Does the theme of the story prompt critical thinking/reflection on the human experience? ■ Is the content developmentally appropriate for the age of the students with whom we work? ■ Does the content and/or theme of the story expand students' worldviews by offering them new perspectives on social and political structures?
Text Structure	■ Does the story follow a sequential narrative arc or are shifts in time incorporated into the narrative arc? ■ Are there changes in point of view or narration that are linked with shifts in time in the narrative arc?

Text Evaluation Considerations for Quality	Ask Yourself...
Language	■ How does the language of the story contribute to constructing a believable, yet fantastical, narrative? ■ Are new vocabulary terms associated with the fantasy elements in the story well-defined and contextualized for readers? Do readers encounter the terms frequently enough to internalize their meanings (to facilitate more fluent reading)? ■ Does the feel of the writing, or the writing style, help to convey a sense of the plot, characters, setting, and themes of the book? ■ Will the readers in my classroom (or a particular reader) will find this writing style engaging?
Visuals: Illustration and Design	■ How does the illustration enhance the reader's understanding of the fantastical events and/or setting of the story? ■ What role do the illustrations play in meaning-making in the book?

Historical Fiction Text Evaluation Considerations for Quality Guide

Text Evaluation Considerations for Quality	Ask Yourself…
Genre Characteristics	<ul><li>What, if any, historical figures are included in this novel? How are they important?</li><li>What events from the novel actually took place and what events are invented?</li><li>How is the protagonist's conflict mirrored by the conflicts within the plot, and vice versa?</li><li>What are the themes of the book and how do they resonate with readers today?</li></ul>
Content	<ul><li>What sources did the author use to research the book?</li><li>Has the manuscript been vetted by an authority on this time period?</li><li>What characters really existed and what characters are invented?</li><li>What parts of the plotline are invented and what parts are real?</li><li>What do I learn about everyday life during this time period? About political or social conflicts? Specific events?</li><li>What do I learn about the different perspectives of this time period?</li><li>What do I learn about gender roles in this time period?</li><li>What do I learn about social class during this time period?</li></ul>

Text Evaluation Considerations for Quality	Ask Yourself...
Text Structure	■ What relationship exists between the plot structure and actual historic events that I know of from this time period? ■ To what extent does the plot progress chronologically and to what extent does the timeline shift over the course of the narrative?
Language	■ In what ways does the language sound realistic to you? Does it sound too modern? Too stilted? ■ Does everyone speak the same way or do people of different social classes have different dialects? ■ To what extent is period-specific vocabulary described in context clues to support the reader?
Visuals: Illustration and Design	■ What, if any, match exists between the illustration style and the time period? ■ What evidence of the past is detailed in the illustrations? ■ Who is in the foreground of the illustrations? Who is in the background? Who is left out? ■ What does the illustrator reveal about his or her research process in the illustrator's note? How does that inform how you approach the book with your students?

Appendix E ▪ Resources for Evaluating Texts

Poetry Text Evaluation Considerations for Quality Guide

Text Evaluation Considerations for Quality	Ask Yourself…
Genre Characteristics	▪ How does the author use sound (rhythm, rhyme, and musical qualities) to convey meaning in the poem? ▪ How does the author create imagery and a sensory experience for the reader of the poem? ▪ Does the poem have multiple layers of meaning, prompting discussion and offering space for multiple interpretations? ▪ How does the shape/physical appearance (pacing and spacing) of the poem serve to convey, reinforce, or enhance the meaning of the poem?
Content	▪ What is the content of the book and how is the content organized? Is it a single poem or a collection of poems? If it is a collection, how do the poems in the collection relate to one another? ▪ What is the author's or authors' intent for the poem, poetry collection, or edited collection? ▪ Is the content of the poem developmentally appropriate and of interest to the reader(s) you have in mind?
Text Structure	▪ What form or forms of poetry are used in the book? ▪ Is the form of the poem well matched with the content of the poem?

Resources for Evaluating Texts • Appendix E

Text Evaluation Considerations for Quality	Ask Yourself…
Language	■ Do the words chosen by the author effectively convey the content and meaning of the poem? ■ How does the author use figurative language to convey meaning in the poem? Will children be able to relate the figurative language to their life experience, thus being able to understand multiple layers of meaning? ■ How does the rhythm and pacing of the poem create and enhance the meaning? What aural devices are used by the author? ■ If it is a rhyming poem, do the rhymes feel forced or contrived?
Visuals: Illustration and Design	■ How do the illustrations convey and enhance the content and meaning of the poems?

Nonfiction Text Evaluation Considerations for Quality Guide

Text Evaluation Considerations for Quality	Ask Yourself…
Genre Characteristics	■ What subgenre of nonfiction is this book? ■ How does the choice of subgenre influence how the content is conveyed to the reader?
Content	■ What content is conveyed in this book? ■ How do I know the author has done an appropriate level of research? What can I learn from the bibliography? Has the book been vetted by an authority on the topic? ■ What does the author's note tell me about the research process and content? ■ How does this slice of content compare to how other books on this topic convey the content? Are important details missing, or does the book cover various elements of the topic? ■ Is the subject of this book a fairly new subject for children's or young adult nonfiction? In what ways?
Text Structure	■ What is the primary text structure used by the author? ■ What are some of the other text structures used within the larger structure? ■ What text features are used to help readers access the information and how well are they matched with the text structure?

Text Evaluation Considerations for Quality	Ask Yourself...
Language	- To what extent is the author's voice included in the work? - To what extent does the language model inquiry? - How are similes and metaphors used to convey conceptual information? - How is source material brought into the language of the text?
Visuals: Illustration and Design	- What media was used to illustrate the text? Does the media feel appropriate for the subject of the book? - If I just read the illustrations, and not the text, what kind of visual narrative is constructed? - What does the illustrator have to say about his or her research process? How did the content of the book shape the creation of the illustrations? - How do the illustrations shape perspectives and point of view within the book?

Guide to Aligning an Evaluation of Quality with an Evaluation of Complexity

How Is It Good?	How Is It Complex?
Genre Characteristics - How does it meet established criteria?	**Genre Characteristics/Levels of Meaning** - How does the book meet and/or differ from genre characteristics? How does this impact accessibility?
Content - What is the book about?	**Content/Knowledge Demands** - How complex is the content for the intended audience? How does this impact accessibility?
Text Structure - How is the book organized? - What is the overall text structure?	**Text Structure** - Is the text structure simple or more complex? How does this impact accessibility?
Language - How is the language rich and interesting? What kind of sentence variation occurs?	**Language** - How challenging is the language? How does this impact accessibility?
Visuals: Illustrations and Design/Structure - How do the visuals engage the reader? How do they enhance the content? - How does the book design reinforce the content?	**Visuals: Illustrations and Design/Structure** - How do the visuals and design impact accessibility?

Evaluating Text for Instructional Purposes Guide

Instructional Purpose	Ask Yourself…
Understanding Content	▪ What is the match between my content standards and the text? ▪ What is the match between my content standards and this text in relation to other texts on the topic? ▪ Is information presented in a way that will hook my students and get them even more interested in the unit topic? ▪ Does the information in this text go beyond the standards? How will that impact how my students read it?
Developing Disciplinary Literacies	▪ Is the vocabulary used in the text authentic to the discipline, but contextually defined in a manner that makes it accessible to my students? ▪ Does the text model the inquiry and/or critical-thinking processes of the discipline either implicitly (for example in an author's note) or explicitly (through direct description in the text)?
Developing Reading Skills	▪ Does this book appeal to students? Will it be worth working on? ▪ How much background knowledge does the book require? Will students be able to comprehend as they decode? ▪ What kinds of words does it contain? What is the balance of sight words, monosyllabic, and polysyllabic words? ▪ How long are the sentences? Too long? Too short? Just right?

Appendix E ▪ Resources for Evaluating Texts

Instructional Purpose	Ask Yourself…
Teaching Literacy Analysis/Genre Study	▪ How does this book represent the genre we are studying? ▪ How does the book represent the genre on its own and how does it accomplish this understanding in the context of other books of the same genre or of different genres that focus on the same topic? ▪ What literary elements are at work in the book? Does the author do anything unique with one or two in particular that stand out as very effective examples to use in instruction? ▪ What is the match between the literary elements that are required to teach according to your school's scope and sequence or state and district standards?
Analyzing Mentor Text for Student Writing	▪ If students are reading "like a writer," what do they learn about genre through this text? ▪ How does this particular text model a particular quality of good writing, for example, varied sentence length, for targeted practice of that skill? ▪ How does this particular text model the ways in which writing can be used to communicate knowledge to the world, by informing readers or informing and persuading readers simultaneously?
Developing Critical Thinking	▪ What are the key ideas and details in this text? ▪ What perspectives and points of view are offered within this text? Which are left out? ▪ What can a student learn by reading just this text? What does the student learn by reading this text in the context of other texts within a text set?

Instructional Purpose	Ask Yourself…
Engaging in Inquiry and Research	▪ Does this text represent "the literature of inquiry"? Does it model the inquiry process, the having of questions, and the ways around stumbling blocks and dead ends? ▪ Will this text help my students persevere through their own research? ▪ Is this text going to help me model how I do research? Or is it one that I will have my students explore? Or both? ▪ How does this text compare to other texts on the topic in terms of all of the above questions?
Developing Reading Habits and Love of Reading	▪ Who is the audience for this text? ▪ What about this book reflects my students' interests, passions, worries, or senses of humor? ▪ Who in my class this year, last year, or maybe in future years, might find this of interest? ▪ If the book is going to be a challenging read, is there enough interesting content to make students to stick with it?

Appendix E ▪ Resources for Evaluating Texts

Evaluating Text for Instructional Practices Guide

Instructional Practice	Ask Yourself…
Read Aloud	▪ Is there a flow to the language that makes it enjoyable to read aloud? ▪ Will the content engage the interest of the whole class? ▪ Is there potential for the text to generate discussion? ▪ Does it contain information that is critical for your unity of study? ▪ Does the book inspire inquiry by prompting students to ask questions?
Literature Circles	▪ Will the text generate student discussion? ▪ Will students benefit from the opportunity to discuss/extend their understanding of the content with peers? ▪ Does the text provide a review of important content information or does the text provide an expansion of information that is well matched to the readers in the group?
Guided Reading	▪ Is the text at a level that students can read and comprehend with some support? ▪ Does the text offer an opportunity for strategy instruction to help students grow as readers? ▪ Does the text provide a review of content study information previously discussed in a whole-group setting, or does it provide an opportunity to expand on content information that is well matched to the readers in the group?

Instructional Practice	Ask Yourself…
Independent Reading	■ Is the text neither too hard nor too easy, offering the reader a chance to develop his or her reading abilities? ■ Does the text provide either a review of information previously learned or an expansion of content study information that is well matched to the reader's particular interests?
Whole-Class Reading	■ Is the text a good match for your instructional purpose and content learning goals? ■ Can enough of the students in the class read and interpret the content independently? ■ Will the text generate discussion among the students?

Appendix E ▪ Resources for Evaluating Texts

Considerations for Instructional Purposes and Text Complexity Guide

Instructional Purpose: Understanding Content	
When considering the text for this instructional purpose, ask yourself: What is the match between my content standards and the text? What is the match between my content standards and this text in relation to other texts on the topic? Is information presented in a way that will hook my students and get them even more interested in the unit topic? Does the information in this text go beyond the standards? How will that impact how my students read it?	**The implications for text complexity are:** It depends on the reader's content and language knowledge. The more knowledge they have, the more complex the text may be. If the content information and vocabulary is essential to the unit of study, the text may need to be less complex so that students access what they need to learn.

Instructional Purpose: Developing Disciplinary Literacies	
When considering the text for this instructional purpose, ask yourself: Is the vocabulary used in the text authentic to the discipline, but contextually defined in a manner that makes it accessible to my students? Does the text model the inquiry and/or critical thinking processes of the discipline either implicitly (for example in an author's note) or explicitly (through direct description in the text)?	**The implications for text complexity are:** A wide range of complexity is possible, depending on instructional practice considerations below.

Instructional Purpose: Developing Reading Skills	
When considering the text for this instructional purpose, ask yourself:	The implications for text complexity are:
Does this book appeal to students? Will it be worth working at? How much background knowledge does the book require? Will students be able to comprehend as they decode? What kinds of words does it contain? What is the balance of sight words, monosyllabic and polysyllabic words? How long are the sentences? Too long? Too short? Just right?	The text should be at a level of complexity such that readers can decode it with little support; unknown words and vocabulary should provide an appropriate level of challenge. The text is at a level of complexity such that the reader can 'work' to interpret the content of the text, drawing on content knowledge and background knowledge with the support of peers or a teacher.

Instructional Purpose: Teaching Literary Analysis/Genre Study	
When considering the text for this instructional purpose, ask yourself:	The implications for text complexity are:
How does this book represent the genre we are studying? How does it accomplish this on its own and how does it accomplish this understanding in the context of other books of the same genre or of different genres that focus on the same topic? What literary elements are at work in the book? Does the author do anything unique with one or two in particular that stand out as very effective examples to use in instruction? What is the match between the literary elements that are required to teach according to your school's scope and sequence or state and district standards?	Generally, in order to analyze genre characteristics, students should be able to access the text with ease in order to focus on critically examining the text. Your selection is also dependent on the readers' prior knowledge of the genre. If they have more experience with the genre, the text can be more complex.

Instructional Purpose: Analyzing Mentor Texts	
When considering the text for this instructional purpose, ask yourself:	The implications for text complexity are:
If students are reading "like a writer," what do they learn about genre through this text? How does this particular text model a particular quality of good writing, for example, varied sentence length, for targeted writing practicing that skill? How does this particular text model the ways in which writing can be used to communicate knowledge to the world, by simply informing readers or informing and persuading readers simultaneously?	The complexity of the text is dependent on whether it is being used as a model for a demonstration of content learning or as a model of genre in genre study. In each case, you have to consider your readers' level of content, genre, and language knowledge). To use as a mentor text, students should be able to access and interpret the text to a degree that allows them to understand the writing process of the author.

Instructional Purpose: Developing Critical Thinking	
When considering the text for this instructional purpose, ask yourself:	The implications for text complexity are:
What are the key ideas and details in this text? What perspectives and points of view are offered within this text? Which are left out? What can a student learn by reading just this text? What does the student learn by reading this text in the context of other texts within a text set?	A wide range of complexity is possible, depending on the content and language knowledge of the reader. Special consideration should be given to the 'levels of meaning' and the perspectives expressed in the text. The complexity should allow students to be able to "dig in" to the content and consider a range of perspectives, and not get bogged down in a reading struggle to access the content.

Instructional Purpose: Engaging in Inquiry and Research	
When considering the text for this instructional purpose, ask yourself: What is the match between the text and the content we are learning about, either individually, in pairs, small groups, or as a class? Is this text well-researched? Does the back matter and bibliography demonstrate to my students how someone does thorough research using quality sources? Does this text represent "the literature of inquiry"? Does it model the inquiry process, the having of questions, and the ways around stumbling blocks and dead ends? Will it help my students persevere through their own research? Is this text going to help me model how I do research? Or is this text one that I will have my students explore? Or both? How does this text compare to other texts on the topic in terms of all of the above questions?	**The implications for text complexity are:** A wide range of complexity is possible as readers may skim or read sections as opposed to reading the whole text. Consider in particular how the text is organized and the access features it includes. A well-organized text can be more complex because readers can more easily locate the information they need.

Appendix E ■ Resources for Evaluating Texts

Instructional Purpose: Building Reading Habits and a Love of Reading	
When considering the text for this instructional purpose, ask yourself: Who is the audience for this text? What about this book reflects my students' interests, passions, worries, or senses of humor? Who in my class this year, last year, or maybe in future years, might find this of interest? If the book is going to be a challenging read, is there enough of interest to make it worth it for students to stick with it?	**The implications for text complexity are:** Text is at a level of complexity that the reader can access and interpret independently. Text content matches interests and motivations of the reader.

Instructional Practices and Text Complexity Considerations Guide

Instructional Practice	Literacy and Content-Area Learning Considerations	Implications for Text Complexity
Read Aloud	Is there a flow to the language that makes it enjoyable to read aloud? Will the content engage the interest of the whole class? Is there potential for the text to generate discussion? Does it contain information that is critical for your unit of study? Does the book inspire inquiry by prompting students to ask questions?	Since the teacher reads the text aloud, the text can be more complex, but the ideas and concepts discussed in the text should be accessible to students with teacher and/or peer support.
Literature Circles	Will the text generate student discussion? Will students benefit from the opportunity to discuss/extend their understanding of the content with peers? Does the text provide a review of important content information or does the text provide an expansion of information that is well matched to the readers in the group?	Consider how students will access the text when determining the appropriate level of complexity. If students will read the text independently, it needs to be well matched to their abilities to decode and interpret. If students will access the text with audio or teacher/parent support, the text can be more complex. Since students will have the opportunity to discuss, analyze, and critique the text with a peer group, the text can be more complex conceptually than if students did not have the benefit of peer support.

Instructional Practice	Literacy and Content-Area Learning Considerations	Implications for Text Complexity
Guided Reading	Is the text at a reading level that students can read and comprehend with some support? Does the text offer an opportunity for strategy instruction to help students grow as readers? Does the text provide a review of content study information previously discussed in a whole group setting or does it provide an opportunity to expand on content information that is well matched to the readers in the group?	The text is at a level of complexity that the reader can access and interpret with *some* support from a teacher. You can identify an aspect of the text's complexity as a focus for instruction that will support the reader's ability to read increasingly complex texts.
Independent Reading	Is the text neither too hard nor too easy, offering the reader a chance to develop his or her reading abilities? Does the text provide either a review of information previously learned or an expansion of content study information that is well matched to the reader's particular interests?	The text is at a level of complexity matched to the reader's abilities, content and language knowledge and interest and motivation. The students should be able to confidently access and interpret the text independently.
Whole-Class Read	Is the text a good match for your instructional purpose and content learning goals? Can enough of the students in the class read and interpret the content independently? Will the text generate discussion among the students?	The text is at a level of complexity that allows for the majority of the students to read independently without frustration and interpret the text on different levels. Classroom instruction in small-group and whole-class settings will provide the scaffolding necessary to allow a range of readers to access the text with success. Like selection considerations for literature circles, the text of a whole-class read can be more complex conceptually than if students did not have the benefit of peer support.

Considerations for Evaluating Your Readers Guide

When considering sociocultural context and how it influences student reading experiences, ask yourself:

- Who are we as a classroom, as a school, as a community?
- What do we value?
- What are our literacy practices?
- How do our values influence our approach to reading instruction?
- How do our values influence the texts that we select?
- How do our values/perspectives influence the meaning that we construct from texts and what we do with texts?

When considering how readers approach a text, ask yourself:

- What are their abilities to access (decode and interpret) the text?
- What are their abilities to analyze and critique text?
- What background knowledge do they have (content area knowledge, knowledge about the world and how it works)?
- What do they know about language and how it is used in different contexts (vocabulary and disciplinary literacies)?
- What are their interests and motivations?

Appendix F • Contents of the Digital Resource CD

Contents of the Digital Resource CD

Page(s)	Title	Filename
34, 216–219	The Quality, Utility, and Complexity Chart Template	chart.pdf; chart.docx
46, 220	General Text Evaluation Considerations for Quality Guide	qualityguide.pdf; qualityguide.docx
50, 221–222	Contemporary Realistic Fiction Text Evaluation Considerations for Quality Guide	realistic.pdf; realistic.docx
54, 223	Traditional Literature Text Evaluation Considerations for Quality Guide	literature.pdf; literature.docx
58, 224–225	Fantasy/Science Fiction Text Evaluation Considerations for Quality Guide	fantasy.pdf; fantasy.docx
63, 226–227	Historical Fiction Text Evaluation Considerations for Quality Guide	historical.pdf; historical.docx
68, 228–229	Poetry Text Evaluation Considerations for Quality Guide	poetry.pdf; poetry.docx
76, 230–231	Nonfiction Text Evaluation Considerations for Quality Guide	nonfiction.pdf; nonficition.docx
92–93, 233–235	Evaluating Text for Instructional Purposes Guide	evalpurpose.pdf; evalpurpose.docx
100, 236–237	Evaluating Text for Instructional Practices Guide	evalpractice.pdf; evalpractice.docx
117, 232	Guide to Aligning an Evaluation of Quality with an Evaluation of Complexity	aligning.pdf; aligning.docx
125–127, 238–242	Considerations for Instructional Purposes and Text Complexity Guide	instrpurpose.pdf; instrpurpose.docx
129–130, 243–244	Instructional Practices and Text Complexity Considerations Guide	instprac.pdf; instprac.docx
140–143, 179–184	Sample *Quality, Utility, and Complexity Chart* for *Those Rebels, John and Tom*	rebels.pdf
147–149, 185–189	Sample *Quality, Utility, and Complexity Chart* for *It's Our Garden: From Seeds to Harvest in a School Garden*	garden.pdf
190–194	Sample *Quality, Utility, and Complexity Chart* for *Dreaming Up: A Celebration of Building*	dreaming.pdf
195–200	Sample *Quality, Utility, and Complexity Chart* for *The Great Trouble: A Mystery of London, the Blue Death, and a Boy Called Eel*	trouble.pdf
201–204	Sample *Quality, Utility, and Complexity Chart* for *Interrupting Chicken*	chicken.pdf
205–208	Sample *Quality, Utility, and Complexity Chart* for *Penny and Her Marble*	marble.pdf
209–215	Sample *Quality, Utility, and Complexity Chart* for *The Port Chicago Fifty: Disaster, Mutiny, and the Fight for Civil Rights*	portchicago.pdf
245	Considerations for Evaluating Your Reader's Guide	readers.pdf; readers.docx

Notes

Notes